"This book did exactly what the narrator promised, and I wanted to hear her truth and her voice in this dreadful assassination of a career and attempted assassination of spirit. Despite the fact that the narrator was incredibly high achieving and hardworking, I found her wholesome, down to earth, and authentic, and the experiences suffered, whilst on a scale that I believe not many could have endured, were still made relatable to anyone who has been bullied at work or affected by discrimination and racism. This meant that I felt invested in the story and also identified with much of the tale. So, I was interested and found myself empathetic, sometimes furious, and other times, like the narrator, completely and utterly flabbergasted. Strong, engaging read indeed!"

—**Ms. Francis,** Reviewer, The Abundant Word

"I liked several things about this book. First, I liked how the author inserted several colorful pictures in the book. This made the book visually appealing. Among the photographs were documents that authenticate her claims. This made the story more believable. Second, I liked how the author used foreshadowing by showing the readers some dialogue that would come later. Third, the creative use of suspense throughout the book kept me hooked in anticipation of what would happen next. In conclusion, there is nothing I disliked about the book. I recommend it to anyone who may have gone through or is currently going through a hostile work environment, racism, or religious discrimination."

—**JM,** Online BookClub Reviewer

"[This] memoir is sad, as it should be. Reading it, I grew angry and frustrated—angry at seeing such behavior from highly educated people who, well into the new century, perpetuate the irrational attitudes of bygone eras, and frustrated because institutionalized racism is so subtle that one cannot expose it easily."

—**Dimitry,** Fiverr Reviewer

"*Naked Truth* is an unflinching and revealing memoir about the abuses that the author underwent at her workplace. Among the great strengths of this narrative is how patiently she dramatizes each of the individual episodes, creating a painful mosaic that brings to life all of the characters and participants in the conspiracy against her from the moment that she made her first complaint about them. It shows how they systematically sought to discredit her simply because she had the gall to call out their illegal biases and recriminations against her."

—**Ernesto Mestre**, Reviewer, The Book Butchers

"I was enthralled with [this] story! [The author] told me some of what was going on during the time it was happening, but reading the completion touched my heart and soul. The way [she] related the story was definitely riveting. I could hardly put the manuscript down!"

—**Eudora Fenty**, Reviewer

"It is no easy feat to offer a balanced perspective—a necessity, if the writer wants readers to glean wisdom and a sense of empowerment from his or her book and not simply consider it an outlet for perceived grievances—but this author clearly establishes herself as reliable in her personal and professional life. Her eagerness to share official documentation at every turn, coupled with her more emotionally driven opinions, instills confidence among readers that they should pay attention to her truth, because if it could happen to her, it's not out of the realm of possibility that it could happen to them."

—**Mark Weinstein**, Editorial Director, Kevin Anderson & Associates

"Loved it! *Naked Truth* is an alarming story about discrimination and racism at the federal government level. I would encourage everyone to read this book. While Dr. Jean Francis tells a very disturbing tale, it is filled with hope and determination, even when everything is falling apart around her. Time and time again, she commits herself to Christ and presses forward."

—**Kareen Hewitt**, Online BookClub

"As a man of color who works in the civil service and who grew up as the first generation in my family not to have been born under colonial rule, *Naked Truth* . . . is the book that I never previously would have allowed myself to read, but in the current political and social climate, I found that it was necessary. First, putting blinders on was not a great move, and I'm so grateful that Dr. Francis came along when I was ready to remove them. Throughout the entire book, it felt like she was speaking directly to me.

"The work on its own is persuasive, and Dr. Francis is clearly a profoundly honest and straightforward professional, but not everyone is going to take her word for it. Well, Dr. Francis kept the receipts. From documented proof of accomplishments that were intentionally left off performance evaluations to emails that contradict the assertions of different officials by their own hand, all of Dr. Francis's complaints have strong legs to stand on. In addition to what transpired, readers are also provided with what should have happened and how to do better in the future. Overall, this is an exceptional memoir with teeth. Very highly recommended."

—**Asher Syed,** Readers' Favorite Review, April 28, 2023

"What an amazing memoir full of faith, truth, and reality of the world we live in. . . . I want to say thank you to the author for sharing her story with the world because it is one that we all need to hear."

—**Janna Herron**, Author of Transforming Tears

"A riveting and explosive account of Dr. Jean D. Francis's twenty-five-year journey through her federal government experiences. Drawing upon her recollection of actual events, Dr. Francis shares her side of the story with raw emotion and candor, providing vivid behind-the-scenes reports and alarming stories of the highs and lows of her career. This book is an eye-opening exposé of the discrimination, racism, and unlawful retaliation that she faced, detailing widespread corruption, lies, and mismanagement. A must-read for anyone interested in power structures within organizations and the importance of speaking truth to power."

—**Sue**, Goodreads Review, April 10, 2023

"There is nothing that hurts me to my core more than injustice, discrimination, immorality, and blatant lies. I was strongly touched by the author's riveting and truthful account, which filled me with respect and admiration for her courage, integrity, and professionalism. *Naked Truth* sheds light on the painful reality of our world and how seeking justice can sometimes be the hardest path one could take. The author, Dr. Jean D. Francis, confidently portrays the reality of her working experiences in the federal government with reference to official documents that tactfully credit her claims against racism and religious discrimination that she endured. Despite all the toxicity and corruption, I saw how the author's faith, optimism, and values kept her strong and helped guide her through the darkness towards the light, which I found very inspiring. I love the relevant and wise quotes that introduce each chapter, capturing the essence of the events and shocking realities that are about to unfold.

"This book resonates with me because I have been in similar situations and I know how painful and nerve-racking it is to stand against evil, and how much courage that requires. There is nothing more touching for me than when someone courageously speaks the truth and keeps going against all odds.

"I am confident that this book will impact the lives of so many people, and will empower them to side with the truth, and speak up in the face of injustice. Our world badly needs more voices like this.

"Dr. Francis closes the book by summarizing her purpose and with words of encouragement, wisdom, and advice to empower those who may be going through a similar situation, because I am sure there are many people who are hesitant to reach out for help. All in all, the manuscript was captivating and kept me engrossed until the last word. I salute Dr. Jean D. Francis."

—**Dina Al Hidiq Zebib**, Author, Transformation Coach

"A powerful and important book that sheds light on the discrimination, racism, and corruption that still exist within our government institutions. Dr. Jean D. Francis's candid and fearless account of her twenty-five-year journey through federal service is both riveting and heartbreaking. Her book is a call to action, challenging readers to be courageous in telling their own truth. This is a must-read for anyone who wants to better understand the power dynamics at play in our society and the importance of speaking up against injustice."

—**Abigail L.**, Goodreads Review, April 11, 2023

"If the roles were reversed and you were the one being discriminated against because of your race, class, gender, or religion, how would you feel? . . .

"Many individuals will resonate with the experience of Jean D. Francis, PhD. They may be facing the same issues in their working environment but decided to refrain from speaking out to avoid losing everything. Jean's story will give them hope, courage, and the motivation to fight for their rights to end corporate discrimination. Her story can create awareness by disclosing the challenges and incidences of racial prejudice prevailing in most human resource departments today. As a result, it is a rallying call for the necessary policies to be implemented to achieve equality in the workplace. I recommend *Naked Truth* to readers facing discrimination in any form, as it will encourage them to speak up for themselves."

—**Grace Ruhara,** Readers' Favorite Review, April 11, 2023

"In her memoir, *Naked Truth*, Jean D. Francis chronicles her journey working in various government agencies, beginning with her entry into the workforce as an Army wife after college graduation. Francis's account is a compelling narrative of her unwavering commitment to her career, family, ongoing education, and religious faith. Unfortunately, the book also shines a light on some of the most insidious and disheartening situations in the workplace, including bosses displaying hostility towards employees who express a desire to pursue growth opportunities elsewhere and the denial of job opportunities based on factors such as race, gender, and religion.

"Francis's storytelling is captivating, drawing readers into her personal experiences and providing insight into the challenges and triumphs of a successful career within the government. I found myself engrossed in her background story, from marrying her high school sweetheart to traveling the world and visiting beautiful places with her family. What I appreciated most about Francis's narrative is her relatable and conversational tone. She connects with readers by sharing a bit about herself, making them feel like they are talking to a friend with a wealth of knowledge to share. Her honesty about the discrimination she faced while pregnant and as a woman in the workforce was shocking and eye-opening. Although we have come a long way in recognizing discrimination and sexual harassment in the workplace, her experiences remind us of the importance of remaining vigilant and steadfast in the face of adversity.

"*Naked Truth* is a thought-provoking memoir reminding readers that while we have made strides in battling racism and discrimination, we still have much work to do. Whether you are seeking to advance your career or navigate challenging situations, this book is an invaluable resource. Francis's experiences serve as a poignant reminder of our rights and innate abilities and inspire readers to persevere. In addition, readers will find Jean's story relatable and get insight into how they, too, can overcome similar challenges in their careers."

—**Karen Almeida** Five-Star Literary Titan Review,
Assistant Editor, May 1, 2023

"The book *Naked Truth: A Fight Against Racism, Religious Discrimination, and Retaliation in My Federal Government Career* chronicles the undeserved humiliations, insults, and hurts meted out to a resilient African American woman at her workplace. If you were in her shoes, would you have suffered through it all or outright called it quits? What Francis did will leave you astonished.

"I loved the carefully selected quotes that strategically preceded each chapter and how this spoke volumes about the content of each chapter. Also, the court dialogues and photographs that further authenticate the author's claims make the story plausible. Furthermore, the organization of the book into four sections, each with numerous chapters, made for a good reading aid.

"The book deserves 5 out of 5 stars. I recommend this book to career warriors who are not willing to throw in the towel and quit on the job but are bent on overcoming workplace toxicity with all the strength they've got."
—**Peace Odii**, Five-Star Online Book Club Review, May 8, 2021

Naked Truth: A Fight Against Racism,
Religious Discrimination and Retaliation
in My Federal Government Career
by Jean D. Francis, Ph.D.

© Copyright 2023 Jean D. Francis, Ph.D

ISBN 978-1-64663-969-4

Published by

3705 Shore Drive
Virginia Beach, VA 23455

800-435-4811

Naked Truth:

A Fight Against Racism, Religious Discrimination, and Retaliation in My Federal Government Career

■ ■ ■

JEAN D. FRANCIS, Ph.D.

VIRGINIA BEACH
CAPE CHARLES

Table of Contents

Prologue

All truth passes through three states.
First, it is ridiculed. Second, it is violently opposed.
Third, it is accepted as being self-evident.

—Arthur Schopenhauer

I sat in deep despair at the hearing. My aching heart's response was to echo the intense hurt I was experiencing as I sat there and watched as they scoffed at my truth and discredited my evidence. I was there because I wanted to see justice flow like it is described in Amos 5:24: "Justice flows like torrents of water, and righteous actions like a stream that never dries up." I believe in justice—I waited for it. But, instead, at the end of the day, I concluded that lies are readily accepted, and truth has become a scarce commodity in our society. And immediately, like a flash of lightning, it came to my remembrance that according to Flora Thompson, "You can lock up from a thief, but you can't from a liar."

I'm certain that you've heard this phrase before. Me? I've heard it countless times. How? Let me tell you the story of my early exposure. This was my late grandmother's favorite phrase, and it has resonated with me throughout my life—leaving me with no choice but to think about my actions and how they affect others in every situation.

My grandmother stood just a little over five feet tall, was in her late forties, and had mahogany-brown, weathered skin. She was petite and slender, with a prominent wart on the right side of her nose. Her name was Mary Burton. However, she was affectionately called Nana. If you had seen her, respect may not have been your first reaction. She may not have been a very impressive woman through the eyes of others. But through the eyes of her grandchildren, she was our remarkable, kind-hearted, and incredible Nana.

Nana was a monumental figure and a phenomenal woman during my formative years. I wouldn't be the woman I am today if not for

Nana. Her positive influence, hardworking spirit, and love for God served as constant inspiration and motivation. These attributes have helped gain strength through adversities and to charge forward when things look to be their worst.

Nana was also a staunch Seventh-day Adventist Christian who taught my four siblings and me to love God first and keep the Sabbath holy from sunset to sunset. As a result, the Sabbath was a high day in our household. Nana referred to Friday, the day before our Sabbath, as *preparation day*. For us, it was like preparing for a wedding or special event. On Fridays as a child, I was always right by Nana's side, helping prepare meals for the next day, with the mouth-watering aroma of her cooking tempting me. The Sabbath could not come fast enough. I could barely wait to partake in the scrumptious meal we had prepared.

As soon as the Sabbath meal was prepared and stored away, Nana ensured our clothes were selected, clean, and ironed, and that our shoes were polished and ready for church the next day. The final phase of preparation day made sure that we were all showered, dressed, and seated in the living room to usher in the Sabbath by sunset. Nana asked each of us if there was a particular song we would like to sing, and we all chimed in like a mass choir. Nana would then recite a Scripture or two from the Bible, and she always ended our worship session by calmly reading Psalm 1.

When she got to the last verse—*But the way of the ungodly shall perish*—her voice rose a notch or two. She grimly stared each of us in the eye as she emphasized the word *perish* loudly, to ensure that we all could hear, shaking her index finger in our faces. One look at her and you would realize Nana was dead serious. My younger brother Lemuel, though we treated each other as though we were twins, would laugh as he hysterically rolled around the floor. I on the other hand, would sit on the edge of my seat and tremble with fear in my dress shoes. After worship, my grandmother ensured that we all went to bed early. She would wake us up on Sabbath for morning worship at daybreak before hustling us off to church.

On many occasions and with her soft brown eyes piercing our little faces, my grandmother also taught us the importance of truth-telling. Nana couldn't stand a liar. So, inevitably, my siblings and I told occasional white lies and got into mischief. Often, it was as though an invisible guest had entered our home, eaten the hidden cookies, drank the last glass of milk, or taken money from Nana's wallet to buy candy. None of us dared confess to the misdeed, though we knew that we would all be punished if the perpetrator did not fess up. We stood in silence, exchanging fearful glances, hoping someone would come forward and take the fall.

"Liar, liar, pants on fire!" These were the words we squealed at each other when someone was caught in a lie. Then, with anger in her voice, fury on her brow, and that index finger pointing at our little faces, our grandmother echoed her favorite words, "You can lock your door from a thief, but you can't from a liar."

As a kid, I did not understand what my grandmother was trying to convey. However, as I grew older, I experienced various ill-fated circumstances that helped with understanding the meaning. As a result, I have grown not only to appreciate, but to share my grandmother's contempt for an individual who lies outright and without conscience. Furthermore, growing up under my grandmother's influence has given me the fortitude to never suppress the truth where lies exist.

■ ■ ■

I was studious and ambitious as a child because of the positive influence of my mother. I was known for my exceptional memory of reciting poems, and under the tutelage of my grandmother—an incredible chef—I was becoming something of a cook. My grandmother may have been the one who provided me with the moral and spiritual foundation I needed early in life, but her daughter and my mother—Viola Estella—became an equally important figure. Hence, as Abraham Lincoln once so eloquently stated, "everything that I am and anything that I aimed to become, I owe it to my Angel mother."

Mom was a statuesque, elegant, and single parent of four children during that time. I remember like it was yesterday that she was intentional about dressing us smartly and keeping our hair well groomed. My sister Arlette and I had long, thick hair back then. And every Monday morning, as we prepared for school, Mom would part our hair with a comb at the center of our heads before plaiting two French braids that hung freely past our shoulders. My face would go numb because of the tightness of Mom's French braids.

On Easter and special holidays, Mom would break out the darkened hot comb—a metal iron comb used for straightening our hair. She would put it on the stove top to heat, then, with a coating of Dax Pomade, she would proceed to straighten our hair. The smoky smell of heated and burned hair permeated the house as the darkened comb hovered close to our scalps, with the occasional burns on our ears. On many occasions, Mom would yell at us to keep still in the process. "Keep still or I'll burn your ears," she'd say when we would squirm under the heat. It didn't matter, she always ended up burning our ears anyway. But it was the price we had to pay for beauty back then.

Mom also kept her home spotless and was also known for her culinary and magical cooking skills. I was convinced that she could produce a gourmet meal from the most mundane ingredients. As a result, the aroma from her kitchen was always stupendous! Above all, my late mother was instrumental in my pursuit of education, making sacrifices to send me to private schools, an opportunity that she herself never had. She spent hours with me after school, going over what I'd learned during the day and helping me with homework. Also, she enrolled me in music lessons and typing classes at an early age.

But Mom dreamed of a better life for her children than the one she'd had. She wanted only the best. Hence, she passed the mothering baton to my grandmother temporarily in search of a better life. I am glad she did. It's the reason why I am here today. Nana did not have to provide for us materially since Mom did; she just loved us unconditionally. She went to extreme to ensure nothing happened to us and would fight for us at the drop of a hat if she had to.

Let me also tell you about my first business endeavor. At fourteen, I operated my Bonnie Bell cosmetics business after school and worked at it full-time during the summer. I had the time of my life taking care of my customers' beauty and advising them on personal care. I was a young entrepreneur and enthusiastic about it. I still feel like the fourteen-year-old who has big dreams. Today, I have founded my own company to solve social problems and create generational wealth. I am confident that I will be an exceptional entrepreneur while also having the time of my life doing so.

Finally, the lessons I learned from my mother and grandmother contributed to my tenacity and drive to succeed, eventually leading me to pursue a career as a civil servant. This would lead to a series of esteemed positions at various US government departments, and a rewarding career in government for eighteen years with a sterling track record. After serving with the Department of Homeland Security as a senior budget analyst, I was offered the position of chief, budget formulation and implementation, for the Department of Labor (DOL), and I accepted. Unfortunately, that marked the beginning of a long and ongoing series of demoralizing and degrading episodes of workplace discrimination. And it was there that my rewarding and successful career came to a screeching halt.

There were discriminatory actions, retaliation, and destructive lies in the coming weeks, months, and years, causing what seemed like irreversible damages to my stellar career and in every aspect of my life. If you can relate to my dilemma, I fully understand your pain. What happened to me was wrong, and I refuse to be silenced. I am determined to set the record straight, speak truth to power, and confront ignorance with facts in this book.

Yet, I found myself with many questions at every crucial juncture.

When had this appalling saga truly begun? Why had it started? How did it get to that point? How would it end?

Well, do you remember the 1950s television series *Dragnet*? If you do, perhaps you are familiar with Jack Webb's famous phrase in it: "Just the facts, ma'am. Just the facts." The facts are what I am intentional in sharing with you. While the names of those involved have been changed, what follows presents the account of what I experienced, including court transcriptions, emails, and letters, as well as my recollection of conversations and events.

I believe that you and I must do our part to fight against racial inequity and religious discrimination in this country and worldwide. This is my intention in sharing my story. I hope to motivate, inspire, and give strength to you and others who have faced discrimination and injustice. Most importantly, I hope to generate change so that others may avoid the injustices that I have experienced. The fight for justice should never be a spectator sport. We should never be afraid to get into "good trouble." The world needs to know my truth—the naked truth.

Part I

■ ■ ■

Beginnings

Chapter 1

A good friend knows all your best stories,
but a best friend has lived them with you.

—Author unknown

I had no interest in working for the federal government. So how did I end up with a career in government? It all started when I met a dashing and debonair young man named Lionel Francis, who was committed to serving God and country. Lionel was one of the most respectable young men in our church, always well dressed, and held our congregation's pathfinder director title. He had a sociable personality and loved mingling and talking for extended periods.

In contrast, I was more reserved and quieter—friendly, but I knew when to walk away. Nevertheless, we became friends, high-school sweet-hearts, and eventually got married. He asked me to join him on a journey as he envisioned a rewarding and adventurous career with the Army. I was hesitant, but eventually I agreed, though I would not become a typical "Army wife."

You may agree that the movie *Titanic,* released in December 1997, received outstanding ratings because of the action-packed love story between a young couple of different socio-economic class. They fell madly in love on the ill-fated first voyage of the Titanic. This is one of Lionel's favorite movies of all times and every year, on April 15, he commits to watching it. I assume that it conjures up memories of our very own love story, among other things. But although our story did not begin on the Titanic, it is action packed, nonetheless. Let me tell you how it began.

Lionel and I met during the summer of 1974, just before my first year of high school in St. Croix, US Virgin Islands. We both sang in our church's youth choir, and one Thursday evening, the youth choir members showed up for choir rehearsal. We were casually standing

outside the church chit-chatting and waiting for the choir director to
show up. Then we got news of the rehearsal cancellation because the
director's wife had gone into labor.

Everyone was beaming with delight upon hearing the news of the
impending delivery of a new baby. So, we hung around for a little while
longer. As I stood under a kidney mango tree gazing intently, listening
to the discussions, and minding my business, Lionel approached
with a smile on his face, trying to capture my attention. And with his
soft brown eyes locked to mine, he flirtingly asked, "Do you have a
boyfriend?"

I gave him the side-eye and nonchalantly responded, "No." He was
quick to say that he was looking for a girlfriend and that I might be an
excellent candidate.

Without responding, I tried to tactfully step away, not looking
for love nor interested in his romantic overtures and continuing our
conversation. But he would not give up so easily. I lived walking distance
from the church, and as the crowd dispersed, Lionel again hurried to
my side and inquired if he could walk me home. I hesitantly agreed. It
would be good company, and he was charming if anything. He talked
all the way home, and after we got to the stairway of my building, he
asked to see me again, said goodnight, and the rest is beautiful history.
We became high-school sweethearts; he was two years ahead of me in
school. Although it was not love at first sight for me, I grew to love my
friend in the coming weeks and months of our relationship, dimples,
and all.

We did not have cell phones back then. Mom was overprotective
and strict when it came to her girls having boys at our home, so we had
to get creative with our communication during our courtship. Lionel
broached the idea of starting a notebook as a two-way communication
component between us. He emphatically called it *the scroll*. The scroll
was a black and white composition notebook (coincidentally, one of
my all-time favorite movies is *The Notebook)*. My would-be husband

wrote his first two pages of a love letter to me and delivered them at choir rehearsal.

After getting home from rehearsal, I would read his love letter and respond in kind. I would deliver the notebook at the next choir rehearsal with my response and the cycle repeated itself. I looked forward to getting the scroll weekly. Choir rehearsal could not come soon enough. In that black and white scroll were words that made us laugh, cry, and fall more deeply in love.

We completed two composition notebooks filled with sweet nothings to each other. Whenever I reminisce on the scrolls, those old memories come creeping back, and I am in full-blown throwback mode. I smile. As someone once said, "Memories are forever." Indeed, they are deathless and priceless. And they have the power to give you joy and perspective when needed.

Following high-school graduation, Lionel enlisted in the Army. I proceeded to Columbia Union College (CUC), in Takoma Park, Maryland, where I began my studies in microbiology with plans to become a lab technician. I enjoyed my college days immensely and continued to remain committed to my education. Lionel and I frequently communicated, wrote letters, and talked on the phone. While stationed in Stuttgart, Germany, Lionel proposed. However, I had no interest in marrying him while he was still in the Army. So, Lionel left the Army after completing three years, and we planned to get married soon after.

After leaving the Army, Lionel traveled to visit me at school. When he arrived on campus, he inquired about me, and someone directed him to where I worked. As a student at Columbia Union College, I worked part-time at the Washington Adventist Hospital (WAH) as a patient billing collection clerk. It was there in the long, white-walled hallway, outside my office, that Lionel and his brother Henroy visited and greeted me with glee. My stomach twisted in knots. I was both joyous and nervous about seeing him again. On the inside, I was jumping up and down on my mom's couch, like we did as kids back in the day. On the outside, I was calm, cool, and collected. We went out for dinner, talking the night away like we always did, and planning a trip to New York over the weekend so that I could meet some members of Lionel's family whom I had never met. On Friday evening, we boarded a Greyhound bus destined for the Port Authority Terminal in New York City. During the trip, he again popped the question, and after thinking about it for a moment, I said, "Yes."

Once we arrived in New York that cold November evening, we took the number two train to Staten Island Ferry and waited for the local bus. It arrived shortly and we embarked on the trip to our destination. We soon disembarked the bus and briskly began walking the final mile.

I've always been a fashionista. My mom had been my inspiration on dressing and fashion from an early age. In elementary school, my best friend Janice Peters always complimented me on my style of dressing. And because of my height, she would say, "I think you should become a model." I'd smile in appreciation for her compliment and gave it some thought a few times. As a teenager, whenever I leave home, I dressed my best and always with matching heels. My trip to the Big Apple with Lionel was no different. I carefully choose my outfit with matching pumps, but the high heels I was wearing were no match for the New England cold we were experiencing. I shivered in my stilettos and my feet and toes were numb at every step.

When I couldn't take another step, Lionel quickly sat me down on his backpack, took by shoes off, and decided to warm my feet under his armpits. It was a sight to see. Awkward though it seemed, in about ten minutes, my feet had warmed enough to complete the final journey. Indeed, I had learned a valuable lesson that day about dressing for the weather.

Over the weekend, I met the rest of his family, who lived on Staten Island. They were a wonderful group of people, and they accepted me without hesitation. A few weeks later, they organized a fabulous engagement party for us, and it was exceptional. In the following weeks and months, I was in full wedding-planning mode.

■ ■ ■

Lionel and I got married on the steamy summer Sunday of July 26, 1981. The two of us stood before our family and friends at the Takoma Park Seventh-day Adventist Church in Takoma Park, Maryland. It was a spectacular day. From the WAH, my supervisor, Robin, helped organized the wedding. Friends and family helped prepare food for the reception. Erlinda Buddy, jovial and in a flowing, elegant blue gown, was my maid of honor. I'd also invited many of my college and work colleagues. We were surrounded by love and well-wishers that evening as we ate, drank, and exhausted ourselves with joy. Since our wedding day, it's been a phenomenal journey, and we've since been married for over forty-one years.

Midway through college and now married, I was working at the WAH. I had hopes of becoming a healthcare or hospital administrator. I was also preparing to transfer to the University of Maryland in the fall of 1981 to continue my studies. After leaving the Army, Lionel struggled to find an alternative career path that was a good fit. One year after we got married, he asked cunningly, "How would you like to be a military wife?" He told me he had contacted a US Army recruiter and taken the test. Therefore, he could re-enlist in the Army as a former service member, keeping his previous rank. I replied, half-joking, "I'd demand a divorce because I told you I didn't want to marry you if you were in the Army." But now we were married, and I would have to compromise. I was committed to partnering with Lionel as we grew together as a team.

Our wedding day, July 26, 1981, one of the happiest days of my life. one of the happiest days of my life.

On October 11, 2016, we celebrated our 35th wedding anniversary with a vow renewal.

Standing with my bridesmaids, maid-of-honor, and flower girls

Chapter 2

*We sleep safely at night because rough men stand ready
to visit violence on those who would harm us.*

—Winston S. Churchill

On January 3, 1983, Lionel departed for Fort Hood, leaving me
behind until he could find military housing. I missed him. When I was
lonely, I picked up extra shifts at the hospital and spent quality time
with my mother and siblings. A few months later, Lionel was back with
a U-Haul for our move to Texas. I was three months pregnant when he
returned. I was happy to see him and ready to move. We packed all our
belongings into the U-Haul, bid goodbye to my family, and headed on
the long road to Texas.

My summer pregnancy in Texas was not easy. I persistently felt
uncomfortable and overheated because of the blazing sun. I stayed
indoors with the rattling and chattering sounds of the air conditioning
system most of my days. I attempted daredevil drives to the mall at
regular intervals. But after exiting the car and walking to my destination,
it always felt as though the heat was radiating off the pavement all
around me. My scalp and other uncovered parts of my body would
start burning in seconds. It was as though I was walking on the sun and
engaging in a marathon training session.

After each outing, I would hurriedly shrink back from the
heatwave, hoping never to experience it again. During the final stage of
my pregnancy, my younger sister Francine came to visit Lionel and me.
She was an exceptional help and good company. Her presence with us
was like joy and gladness during Christmas.

After two years of marriage, on September 23, 1983, our
daughter—Jeanelle Darlene—was born at the Metroplex Hospital in
Killeen, Texas. She was Daddy's girl from the start and the days and
months to come were pure bliss.

Motherhood became my motivation for everything I did and continue to do. Fortunately, it took me no time or thought to fully engaged myself into my new role as a mother. I was my mother's first born and was often the caregiver for my younger siblings; hence, it was a natural undertaking for me. However, with having my own daughter, embracing motherhood was a life-changing experience. Whenever I felt like I should focus on my own hobbies or interests, my daughter always reminded me that she was waiting for my attention. Nevertheless, it was one of the best experiences for me—the feeling that someone truly needed me. Likewise, Lionel was intimately engaged in the process of taking care of our daughter. He often bathed her, swaddled her, and kept her pressed to his chest. He was a doting father to his daughter.

Killeen, Texas, home to the largest military installation in the world, Fort Hood, felt rife with possibility. We became charter members and founders of the Killeen New Hope Seventh-day Adventist Church, and our fellow church members were like family. I applied for and landed a position at the Metroplex Hospital six months after our daughter's birth. However, the position was short-lived because Lionel received overseas Permanent Change of Station (PCS) orders in July 1984, to Hanau, Germany.

Although I enjoyed traveling, I was not ready for another move. What would life be like for my family while we were living overseas? Would I find a hospital in Hanau where I could continue my career path and a university to complete my education? How long would the tour last? These questions baffled and troubled me as we prepared ourselves for the move. Despite the questions, I was ready to take the chance at living overseas, instead of, at some point, regretting the opportunity I didn't take. I decided to make the leap as an adventure for the family.

After our move from Texas, my daughter and I stayed with my mom in Maryland, until it was time to join Lionel in Germany in the summer of 1985. I was intentional about getting acclimated to my unfamiliar environment quickly. Our daughter was still noticeably young, and—after joining Lionel—we decided that I would put off returning to work and be a stay-at-home mom until she was of school age. I cherished the time with her, marking new milestones and bringing new wonderment each day. At the same time, living far from family and friends back home was difficult. Mainly when Lionel was deployed for between two weeks to forty-five days, we could not see him. I struggled with solo parenting and loneliness during these periods, particularly in a foreign locale where I did not know the language and had no friends. So, like many times in my life, I took solace in my faith.

We soon developed close relationships with other military families of like faith at the Atterberry Chapel and Servicemen Center in Frankfurt, Germany. The Atterberry and Servicemen Center represented a spiritual oasis for soldiers and their families assigned overseas. We enjoyed Sabbath potlucks at each other's homes and visited magical destinations throughout Germany on weekend picnics and vacations. Most importantly, we supported each other with weekly calls, checking in to ensure each family member was doing well. We had formed an exceptional bond and a solid support system while serving overseas.

When we traveled back to the US to see my family in the summer of 1986, it was exhilarating. After a brief and enjoyable visit with them in Maryland, Lionel, my four-year-old daughter, and I were flying back to Frankfurt, Germany, from Dover Air Force Base, Delaware. The C-5A Galaxy military transport aircraft flight had been smooth, and our daughter was fast asleep. Then, halfway through the flight, we heard unusual sounds, and the plane began making jolts and lunges. Suddenly, it began to rapidly descend from 37,000 feet.

"Please tighten your seat belts. The plane is experiencing hydraulic failure," a voice from the cockpit said.

The cabin pressure changed. Then suddenly, oxygen masks dropped down. Passengers hurriedly put their masks on. Lionel and I sat terrified in our seats, as we focused on masking our daughter. Then, a flight attendant came by and asked us to take care of ourselves first by putting on our masks before taking care of our daughter. We hastily did so. Then, Lionel and I looked at each other and I could see the fear in his eyes. I'm sure he saw the same in mine.

We prayed intensely and hugged each other as though it was our last time. The pilot soon announced over the loudspeaker again that there was indeed a problem with the aircraft and that they were considering going back to Dover. However, they decided to continue to Germany because the distance was the same. This was not comforting. We needed a miracle.

All the passengers looked tense and fearful. Everyone except for my daughter. She was still sound asleep. The pilot had to fly the aircraft below 10,000 feet to Germany for us to breathe. It was a rough flight flying below altitude, but we eventually made it. After the plane's safe landing, everyone onboard clapped and cheered loudly, relieved to be back on the ground. I was immensely thankful and grateful to God for divine intervention, which allowed us to see another day.

On March 12, 1988, our second daughter, Latisha Erica, was born in Hanau, Germany. I'd scheduled an appointment to see my doctor earlier that day. And during the examination, my doctor was concerned because he detected that my baby had an abnormal heart rate. I was worried and so was Lionel. "Lord, please bless us with a healthy baby," I prayed.

Before I could say another word, my doctor informed me that I would need an emergency cesarean delivery. I was scared, but when he told me that failing to undergo the procedure may result in brain damage or death to my child, I decided to make the best decision for my baby and me. I agreed to the C-section. I don't remember how it happened. All I know is that I woke up in excruciating pain early the next morning. It was as though a tractor truck had run over my entire body. I couldn't move. Then later I was introduced to my six-pound, five-ounce baby girl. My heart was overwhelmed with joy because she was healthy and stunningly beautiful. Immediately, she also won the hearts of the attending nurses, her dad, and big sister.

We grew as a family and became well acclimated to our overseas environment. My mom agreed to come and stay with us for a while after the birth of our daughter. Her presence in our home was like a breath of fresh air. It was a beautiful thing to have three generations of strong, beautiful, Black women under one roof. We traveled together, and the girls loved having Grandma around. Mom specifically wanted a mother-daughter trip to Paris. We left the girls behind with Lionel, and the two of us traveled there like sisters. We had the time of our lives.

One year after the birth of my second daughter, I began my career with the Army as a civil servant. I was excited about going back to work and mastering my new role. However, I also wanted to make good impressions on my new colleagues. Therefore, I was prepared to use every interaction as an opportunity to demonstrate that I was respectful, professional, and hardworking—someone my colleagues would enjoy spending eight hours with on the job each day and could rely on during challenging situations.

I will never forget the morning of July 17, 1989, which started out gorgeous and sunny. I miraculously survived a near-fatal car accident when my car was struck by another car that was speeding excessively through the city of Hanau. I was on my way to work. I stopped at an intersection. There was no car in sight, and I proceeded to cross the street. Instantly, a car smashed into the driver's side of my car—a 1984 black and silver Mercury Cougar that we had brought with us to Germany.

It was the mayor of Hanau's driver who had hit my car with his large silver S500 Mercedes Benz. I felt the sudden impact to my left hip. I quivered. "Lord, please don't allow this accent to leave me crippled," I prayed. Then my car was thrown across the street against a pole. The impact smashed the passenger side of my car and hurled me back across the street. Both doors were crushed. The entire car was mangled badly on impact. And I was devastated as I sat trembling in the driver's seat.

Many bystanders stopped to help. Someone called the ambulance, and it arrived in a hurry. The drivers and medical technicians emerged from the ambulance and rushed to my aid. Because the driver's side door was totally smashed, I managed to escape through the passenger side. But as I emerged from the car, I realized the passenger door was also crunched against the pole on impact. Then I was rushed to the 92nd Medical Detachment Hospital Emergency room for a complete examination. Despite the trauma and a neck fracture, I was a car accident survivor. And I owed it to God, who had protected me.

A few weeks later, my family and I decided to visit the junkyard and final resting place of what was left of our car for one last look. It was the first time after the accident that I had seen the car. I was overcome with emotion. It was the first time for my mom too. Tears came to her eyes as she examined the car. She was shocked that I had survived the accident. Then I heard her say a prayer of thanksgiving to God for protecting me. As we left the junkyard, I was grateful to God for protecting me. And I concluded that it wasn't my time to go. God still had work for me to do, and I was thankful to Him for a second chance at life with my family.

I returned to work a few weeks later. And I was thankful and hopeful for the wonderful future that was ahead of me.

Jeanelle, and Latisha and my mom in Hanau, Germany.
It was a breath of fresh air having Mom with us. .

Part II

∎ ∎ ∎

My Working Experiences
in the Federal Government
System as a Black Woman

Chapter 3

It's the most rewarding thing to a be civil servant.
—Sargent Shriver

My civil service career officially started on April 8, 1989. You may recall that I had never envisioned working for the government. However, as a military spouse overseas, the available career options seemed to be childcare providers or employment with the Department of Defense, and I chose the latter. Having previously worked in the private sector, specifically in healthcare, I had learned that you can never fully understand the expectations of a new work environment. It was a challenge getting accustomed to the military practices and acronyms, for example. However, I had always been versatile and an adaptive learner, and I eagerly rose to the challenge.

I initially worked as a secretary for the 92nd Medical Detachment, Dental Services. Here, I was first introduced to the Department of Defense security clearance system and its importance. I learned that a security clearance was necessary to access and manage classified documents. Soon, I became acquainted with the military business system. For me, it was a challenge. But I learned to enjoy my new position. Less enjoyable were the challenges of life as a military spouse and working mother. At the same time I was trying to learn all these new skills, Lionel was deploying for extended periods.

During these deployments, I devoted my time engaging in various outdoor activities with other military wives whose husbands were also deployed. I also participated in exercising sessions at the gym with my children. Additionally, I took them shopping occasionally and visited various historic sites, which aided in making life more pleasant during the separation. I was also enrolled at the City College of Chicago, in Hanau, Germany, pursuing my bachelor's degree in business and management.

After work, I attended classes while Lionel took care of the girls. I enjoyed my classes immensely; business law was one of my favorites. But a year and a half into my studies, I could barely keep my eyes open in class. I also felt extremely tired after work and just wanted to go home and crawl into bed.

A visit to the doctor revealed that I was pregnant with our third child. The entire family was excited to hear the news, and we all hoped for a boy. After the semester ended, I decided to focus primarily on my pregnancy and continue my studies later.

In mid-October 1990, Lionel informed us that his battalion was being deployed to Iraq to support Operation Desert Storm. Although I was ready for many of his prior deployments, no one could have prepared me for that one; he had never been to war before. My heart was in my throat when I heard the news. I was immersed in fear for Lionel.

I was three months pregnant with our son during that time, and the immensity of this deployment weighed heavily on my heart. In addition, our two young daughters needed constant care. I would be juggling these responsibilities with the demands of my new job, plus the concern of my young husband now deployed in a war zone in the Middle East.

Although the prospect of Lionel's departure caused me great anguish, I promptly came to terms with his deployment. I began strategizing on making the best of the situation for our family. Preparing for his departure was the hardest thing I had to do. Knowing that my soulmate and companion was going into an unknown war zone was devastating. We constantly reassured each other that we would be together again to prepare mentally for his journey.

The day finally arrived. As Lionel prepared to board the bus, he whispered gently in my ear, "I'll be back—before you even know it!" I was no longer worried, and I kissed him goodbye. I was confident that God would answer my prayers, protect him in war, and safely bring him and the other battalion members back home. I hired a nanny to help take care of our children and to do household chores that I was unable to manage due to my pregnancy. In addition, I served on the committee to support the soldiers' wives who were participating in Operation Desert Storm to keep my mind occupied.

During this time, I never missed a day of work, aside from my prenatal doctor's appointments. However, I worked for a Colonel who had heartburn whenever I had to leave the office to attend my scheduled prenatal appointments. One day, I presented a leave slip for his approval and to let him know of my appointment. At that time, I was at the point in my pregnancy where the doctors wanted to see me for weekly check-ups. He wasn't having it. He said, "You have been taking off quite a bit and leaving the office for these appointments." He seemed rather upset. I calmly said, "Sir, I am pregnant. These appointments are important for me. Moreover, my husband is away fighting in Operation Desert Storm. Therefore, I must take care of me and my unborn child." Then I asked, "Have you ever had to leave your pregnant wife behind to fight in a war?" My boss, the Colonel, did not answer; neither did he ever talk to me about leaving for any other appointments after that day.

It was rather interesting, however, that a few weeks later, I walked into his office—which was right next door to mine—to place some documents in his inbox. I noticed right away that there was a crisp twenty-dollar bill strategically lying right in front of his desk. I thought it unusual for a twenty-dollar bill to be lying on the floor in that manner. I picked up the bill and said, "Sir, I think you may have dropped your twenty-dollar..." Before, I could say "bill" he jumped out of his chair as though surprised, walked to towards me, and said, "Oh, wow, I wonder how it got here?"

I side-eyed. Then I said, "Well, it sure didn't come through the window. It's closed!" Then he said, "You know what, let me hold on to this to see if anyone will come by and claim it." I walked out of his office, giggling inside. I thought to myself, *"Come to claim it? How about just sending an e-mail inquiring as to whether someone had lost the money*." To this day, I can't explain the phenomenon. However, one thing I knew, my grandmother taught me to be ethical, and I wasn't going to take a twenty-dollar bill lying strategically on the ground in front of my Boss's desk. I don't believe anyone came to claim the money, but that was not my problem to figure out.

■ ■ ■

I was thrilled when my sister Arlette moved to Germany to spend time with the girls and me and to ensure everything went well in the absence of Lionel. My family and my faith have always been the fountainhead in my life during difficulties. My sister and I had been remarkably close growing up, and we stayed up late into the nights talking like we were girls again. My marriage and travels had separated us, but her visit had brought us back together and in an unusual way. Her presence with me and my girls made an enormous difference, for which we will always be grateful.

One February 13, 1991, I delivered a baby boy at the Hanau Stadtkrankenhaus. We'd planned to call him Lionel Jr., which I did. It was sweet because God had blessed me with the joy of the baby boy I always wanted. It was bitter because Lionel was not by my side to support me through the delivery. I held my son in my arms for as long as I could before allowing the nurse to take him to the nursery. After seeing and holding my son for the first time, I was overcome with emotion. And I smiled graciously.

Many of my colleagues and friends from the 92nd Medical Detachment, Dental Services, and my loving sister wanted to make life bearable and feasible for me in Lionel's absence. They were all there to support me and ensure that my baby and I were offered the best medical care possible. And they did so exceptionally.

In July 1991, Lionel and his battalion returned safely from

deployment. We waited excitedly with the other military spouses and children as the buses finally arrived at Hessen-Homburg Kaserne in Hanau. Finally, finally, the men were all safe and in good health. As they emerged from the buses, weapons in hand, they were greeted with joyful shouts, screams, and hugs.

The girls were not shy about welcoming their dad home, though our six-month-old son was more apprehensive. I was thankful and relieved to have their father back, and I quickly yielded the baton to him after being in the lead at home for eight months.

After this deployment, adjustments were made when we were done with the well-deserved celebration and reintegration. Our son had to adjust to having his dad around whom he had never met. This process was emotionally stressful for both Lionel and my son. Still the relationship began to turn around for the better.

Shortly after Lionel returned from Desert Storm, there were talks about an enormous drawdown of troops and base closures in Europe. The base in Hanau where we lived and worked was scheduled to close. As a result, we decided to take advantage of last-minute travels before leaving Germany. So, we loaded up the car and traveled across Europe for some of our final escapades.

Our favorite stops on the trip were Switzerland with its beautiful alps, rivers, and lakes; Italy, with its long Mediterranean coastline and delectable cuisine; Austria, with its impressive imperial sights and well-kept historical gardens; Holland, with its radiant tulips; and the Czech Republic, home to impressive national parks and chateaus.

There were many unforgettable experiences on our trips. But one of the most memorable experiences was on our trip to Czechoslovakia— the chandelier and crystal hub for the US Armed Forces personnel serving overseas. Many of my friends and associates would say, "If you want to get the best deals on crystal chandeliers, go to Prague." It sounded like an enjoyable experience to me. So, we decided to make it a vacation spot. We packed the car and began our vacation from Hanau,

Germany to Czechoslovakia. It was a stunning sight driving toward the city of Prague, particularly at night.

It was a rumor that border-guards might search and take some or all your purchases on the way back. We were determined not to let it happen to us. My sister was with us, and we went intending to shop for chandeliers and crystal. The Czech chandeliers are well-built and not easily broken on contact. The many small parts that make up the chandelier are stored in their own sturdy packages, so we devised a plan to prevent the border guards from confiscating our purchases by having everyone sit on chandeliers parts and crystal. We took the small parts out of their boxes, wrapped them carefully, and executed the plan.

On our return to Germany, we had to drive past the border guards. We stopped, and the guard came to the car. He began to walk slowly around the car. Lionel and I traded furtive glances, just waiting for the command to perhaps "search" the car. There was silence. I thought, *Will he ask us to get out of the car?* in the silent moment. He took another look at the back of the car; my heart began to beat uncontrollably. He returned to where I was sitting, then looked at me, signaled to us, and said, "You can go." He didn't have to tell us twice; we were happy to get out of there. We stopped at some point and put the items back in their respective boxes, then joked and laughed about the entire escapade on the way home.

Our European tour truly broadened my perspective in a meaningful way, allowing me to work and associate with people of diverse backgrounds. As a Black woman in Europe, I always felt welcome, and I cannot recall a single incident of racism or discrimination. My German colleagues taught me how to work hard, but also to take vacation time often.

"Make sure you take a visit to Baden-Baden," my friends would often say. Baden-Baden is a spa town, with a reputation for its healthcare offerings, among other things. As a result, many of our German friends would vacation there often. I was also introduced to *volksmarching*, a more formalized version of a hike, known as the "people's sport" and one of Germany's most popular activities.

My family and I often looked forward to volksmarching as one of our weekend rituals. We enjoyed the exquisite countryside nestled around beautiful clear lakes, and we gleefully chatted with walkers on the beaten paths. Most importantly, we looked forward to earning our Volksmarch Medals at the end of the journey.

You'd always hear a saying among military personnel overseas: "When a military family leaves Germany, they must leave with three things: a child (born in Germany), a *shrunk* or wall-unit, and a grandfather clock." We were leaving with not only one, but three kids, the shrunk, and the grandfather clock. God had been exceptionally good to our family throughout our time abroad.

At the end of my service with the 92nd Medical Detachment, Dental Services, I earned outstanding reviews, I found the work fulfilling, and I left with the desire to continue serving as a civil service employee. My ambition was to work at the Pentagon once we returned. In May 1992, Lionel was assigned to Fort Sill, Oklahoma. And after eight wonderful years in Germany, we were ready to return home, finally.

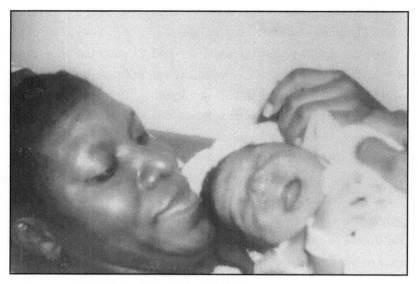

My son and me immediately after his birth.

 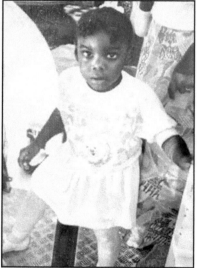

Our Daughters Jeanelle and Latisha on our Amsterdam tour.

Chapter 4

It's a funny thing coming home. Nothing changes.
Everything looks the same. Feels the same. Even smells the same.
You realize what's changed is you.

—F. Scott Fitzgerald

Following our German tour of duty, our family was eager to return to the United States. Still, we were not as keen about moving to Oklahoma for multiple reasons, including being far away from family again. Lionel requested and was granted a reassignment to Fort Bragg, North Carolina. I stayed in Takoma Park, Maryland with my mother and siblings because we wanted to give our children a stable and consistent school environment, among other things. Lionel reported to his new duty station, Fort Bragg, and he drove home to Maryland to spend time with us on weekends.

In those days, military spouses were granted *spouse preference*. In early August 1992, I applied for several positions utilizing that benefit. However, with the prospect of working at the Pentagon still in the back of my mind, I also applied for the position of secretary for the Pentagon's Secretary of the Army Office, Deputy Chief of Staff for Operations and Plans (DCSOPS). I was invited to interview for this position, and I was offered the job the following week. I was ready to begin my new assignment with the Pentagon. It felt like the beginning of a dream come true.

In mid-November 1992, I started my new job with the secretary of the Army, DCSOPS. The Pentagon was an energizing and rewarding place to work, with a fast-paced environment, affording access to the highest levels of the Department of Defense (DOD) operations on any given day. There were no advancement opportunities in a particular department at the Pentagon. To shift to the next GS grade level you would have to move around a lot. I got myself acclimated to my new position, quickly mastering the day-to-day functions of my job. And I developed an excellent rapport with my coworkers and supervisor.

My direct supervisor was impressed with my performance and growth. He offered positive feedback in my reviews and increased my duties and responsibilities in my role. I was ready for a new challenge at the three-year mark, so I began seeking new career growth and development opportunities. I found a good fit position in another DCSOPS office and started the application process.

Still, a supervisor had to sign my application to make it complete. I met with him to let him know that I was considering applying for a new position and that the application would also require his signature. I was stunned by his response: "I hired you, trained you, and now you want to leave?" Even though he knew that there were no opportunities for career advancement at my current position, not to mention the highly unprofessional nature of such a response.

In the weeks that followed, he displayed his dissatisfaction with my decision to move forward with my career. He refused to sign the application. Every morning, before I arrived at the office, he would send me an email expressing his dissatisfaction over minor office details. The constant unnecessary emailing became overwhelming. Finally, one morning, I walked into his office, closed the door, and demanded that he cease the continuous nagging and messaging. I also let him know that I would be okay with or without his approval if he refused to sign the document. He sat at his desk in silence, staring at me as his complexion went beet red. I gently opened his office door and left.

Karen, a colleague who sat in a cubicle outside his door proceeded to tell me as I exited, "You shouldn't have done that." This I didn't understand. As federal employees, you had the responsibility of making the best choices for your career path and individual development.

Ignoring her, I continued to the Human Resources Office (HRO) to voice my concerns and to ask for a transfer. I met with the HRO representative on Friday, February 11, 1994, shared my concerns, and politely requested a transfer just in case there was another position available within the department. As fate would have it, there was a vacant position, and I was transferred immediately.

I reported to my new assignment with DCSOPS, Resource Analysis and Integration Office the following Monday. When my supervisor was notified of the proceedings, he hurried down the hall to HR, demanding an explanation for the transfer. I'm not sure if he was given a satisfactory explanation, but that was not my concern. He had begun to behave as if I needed to sacrifice my career and growth prospects because he had trained me, which was part of his job.

On Monday morning, bright and early, I reported to my new office. After the transfer, I would occasionally walk pass my former supervisor in the hallway. Still, he would walk with his nose in the air without making eye contact. Nevertheless, that was fine with me. I was grateful to have been transferred to a new agency that was a good fit.

■ ■ ■

My new assignment with DCSOPS, Resource Analysis and Integration Office, was refreshing. God must have been orchestrating my career path. Not only that, but my new supervisor, Lt. Col. Donna Gamboa, a native Guamanian, exceptional leader, and the budget team chief, would eventually become one of my cherished professional mentors. Lt. Col. Gamboa took an active interest in my career growth and success, which was a new and enriching experience. In addition, she introduced me to the federal budget process, allowing me to collaborate with her on the budget and on projects and action items that expanded my horizons.

Lt. Col. Gamboa dedicated time to meet with me for an hour each week to discuss my career path. This was the model of an effective boss. After our first meeting, she gave me a copy of the bestselling career workbook, *What Color Is Your Parachute?* The importance of this book is to provide timeless advice for career change. Next, we discussed what

I had learned based on the book and performed the workbook tasks at our weekly meetings. Finally, we talked about the next move in my career and what it would take to get there.

Additionally, I received exceptional performance evaluations from Lt. Col. Gamboa, various awards in my position, and invaluable support and encouragement. She eventually retired, which was bittersweet for me, but I was grateful our paths had crossed. She had taught me to maximize my full potential and to challenge and outperform my own best self. A genuinely great boss like Lt. Col. Gamboa is hard to find. It was difficult to see her leave, and it has been impossible to forget her.

Soon after her departure, on January 22, 1995, I was promoted from the DCSOPS Program and Budget Team to the Resource Analysis Integration Office as secretary. In this position, I had the opportunity to interact with military personnel from the highest to the lowest ranks. The camaraderie was exceptional, and the working environment was familiar. In this role, I also received letters from generals such as Major General David A. Whaley and Lieutenant General Thomas N. Burnette, Jr., congratulating me for a job well done and my exceptional performance on extracurricular projects.

My performance was always rated "excellent" by various colonels who served as the chief of the agency and my bosses. On February 15, 1998, I was again promoted from the Resource Analysis Integration Office to the Assistant Chief of Staff for Installation Management Office as secretary. I was eager to begin my tenure with the new agency and to work just as hard to add value to the organization. Someone once said, "Promotions will come and go, but your hard work will always shine and show." I honestly believed that to be true.

Chapter 5

True winners remain winners because they truly believe that
challenges, struggles and obstacles can all lead to big blessings
through persistence and perseverance.

—Edmond Mbiaka

During my time at the Pentagon, Lionel served at the 37th Engineers, Alpha Company, in Fort Bragg. Although we were no longer overseas, the challenges of being a military spouse remained. Although Lionel returned home on weekends, he was frequently deployed for extended periods. As a result, I had to parent our three children alone while also working full-time.

Additionally, we had decided to purchase a home, and I managed finding the property and working with our realtor all on my own. My sister Francine accompanied me often on my house hunting adventures. I was grateful for her support and commitment. Unfortunately, at the time of the scheduled closing date of the house, Lionel was selected for a semi-automatic precision rifle (SAPAR) training deployment in Fort Leonard Wood, Missouri, and he could not be there. I had to undertake the task by myself.

With the power of attorney in my hand, the check to pay for the closing costs, and my realtor at my side, I sat in a conference room, settling on the biggest purchase of my life. The ritual of the closing meeting and all the formal signatures took a toll on me. At the end of the settlement proceedings, I was exhausted and didn't even want to see the keys to our new house.

After Lionel returned from the SAPAR training, we moved into our new home. However, I would contend with many more deployments and long absences in the coming months and years. This caused me loneliness, stress, and difficulties in maintaining the children's discipline when he was stationed in the United States. Nevertheless, his returns from deployment were always cause for celebration.

In addition to keeping things together on the home front, keeping our children occupied and on track, and ensuring things went smoothly at work, I decided to enroll at the University of Maryland to continue completing my bachelor's degree and to position myself for a more lucrative and rewarding career at the DOD. In addition, all my course credits from City Colleges of Chicago were transferable, which was a big plus. I eventually received my Bachelor of Science degree in business and management with a concentration in computer sciences. Subsequently, I enrolled in a master's program as well. The Army paid for my courses because they were directly associated with my day-to-day responsibilities at the DOD.

After approximately three and a half years of assignment at Fort Bragg, Lionel received PCS orders to Fort Belvoir, VA. It was one of the happiest days of my life when I received the news.

■ ■ ■

Life became less stressful and more manageable after Lionel was reassigned to Fort Belvoir, VA., in April 1996. He was finally home to help with our children and all the other day-to-day problems that kept popping up. Additionally, we could carpool to work each morning, which was a welcome amenity. Then, on October 29, 1998, in response to a resumé I had submitted, I was offered a position as program coordinator with the Pentagon Renovation Program (PENREN), to manage the budget of a $581 million project for renovating the telecommunication infrastructure of the Pentagon. And I graciously accepted the offer.

My supervisor was Ms. Angela Lewis. She was a blond-haired, blue-eyed, elegant young lady who always had a lovely smile. She was the resource manager and an exceptional leader as well. She ensured that I was equipped with the necessary tools for success. I was the only other government employee in the budget office of eight employees. I worked together diligently with the contractors to get the work done daily.

In this position, you had to train and become an expert with the new defense financial system called the Standard Operations and Maintenance Army Research and Development System (SOMARDS). In addition to becoming a SOMARDS expert, my other duties entailed: managing, directing, and conducting contract negotiations, preparing contract modifications for the Pentagon Renovation project, coordinating government-wide purchase-card programs, continually providing training, monitoring the agency credit-card holders, and managing supply acquisition. Most importantly, I also oversaw and managed the agency's budget formulation, execution, and end-of-year close-out budget processes. However, I quickly grasped the current information and continued to accept increasing responsibilities in my new career path.

Angela and I had developed a good, friendly rapport with each other. She was intentional about boosting morale among the team.

Specifically, she was also intentional about helping her staff stay focused on completing the work and ensured that we had all the resources and training needed to achieve results. It was a breath of fresh air working on projects with an efficient supervisor. Angela was not only interested in ensuring that I was successful in my day-to-day work performance, but she was also most noteworthy, for encouraging her staff to make sure that we maximized our retirement contribution to the Thrift Savings Plan (TSP) in preparation for retirement in the future. I counted it a blessing to have had her as one of my best supervisors. She truly set the example of an exceptional leader—one I was training and aspiring to be.

I was promoted to the next grade level of my position as program coordinator one year later. At each promotion level, it was a requirement for the individuals in my field to be certified in the acquisition arena and to establish consistent competencies and standards for performing acquisition-related work and career development. I attended the

Defense Acquisition University (DAU) and attained Level I certification in acquisition. Additionally, I was also fully engaged in the master's of science program in business and management with a concentration in finance. Finally, I juggled and created a balance between taking care for my family, attending college, and meeting the requirements of my job.

■ ■ ■

My time at PENREN was rewarding, despite the challenges of mastering the new budget formulation and execution system and collaborating with contractors to deliver products and services on time and on schedule. In the fall of 1999, Angela announced that she had accepted another position and was leaving our department. The day she left was one of the saddest days of my career because I knew I would miss her greatly. In addition, her departure meant that as the only other government employee in our area, I would have to fill the void as resource manager until someone was hired to fill the position. I did that to the best of my abilities.

I was learning on the fly, and I had to make tough decisions as an acting resource manager from time to time. For example, I remember facing the daunting task of dealing with a shortfall of eight million dollars. The situation required tough decisions on which activities would be spared funding.

Before making the decision, I met with project managers and stakeholders to gain insight into the impact and unintended consequences of the projects that would be underfunded. I also presented my suggestions to efficiently deal with the shortfall. In the end, my suggestions helped us decide which activities were to be zeroed out. In addition, my background in federal budgeting allowed me to control costs effectively through economical utilization of personnel and materials, while at the same time striving for maximum return on the taxpayer's investment.

On November 23, 1999, Lionel retired from the military after twenty-three years of service. Our marriage had survived twenty plus years of military life. Though Lionel was ready for a return to civilian life, the transition for all of us was significant. It required medical paperwork, careful budgeting, and job searching.

I continued working for the Army. However, the sense of disconnect from the military spouse community was something I did not foresee. This community had been part of my life for two decades. The military spouse's life will always be a part of the fabric of who I am. At Lionel's retirement, he was acknowledged for his stellar service to the military. Furthermore, the Army acknowledged my outstanding service to Lionel that made possible his lasting contribution to the nation. That meant a lot to me.

After Lionel's retirement, I had expected different companies to come knocking at our door to offer him opportunities. Instead, it took a few years before he landed the right job. Finally, his career at Julien Enterprise & Science Applications International Corporation (SAIC) catapulted him into a position with one of the US government's major intelligence agencies. He is now in a senior position. Meanwhile, I was steadily climbing the ladder of professional success.

In March 2000, a new PENREN resource manager was hired to fill the position. I was more than ready to hand over my temporary duties. However, in the early weeks of my new supervisor's tenure, the work environment suddenly became hostile and disrespectful, contrasting the atmosphere Angela had cultivated so carefully.

In September, I had a reprieve from the office environment. I was on Temporary Duty Travel (TDY) to Fort Monmouth, New Jersey, for the Level II Acquisition Certification training. When I returned, I began seeking employment elsewhere because the hostility and stressful work conditions were too much to bear for the first time in my government career.

I submitted my resumé to various departments such as the Department of Veterans Affairs (VA) and the Department of the Interior (DOI). In December 2001, I was invited to interview for a budget analyst position with the Veterans Administration. The interview went well, and the following week, I was offered the position as a budget analyst (GS-12).

As I prepared to fill my new role at the VA, which would begin in mid-February 2001, I also received a call from the DOI personnel staffing specialist stating that I had been selected for the position of budget analyst GS-12/13.

Although it was not the job that I had been interviewed for, I was selected as the best qualified candidate. The decision to accept it was an easy decision because of the double promotion. I negotiated and set the start date on April 8, 2001. And I notified the VA that I had accepted another position. I subsequently began preparing for my new job with the DOI with great delight.

Chapter 6

The best time for new beginnings is now.

—Author unknown

On April 8, 2001, I began my new job as budget analyst GS-12 at the Bureau of Indian Affairs (BIA), which is part of the Department of the Interior. The BIA was the first civilian government agency that I had joined after working for the DOD for fifteen years. I immediately felt like a fish out of water. I was surprised to find that I missed the military formality, structure, and camaraderie of the DOD, including the regular hail-and-farewell events that were thrown for active-duty military employees transferred to new departments or duty stations. I also missed my morning workouts at the Pentagon Officers' Athletic Center (POAC) and occasional morning runs from the Pentagon to National Airport, Clarendon, or downtown DC. However, this was a new day, and I was determined to succeed in my job and working environment.

As time passed, I recognized BIA as a unique organization within the federal government. So, I positioned myself to learn all that I could about its mission to enhance the quality of life, promote economic opportunity, and protect and improve the trust assets of Native Americans, Indian tribes, and Alaska Natives.

I had Native American colleagues who were also close friends. Whenever we traveled together to an Indian reservation, they were intentional about educating me on the history and culture of their community. Often, community members from the reservations we visited would offer me handmade tokens as gifts. These were gestures that I honored greatly and appreciated.

As a budget analyst, I quickly grasped the essence of how the agency operated and did business. Among other responsibilities, I formulated and executed a $541 million budget for funding of one hundred and

December 31, 1977, my husband's basic training photo.

December 31, 1999 At Lionel's retirement ceremony

eighty-seven bureaus and grant-operated Native American schools, two post-secondary schools, twenty-four tribally controlled community colleges, and various other tribal organizations. In addition, I formulated policies and procedures relating to budget, acquisition and grant management functions that applied to tribal colleges and university operations.

I also conducted annual budgetary and acquisition management training. I was enjoying my assignment at the BIA and mastering my craft. I often had to work long hours during the week. If additional work were to be done, my supervisor would ask me to come in on the weekend on whatever day worked for me. I would always choose Sundays to accommodate my religious observances. I would come in and work for however long it took me to get the job done on those days. Before I knew it, five months had gone by.

On the morning of September 11, 2001, I was in the elevator heading back to my office after a brief meeting. Everyone appeared to be in panic mode. I wondered what had happened, and one of the women in the elevator with me asked, "Did you hear what happened at the Pentagon?" With a puzzled look, I quickly said, "No. What happened?" She responded with, "The Pentagon had been hit by an aircraft."

The shocking news triggered feelings of fear, sadness, and powerlessness within me. I had just left the Pentagon that same year. The thought of such an elaborate edifice under attack seemed unreal. Moreover, many of the individuals I had worked with were still there.

I hurried back to my office in shock, and no sooner did I get there than we were all told to evacuate the building. That morning, getting out of the district was mayhem, as cars were blocked from driving downtown. The city was filled with pedestrians and government workers rushing to find the nearest Metro heading out of town.

Lionel worked in Northern Virginia in his lucrative position as a government contractor. He began frantically calling my cellphone to ensure I was safe and to figure out the best place to meet since we were carpooling to and from work. Finally, we maneuvered our way out of the city, and once we were finally home, we sat in front of the TV watching the events that had unfolded in New York. We watched the scenes of American Airlines Flight 27 as it circled over downtown Washington, DC, before crashing into the west side of the Pentagon. We were totally at a loss for words that day.

The experience for me was shocking and surreal. That had been my longtime place of employment. I could not stop thinking about what might have happened to me that day had I not taken the job with PENREN, which eventually led me to the BIA. American Airlines Flight 27 had hit the west side of the Pentagon, right where I had worked. I later found out that many of my former colleagues whom I had worked and laughed with had lost their lives. When I saw the names and photos of those, I had known whose lives had been lost, I felt my gut wrench. All I knew was that I felt the pain. It was a day that would never be forgotten in the United States and would remain in the hearts and minds of all Americans.

I considered my good fortune once we all returned to work at the BIA, striving to be the best that I could be in my role. My colleagues and anyone who knew me recognized that I was a very diligent and ambitious person. A few of my colleagues would make fun of me and say, "Girl! Every time I look around, you're always doing something."

This was a joke among friends, but I was serious about what I did. I was determined to use all the talents and gifts that God had given me while on this earth. I wanted to maximize my potential to benefit others and improve the world. I wanted to give back to others in appreciation of my own success and good fortune.

■　■　■

I continued to pursue my master of science degree in business and management, with a focus on finance. Additionally, my department paid for numerous budget and financial management courses to keep me up to date in my profession as a budget analyst. The stress of juggling family, work, and school had lessened with Lionel no longer in the Army, and we continued to carpool to work each day. As a result, I arrived at my office at around six o'clock every morning. This was nothing new because I had adopted early morning arrivals while working at the Pentagon. This was especially useful for fitting in morning exercise and getting refreshed and revived to my office.

On the morning of October 30, 2001, I arrived early to the office as usual. I was reading a book by Willie Jolley titled, *It Only Takes a Minute to Change Your Life*. After my arrival around six, I found time to read a section of Chapter Three, called "Goals: Dreams and Deadlines." After reading a few pages, I was inspired to get a piece of paper and write down some of my own dreams and aspirations. Before I knew it, I had written a timeline into my future. Eventually, I folded the written timeline and tucked it into the book on page forty-nine. I would finish reading the book in the following days, placing it on the shelf in my library and forgetting about what I had written. It was out of sight, and hence, out of mind, at least for the time being.

On April 8, 2002, I was promoted to budget analyst, GS-560-13, and I was still enjoying my assignment at the BIA. I traveled with my supervisor and coworkers to Indian reservations in Washington State, New Mexico, Minnesota, and Maine twice a year. We traveled in the spring and fall to facilitate budget, fund management training, and ensure proper control and accountability in the utilization of funds.

This department was one of my favorite job assignments. I appreciated getting to know the Indian reservations and understanding more about Native American culture. I was treated with respect and professionalism and always given positive feedback on my job performance. The BIA was indeed a place to work and learn. However, by the summer of 2003, many of my colleagues were either retiring or leaving the department for other roles. In addition, there was chatter about a newly formed government agency named the Department of

Homeland Security (DHS). A few of my former colleagues had applied for jobs and had begun working for the newly formed DHS.

The idea of working for a newly formed department piqued my interest. So, in April 2004, I submitted my resumé for the position of a budget analyst GS-14 with the Under Secretary for Management, Chief Financial Officer, and Office of Financial Management at the DHS. The director invited me to interview for the position, and two weeks later I was offered the job.

Leaving the BIA was bittersweet, but I felt that I had accomplished my mission there and learned much in my three years. Moreover, my knowledge, skills, and abilities in the position I held at the BIA were transferable to my position at the newly formed DHS. It seemed as if the wheels of my career were spinning full speed, and I couldn't wait to roll my sleeves up and get ready to work in the new department.

Chapter 7

As you climb the ladder of success,
be sure it's leaning against the right building.

—Author Unknown

In mid-June of 2004, I began my tenure as budget analyst with the DHS, working with the undersecretary for management, chief financial officer, Office of Financial Management. Once again, I felt like a fish out of water because of the unstructured culture of the new department. But, to be honest, I had expected that.

Although I had acclimated to the organizational environment at the DOI, I still had a bit of the DOD structured work culture running through my veins. But I was again prepared to do whatever was necessary to fulfill the requirements of my new role and contribute to the newly formed department.

I was delighted to bond with a new colleague named Deanean Bullock. When I first saw her, she was impeccably dressed in a powerful navy-blue suit and matching sling-backs. She seemed shy, but friendly, nonetheless. She gingerly smiled at me and said hello. I smiled back and said hello. And from that moment we were inseparable in the workplace.

We started together as budget analysts around the same date, and we immediately developed a dynamic working relationship. As budget analysts for our agency, we worked tirelessly to develop a $581 million working capital fund (WCF) and managed approximately twenty-four E-government initiatives under the President's Management Agenda 2004. We were like the Bobbsey twins.

Wherever Jean was, Deanean was and vice versa. Even the security guards at the door knew this and would ask me about her whereabouts whenever I left the building without her at lunchtime. At regular intervals, our lunchtimes were spent walking together for exercise, stopping to smell the cherry blossoms during the spring, and taking pictures of each other along the way. I was grateful for our friendship. Deanean was like a sister to me, and she is one of the best and hardest-working budget analysts I have ever known. She continues to be an inspiration to. Her weekly motivational messages on a weekly basis help to empower and motivate me along the way.

In addition to my friendship with Deanean, one of the highlights of working at DHS was the occasional visit we would receive from DHS Secretary Thomas Joseph Ridge. Ridge was the department's first secretary, and he was one of the most inspiring leaders I had worked with. He frequently took time out of his busy schedule to visit the financial management team and scheduled one-on-one meetings with us. So naturally, the finance team always looked forward to a photo-op with Secretary Ridge, and he was happy to oblige. He was an effective leader in the truest sense, and we were delighted to have him at the helm of the DHS.

At the DHS, part of my role was ensuring that our policy decisions complied with the president's management agenda and the DHS's mission. Since the DHS was a new department, it could be challenging to bring members from each agency to the table to develop policies and procedures. Most of the other agencies had been operating independently for years. Therefore, giving up their policies and procedures regarding day-to-day operations was unthinkable. It was a challenge getting each agency representative to agree to blanket policies and procedures without a lot of kicking and screaming.

Both my DHS supervisor and our director were great about ensuring that all employees had the opportunity to contribute to the department based on their varying skill sets. However, one area that was lacking at DHS was financial policy. As a result, I volunteered to serve on a team of experts developing new budget and financial management policies for the department. I met Mary Lou Alderman as a colleague, who we called "ML" on this policy management team.

She was an exceptional teacher who taught me a thing or two about the policy department. ML indicated that the department's debt-collection regulation was a foremost concern and top priority when I began working on the team. "It would be a good place for you to start," she said. With her guidance, I developed the DHS Debt Collection Regulation with our legal team for a thorough review and approval of the document. On January 20, 2007, the DHS Debt Collection Regulation was completed and published in the Federal Register, and it was one of my proudest accomplishments while at the DHS.

In addition to working hard to develop policies for the department, I had the opportunity to travel on training to Jacksonville, Florida, with ML. After the training, we visited the surrounding area. We scoped out the most desirable real estate nearby and had the time of our lives, and I was sold on moving to Jacksonville after retiring. However, Lionel was not. Mary Lou retired shortly after our trip to Jacksonville, and I missed her greatly. Nevertheless, I learned from ML that you are never too old for Walt Disney World after retirement.

During my time at DHS, I finished my master's degree in business and management with a concentration in finance. I was happy I'd completed my journey. After many finance, statistics, and math classes, I was exhausted. As a result, I wanted to take a brain dump on the beach in the Caribbean somewhere and Netflix-and-chill with Lionel.

A few weeks after graduation, Lionel told me one of his coworkers had invited us to his wedding. I was excited to attend. On the appointed day, we dressed appropriately, got in our car, and headed to the event. As we walked into the venue, to my surprise, my sister, Francine, was walking toward us. She was shocked to see us. Then she frantically turned in a hurry and disappeared around the corner. I was confused. I started to run after her, but Lionel held me back. *Why was my sister running away from us?* I wondered. And what was she doing at this event? I asked Lionel. He quickly stated, "Oh, maybe she knows my coworker."

I was even more confused. But before I could ask him another question, Lionel paused in front of the door, wryly smiled, and whispered, "Are you ready?" To which he then burst open the door of the hall to a full suite of attendees yelling "Surprise!" It was my graduation surprise party. And I almost fainted. It took me a few minutes to gather my composure. Then, I took a few tentative steps into the crowded room.

The attendees included colleagues, friends, family, my mom, children, in-laws, and my sister Francine. She was standing and laughing hysterically. I was surprised by the large turnout and after greeting everyone, I settled down in my seat. Looking around, I saw people hugging and greeting each other—some pointing at others from across the room. Squeals and laughter could be heard over the DJ's music. There was a table covered with gifts. And an easel was right beside the table holding a large picture of me. Finally, as the evening progressed, my brother, Lemuel, who had practically been my twin in our childhood, walked into the room and surprised me. And a surprise it was indeed! The celebration was splendid, and everyone congratulated me. I was grateful and thankful to my family for making the evening unforgettable.

I started applying to different universities to pursue my doctorate in the fall. In mid-February 2007, I also applied to the Department of Labor (DOL) for a GS-560-15 position as chief, budget formulation and implementation, Employment Standards Administration (ESA), Office of Management and Planning (OMAP). The job description had all the features that I had been looking for.

I could use my experience, knowledge, and education to lead others and manage resources, I thought. And it would be a promotion from my status at DHS. Up until this point, my federal government career had been rewarding.

But now, let me share the rest of my story with you.

■ ■ ■

When Lionel and I had first met, our religious faith was one of the key things we had in common. This sowed a deep bond between us and helped contribute to a lasting and fulfilling marriage. In addition, my grandmother had taught me to honor and keep the Sabbath holy, and Lionel's mother had taught him to do the same as a youngster. As a result, I'd never had any problems or competing priorities with Sabbath observance in my entire career. But let me tell you about Lionel's Sabbath observance story.

Before we were married, in the summer of 1978, Lionel was stationed in Fort Campbell, Kentucky. He was a private in the Army at the time, and he was faced with pulling duty on the Sabbath.

One day, Lionel summoned up the courage to tell his platoon sergeant that he could no longer work on the Sabbath. The sergeant told the first sergeant, and he scheduled an appointment for Lionel to see the commander, who was a first lieutenant at the time.

The day came for Lionel to see the commander. During the meeting, the commander asked Lionel, "What's going on?"

Lionel replied, "Sir, I am a Seventh Day Adventist. Saturday is my Sabbath, and I will no longer work on my Sabbath."

His commander said, "You will do what you're told. You will not get out of any duties. But, on the other hand, if you do not do what you are told, you will get into a lot of trouble."

My husband responded, "Well, you might as well punish me now. I will not work on my Sabbath anymore."

The commander responded, "We will see. That will be all!" My husband saluted respectfully and left his office.

Two weeks later, Lionel's military company deployed from Fort Campbell to Eglin Air Force Base in Florida, arriving on a Friday night. On Saturday morning, everyone was preparing to go to work. My husband sat with the equipment knowing he was not going to work on the Sabbath.

The platoon sergeant came over and said to Lionel, "Francis, you don't have to go with us," as he was sitting there. "You just stay here and watch the equipment," he directed.

My husband sat in the shade all day and watched the equipment. He believed that the commander had sent a message to the platoon sergeant to tell Lionel he did not have to work that day. That was the end of his problems relating to working on his Sabbath in the Army for the rest of his career.

Sixteen years later, Lionel happened to meet that same commander, and—believe it or not—he had become a born-again Christian. Did Lionel's influence have an effect on the commander? We'll never know for sure, and Lionel's experience may be the exception. However, what I do know is that my experience with defending my Sabbath and my religious beliefs at work was completely different. It came with negative consequences for my career as it reached a climactic moment—one that I never could have imagined in my wildest dreams. No amount of training and no problem that I had solved previously in my career path could have prepared me for the next chapter of my government career.

I am standing with Secretary Ridge, and Deanean for a photo-op

Part III

. . .

My Experiences
with Systemic Racism
and Retaliation in the
Federal Government System
as a Black Woman:
The Highs and Lows

Chapter 8

If it costs you your peace, it is too expensive.
—Author unknown

I remember as if it were yesterday. On the evening of March 20, 2007, my cell phone rang suddenly while shopping casually at Costco with Lionel. I did not recognize the number and Lionel advised me not to take the call, but I decided to take it anyway. The caller introduced herself as Georgia Tempest from the Department of Labor. She was inviting me to an interview the next day for the position of chief budget analyst. I asked her to hold on for a minute and conferred with Lionel.

He vehemently advised me to decline the interview invitation. "No government agency should be calling after duty hours to attend an interview on the following day. That's unusual," he stated. He sensed something right away.

I agreed that the timing of the call was a little odd, and an invitation to the interview the following day was somewhat weird. However, I got on the phone with Ms. Tempest and agreed to the interview. My husband was not pleased. He said that he was convinced that something fishy was going on. Moreover, I was not ready for an interview the next day. Nevertheless, I returned home and prepared in the best way I could.

The interview was scheduled for the following day, Friday, March 21, 2007, at three o'clock. I was interviewed by Financial Management Director Georgia Tempest, and ESA/OMAP Director Hattie Browne-Deville. The interview started a little late because Tempest and I waited for Browne-Deville to join us in the conference room. After about ten minutes of waiting, Tempest decided to begin without her colleague. Eventually, Browne-Deville walked in and looked at me with a stony-faced expression, as though she was displeased to see me there. I felt uneasy. She sat down wordlessly.

Throughout the interview, Browne-Deville sat there silently, her face expressionless. At regular intervals, Ms. Tempest would ask, "Do you have any questions for her, Hattie?"

She would barely shake her head in saying no. The atmosphere was awkward, and I felt radically out of place. But I could not pinpoint why.

Why was the director of the agency not asking questions of a potential candidate for a prominent position under her leadership? I wondered. I later found out through Browne-Deville's testimony in the investigative records that I "was not the one" she wanted to fill the position. She wanted someone else. In retrospect, how I wish I had known this. I was about to step into a workplace where I was not wanted and had no knowledge of it.

During the interview, Tempest provided an overview of the position. She also allowed me to share my experiences and the various managerial theories that might apply to organizational management. After my presentation, Tempest stated, "I can see the doctor coming out in you." I imagined she said this because I had mentioned that I was pursuing my doctorate.

According to Tempest's job description, the role did not require weekend work, just occasional long work hours on Mondays through Fridays. In our interview, she cited an example of a time when a team had worked late on a Friday evening to complete an assignment. However, she did not indicate that working on Friday nights or Saturdays, was a job requirement.

But even if it was, this was the US government, and its respect for religious freedom was engraved in its Constitution. In any case, all this was presented as a worst-case scenario. As part of the budget team in other departments, I understood that occasional late work hours were the norm, and I had navigated this successfully in my past positions. Therefore, I did not sense the need to state that my religion would prevent me from working on Friday nights and Saturdays. At the end of the interview, Ms. Browne-Deville still had not said a word.

I thanked them both and said goodbye before leaving the room.

■ ■ ■

The following week, Ms. Tempest invited me back for a second interview with the team I was to lead if selected. I accepted the invitation and met with three team members on the designated day and time. We talked about what the agency was looking for in a leader. I discussed what I would bring to the position to improve day-to-day processes and to help maximize everyone's potential, including continuous training and development. I left believing that I was a good fit for the team and that the interview had gone well.

After leaving the room, I would later learn that the group discussed the interview. Ms. Abigail Brooks, who served as the Freedom of Information Act (FOIA) specialist with the budget team, was present at the interview and for the discussion. In her response to the investigation report, Brooks stated: "[One of the] candidates looked, acted, and had the same mannerisms as Ms. Browne-Deville. Branch Chief of Financial Management Georgia Tempest said that Ms. Browne-Deville wanted to hire the candidate that looked like her. After participating in the interviewing process and meeting the candidate, we agreed that Ms. Browne-Deville would probably want to hire that person."

I was not that person.

Brooks also stated in the investigation report that: "At the time, Ms. Georgia Tempest, the Branch Chief of Financial Management at the time told all of the Budget staff that Ms. Browne-Deville was concerned about hiring Mrs. Francis because of a grammatical error on Mrs. Francis's resumé. Ms. Tempest went on to say that Ms. Browne-Deville wanted to have Mrs. Francis submit a writing sample."

According to Brook's testimony, "the Budget staff unanimously chose Mrs. Francis for the position. We felt that Ms. Browne-Deville was searching for flaws in Mrs. Francis's resume in an attempt not to hire her."

I did not hear anything else about the job until two months later, in mid-May 2007, when I received a call from Tempest. By this time, the possibility of me filling in the position was out of sight. I thought another candidate had been selected for the position.

During the call, she asked for contact information from my supervisor. She also requested three writing samples. I emailed the information as requested. On May 21, 2007, I received a phone call from the DOL, ESA, Human Resources Management, informing me that I was selected for the position. I was elated about the new job and graciously accepted the offer. I was also happy to meet the staff again, particularly those with whom I had interviewed. It appeared we had connected, that we had a lot in common and that they truly wanted me to be a part of their work environment. However, given the unusual interview process and bad vibes I had received during the interview sessions, particularly from Hattie Browne-Deville, I felt somewhat apprehensive and uncertain about what I was about to face in the new job.

My start date was to be June 8, 2007, on my birthday. Two weeks before my official start date, I received two big boxes at my home address from the department. They contained copies of previous budget documents, policies, the departmental E-budget system manual, and other budgetary materials. Never in my eighteen years of government service had I experienced such a thing. I was at a loss for words when I received the boxes of documents. According to Georgia Tempest, the information would serve as a means for me to come in on the first day and "hit the ground running."

Outrageous! I thought. At the Department of Defense and any other agencies where I had worked, this was not how classified government files or materials for new employees were managed. Moreover, I was being asked to use my personal time to review the materials for a job I had not yet started. Also, I was still employed with the DHS, which did not provide me with the luxury of reading and getting acclimated with two boxes of a prospective employer's documents to come and "hit the ground running."

The request was totally unacceptable in my view. It was undoubtedly one of the red flags I totally ignored.

Chapter 9

You don't have to compromise to be recognized.

—Wintley Phipps

The past eighteen years of my federal career had been in preparation for landing a job like this one. The new role was cause for celebration, and my family and I planned a promotion party the week before I started. The event was held at my alma mater, the University of Maryland. Family, friends, and coworkers came from near and far to celebrate my professional achievement with me.

Everyone had fun, and even my childhood pastor was in attendance. He gave an inspiring speech and said a prayer for my success. I was humbled by the kind words and good wishes. But the best gift he gave me that evening was a framed inscription that said *Set Your Standard High*. After reading the words, I was fired up and ready to work! It is still a prized possession in my office today.

On June 11, 2007, I started working at ESA/OMAP, Branch of Budget Formulation and Implementation (BFFI), as the chief of budget formulation and implementation (GS-560-15). Excited and filled with lots of emotions and first-day jitters, I walked down the hall to my office. I had already met much of the staff, and they were there waiting to greet me with big smiles on their faces.

The excitement was overwhelming as one of the budget analysts reached out to me with a hug. I replicated the kind gesture. Georgia walked past me, and vehemently said, "We don't do that here." The excitement of the moment quickly waned.

From day one at the DOL, ESA, I had no support from upper management. I was on my own to sink or stay afloat in this new position. Asking my supervisor for information and direction was like pulling a tooth from the root. Therefore, I had to depend on my staff to help me along the way. I sensed that Georgia did not care to meet. She did not ask to meet with me regarding office procedures or information that would have been helpful to me as a new employee. She typically got to the office between ten thirty and eleven each morning, and she kept her office door shut, it would seem, to avoid speaking with me. Therefore, I communicated with her via email if there were any questions or concerns. However, the responses to my communication were always short and abrupt.

For example, if I asked what the procedure for a particular action was, she would respond, "Barbara and Margaret know how to do this. They have done it before."

When I asked about the process for completing the manual timesheet, her response was, "Speak with Kenny and Rachel."

If she received an action needing to be completed, she would forward the email to me stating, "Jean, please cover this," or with the subject heading *For action*. These are some examples of what communication was like from her in the first two months of my tenure. To say that apprehension had started to raise its ugly head during that time is an understatement.

In my first two weeks, I did not have a working computer, which made matters worse. Instead, I had to review hard copies of the budget, edit them manually, and give the documents back to the staff to make the necessary corrections. Additionally, Georgia had agreed to oversee the departmental budget formulation process, and I took over the Office of Management and Budget (OMB) budget formulation process. The departmental budget formulation lasted two weeks, and I started collaborating with the staff to expedite the process.

June 22, 2007 was the Friday of my second week on the job. I worked over the required core hours beginning at 9:30 a.m. and ending at 7:30 p.m. Further, the DOL budget was completed by 6:30 P.M. However, the analyst was waiting for the new Departmental E-Budget System (DEBS) to generate the budget and to upload the final product into the DEBS library. This was the very last action of the budget submission process, and it did not require my presence.

The DEBS database was slow that day, causing the process to take longer than usual, and waiting for the budget to upload did not require the presence of the entire team. This would equate to paying overtime to employees for just sitting around doing nothing. One analyst could have completed this part of the budget process because the DEBS administrator was also on site. I worked ten hours that day. Once the budget was completed, I told everyone, including Georgia, that I was heading home, leaving the office at 7:30 p.m. Regarding my departure, in a later deposition, Georgia stated, "I thought it was very unusual."

Chapter 10

*Trouble no one about his religion; respect others in their views
and demand that they respect yours too.*

—Tecumseh

When I arrived at work the following Monday morning, I was immediately called into a meeting. Hattie Browne-Deville, the director, Noah Ralston, her deputy, and my first-line supervisor, Georgia Tempest, were all present. I was told that we were meeting to discuss why I had left at 7:30 p.m. the previous Friday, before the rest of the staff. I was puzzled. One important thing to mention here is that the staff members were seasoned budget analysts. They had worked in their positions for twenty-five to thirty years before I got the job with the agency.

I told Hattie that I had left because the budget was completed. I also left because I observed Sabbath hours that began at sunset on Fridays and ended at sunset on Saturdays.

"I didn't know you observed a Sabbath," she said with a puzzled look.

I was baffled at her response. *Why is she puzzled*, I wondered? *I didn't think I had to tell her that I had a Sabbath.*

"Yes." I replied. "My Sabbath hours begin at sunset on Fridays and end at sunset on Saturdays."

"So, if I ask you to come in on Saturdays, you mean you are not going to come in?" she asked with her voice raised.

I was not sure if Hattie had understood my initial explanation for why I had left when I did. So, I reiterated, "No, I would not come in on my Sabbath hours, even if you required it. However, I would be willing to come in after my Sabbath hours or on Sundays, if needed."

When I presented this accommodation request, Hattie seemed

shocked, and said she would not have hired me if she had known this at our interview.

I told Hattie that the interview was not for me to speak about my religious belief or my Sabbath. Still, I would bring the position's knowledge, skills, and abilities.

She continued, "So as the branch chief, are you telling me that you would have your people working on Saturdays, but you are not?"

I had never said that I would ask a staff member to work on weekends, yet she was persistent in wanting me to work on my Sabbath. Hattie said she wanted me to get the job done "whatever it took." She looked at me and said, "Your performance will not be satisfactory, then." She dismissed me from her office.

I was stunned and could not believe what I was hearing. Not just that she had brought the issue up, but that she had followed it with a threat. In the coming weeks, months, and years at the DOL, it became clear to me that this supervisor, and others, were determined to eliminate me from my position.

I was utterly dismayed and sincerely baffled by our conversation, to say the least. I had served in numerous government agencies throughout my eighteen-year career while maintaining observance of my Sabbath without a single issue. I had worked many weekend hours as a budget analyst in other organizations. Still, I was never pressured to work on Friday nights or Saturdays.

My performance had always been commended, and my religious requirements had never interfered with my work. Yet, after two weeks with the ESA, Hattie was saying, in no uncertain terms, that my performance hinged on my willingness to work on my Sabbath. Neither she nor Georgia were willing to accommodate my request or offer any compromise. It appeared to me they had decided that this accommodation meant that I would not be able to fulfill the duties of my position.

It appears that my career was crashing because of my religious beliefs. This could not be the same country my Lionel had risked his life to defend. And my sense that I was being penalized for my religious observances was verified during Georgia's deposition with my attorney, Mr. Hung, on March 4, 2011, when the following conversation between them ensued:

Mr. Hung: "What was Ms. Francis's response?"

Ms. Tempest: "As I recall, her response was that Friday was her Sabbath, which was a surprise to both Ms. Hattie Browne-Deville and myself."

Mr. Hung: "What was Ms. Hattie Browne-Deville's response to that statement?"

Ms. Tempest: "My recollection was she was very shocked, as we both were, and she said, if I had known that during the interview, I would have made other arrangements . . . And by that statement, she meant Ms. Francis would not be able to fulfill the duties of her position."

■ ■ ■

Let me be clear here; the position did not actually require weekend work. The job description did not state, "Work on Friday nights and Saturdays is essential to the position." I knew of no other employee at the DOL who was being pressured to work on the weekend or on his or her day or worship. And as I've mentioned, no discussion of the need to work on weekends took place during our interview. So, it seemed that now they were changing my job description in a kind of bait-and-switch.

During her deposition on March 4, 2011 with my attorney Mr.

Hung, Georgia stated, "When people who work in the budget arena see the term *long hours* in a job announcement, they understand that they could continue to work through weekends and holidays."

This explanation was new to me. However, as my attorney continued to seek clarity on the meaning of *long hours* as stated in the announcement, the following conversation ensued:

> **Mr. Hung:** "So, when you write 'long-hours' in a job announcement, you leave it to the reader's interpretation to dig out weekends and holidays?"

> **Ms. Tempest:** "Well, we don't leave it to the reader's interpretation. It is assumed in. As I said, in the budget world in Washington, DC, a GS-15 budget level, anyone reading this that has been doing budget formulation and understood the demands of the position would understand that long hours could encompass any time. And I've applied for budget positions where it has said the same language, and I immediately knew what that meant. You must do whatever it takes to get the budget done."

■ ■ ■

I had worked as a budget analyst for other federal agencies before I took the job with DOL, and I had never heard of such a thing. Moreover, I often worked long hours during budget formulation in my previous jobs. However, I have never had a supervisor who demanded that I worked on my Sabbath hours. If weekend work were imminent in other agencies, the supervisor would check to see if the agency director would approve weekend work. No overtime or weekend work was charged to the government unless it was approved. If approved, the supervisor would check to see which employees were available to work on Saturdays or Sundays and make appropriate arrangements with them based on their availability.

The agency's change in the requirement section of the job description to include Saturday and weekend work was after I had accepted the position and told the management that Saturday was my Sabbath. This is why I consider it to be misleading and a form of discrimination.

In the March 2011 deposition, when my attorney asked Georgia about how I had been selected for the position, the following exchange transpired:

Mr. Hung: "What were the criteria you relied on or, I guess, why did you choose Ms. Francis?"

Ms. Tempest: "Because at the time, based upon the information in her application and based upon the checks of her references, it appeared as though she would be able to perform the duties and requirements of this position."

Mr. Hung: "Better than the other two finalists?"

Ms. Tempest: "Yes."

Georgia admitted in the above proceedings that I was chosen for the position based on my application and reference checks. However, in week two of my tenure at the job, my religion became the center of attention, to the point that there were talks that they would not have selected me for the position, which in my view was discriminatory. Freedom of religion is considered a fundamental right of all Americans, and this was a US government job. However, my religion was being used against me.

In the following weeks and months, I was treated less favorably. Perhaps the most disappointing aspect, in this case, was that the OMAP agency was a part of the Department of Labor, whose Strategic Goal Number Three assured fair and high-quality work-life environment. Strategic Goal Number Five assured fair working conditions in the workplace. I had only been a DOL employee for two weeks. The constant reprimands became overwhelming and seem hostile.

Working on my Sabbath was non-negotiable. It was crucial to me that I never compromise my religious beliefs. My grandmother taught me at an early age to keep the Sabbath holy. As an adult, I have come to a personal understanding of the importance of keeping the Sabbath and continuing to employ the lessons learned from my grandmother. My family continues the tradition, and I have passed it down to my children. Sabbath-keeping had long been a source of peace and tranquility in my life. However, now it was front and center in a conflict that threatened to derail my stellar career at the DOL. I was gravely concerned and feared for what would come next. However, losing my job was not my biggest concern; faithfulness to my religious beliefs was.

Chapter 11

My key for dealing with stress is simple:
just stay cool and stay focused.

—Ashton Eaton

Despite the stress at my new job, I was still managing to keep my spirits up through interests and pursuits outside of work including working as the health ministry leader for my church. In this position, I focused on keeping our church members and surrounding communities aware of the importance of health and wellness by organizing physical activities and health and cooking seminars. Helping others to become healthier versions of themselves did a tremendous amount to counteract my stress in the workplace, even if my situation did not change.

In the weeks following the initial meeting with Hattie and Georgia regarding my Sabbath, other conflicts arose—seemingly in retaliation for my schedule restrictions. On Friday, July 13, 2007, at around noon, I notified Georgia that I would need to leave work at five o'clock for an appointment.

I had worked over eight hours that day, so, leaving at five was not an early departure. Notifying Georgia was a display of courtesy. She did not respond. When I returned to work the following Monday and checked my email, I saw that Georgia had forwarded an email to me at 6:52 p.m. the previous Friday, reprimanding me for leaving "early."

In her email, she said: "Friday nights are usually busy in BBFI, and this night was no different."

In addition to this petty stress, Lionel also seeking new employment because of a reorganization of his company. Hence, there was the uncertainty around whether Lionel would have a job or was able to find a new position elsewhere in a timely manner. Moreover, I was also enrolled in my doctoral studies. Therefore, this stress from my place of employment was not a good complement.

I told Lionel about what was happening, and he became my sounding board when he picked me up from work in the afternoons. He empathized and provided advice on how to manage my work situation. Personally, and spiritually, he was a big part of my support system. I also confided in my mom. She was incredibly supportive, calling me each day with encouraging words and motivational thoughts. After getting off the phone with her, I was always empowered and inspired to make it through another day.

I also confided in a couple of friends who worked in ESA HR. They emphatically encouraged me to get my resumé ready and begin my job search. From what they knew, prior to my hiring, the position had been announced many times, but no one at the DOL had applied. Hence the job was vacant for at least three years, and Georgia had been filling my position and hers until I was hired.

One of the budget analysts later told me that if Georgia had allowed her to walk me out of the building after the interview, she would have told me not to take the job. I liked the work but hated the work environment; the stress of going to work at the DOL ESA had become overbearing in just a few short months.

In getting acclimated to my position, I was required to attend a supervisory training course for new employees to become familiar with specific potential employee issues, union issues, and other factors governing employee supervision in my new role. Employees were automatically enrolled in the course and would receive several reminders to attend the training. One week before the training, I told Georgia I was enrolled in the training and would be attending on July 19, 2007. She gave her consent. The training day arrived, and I forwarded an email reminder to Georgia before leaving the office.

After I left for the training, Georgia responded to my email stating, "Your concentration should be on the budget and not on the supervisory training." The training was a part of the department's new supervisor onboarding process; however, I was denied attendance. Later, I was reprimanded in a memorandum for attending this mandatory training for new DOL supervisors. At this point, I had only been with the DOL for a little over a month, but I had already begun to put feelers out for new employment.

On July 24, 2007, I was called into Hattie's office, along with Georgia, and Noah, for a meeting. Once we were behind closed doors, Georgia looked at me and said, "She is the most arrogant person I have ever known."

I was flabbergasted. I had no idea where this comment was coming from. I had not given Georgia any motive for labeling me as arrogant as far as I knew. The meeting convened after her insulting statement about me. Subsequently, Hattie announced that Georgia was leaving the department. I sense a slight relief.

At the meeting, Georgia had expressed that she didn't trust me to put the budget together without her there to supervise. I was astonished at her remarks because she never mentioned fears or reservations about my inability to put a budget together at the interview. I responded that I had formulated numerous budgets for various agencies and that this would be no exception.

Hattie said, "But you have not put an ESA budget together."

I smiled and assured Hattie that I was able to formulate the ESA's budget and would do all that I could to ensure that the process ran smoothly. After sharing my experiences with formulating numerous budgets at other agencies, she stated that she was not encouraged. She repeatedly stressed that I must do "whatever it took" to get the budget done, and I assumed she was implying that I must be willing to work on my Sabbath when she said this.

On July 27, 2007, almost three weeks into my tenure, Hattie sent me a follow-up memorandum to the July 24 meeting. The memorandum documented items from our discussion on July 27, which had centered mainly on how my performance would not be satisfactory if the "requirement" of working on my Sabbath was not fulfilled. In the memorandum, Hattie also stated that my actions were questionable when I left "early" on Friday June 22, 2007. She further said that my actions were questionable on July 13, 2007, when I left at five for my appointment.

In this memo, Hattie also documented other alleged performance-related issues, including that I was "not jumping into the DOL process." However, this was false. When I joined the team, the DOL formulated the agency's budget during the first two weeks of my tenure. As a result, I "jumped into the process" wholeheartedly as instructed by reviewing the budget documents and providing input to finalize the budget. That is why I stayed at the office working until 7:30 p.m. on my second Friday.

Additionally, Hattie said she "had questions in her mind" as to whether or not I was engaged in "program orientation," which was also false. One month into my tenure at ESA, I began circulating a memo to the six program offices. They regarded monthly budget meetings that needed to be set up, since there was no schedule for such meetings in place. This was a process of bringing individuals together to address existing problems or concerns and to share ideas for making improvements.

Related to Hattie's complaints about me not scheduling my orientations with the program offices, orientation is always part of the onboarding process used to make employees feel welcome and integrated into the new organization, to help them perform their jobs successfully. From previous experience in the workplace, I understood that the orientation process was spearheaded by human resources management or the agency and not the responsibility of new employees. For Hattie to cite me for not arranging orientation with the program offices as a new employee made absolutely no sense. It also seems like a projection of her own flaws in integrating new employees and welcoming them into the fold.

Hattie's final critique was that I was "relying upon staff instead of supervisor and upper management." As mentioned, when I accepted the position, I received two big boxes of documents at my home. I was expected to review them to "hit the ground running" on my first day. I take it that Hattie and Georgia may have thought I had committed those two boxes of documents to memory and needed no further training on the job. Hence, whenever I had questions regarding work-related issues and processes, Georgia would respond in less than a sentence. She told me that I should ask staff members or other individuals for help. Yet, Hattie had criticized me for relying on the staff.

Interestingly, Hattie stated the staff wasn't a good source of information. They had "not been involved in policy-making processes and weren't well-versed in those areas." It begs the question, "Why not?" The budget analyst staffs had been formulating and executing ESA's budget for twenty to thirty years. It made no sense that they were never involved in policy issues.

Hattie concluded the memo by saying: "Noah and I will do whatever is necessary to help you succeed." This seemed like a joke, because Hattie had done everything she could to create a work environment that would prevent my success in the role.

In the subsequent weeks and months, the work environment got even worse, which I would not have thought possible. To be in that close proximity to, and even to work with someone whom you didn't want to fill a position would inevitably lead, sooner or later, only to trouble. However, Noah Ralston was regularly supportive and helpful to me during the chaos. After the July 24 meeting, I was stressed, overwhelmed, and frankly had had enough of the constant criticism. Noah noticed and called me into his office to assure me that everything would be fine. I remember him saying, "I believe in you. I believe in you."

Noah asked if anyone had taken me around to the program and other offices for an introduction.

I replied "No."

He quickly scheduled time on his calendar to take me around, making me familiar with the program and other offices.

Specifically, on August 3, 2007, I worked on appeals and object class adjustments requests with the program managers and the Office of the Assistant Secretary for Management Leadership, Mr. Willis. Noah was working remotely that day; however, he emailed me to ensure that everything was fine.

After giving him a brief update on my day and what had been done, he responded, "You're getting some good face time today! Enjoy your weekend. You earned it."

Noah had provided a tiny glimmer of hope at ESA just when it was needed most.

■ ■ ■

One of my first personnel actions as chief for the Budget Formulation and Implementation Office was to select a budget analyst team lead—a right-hand person who would help with day-to-day operations. Hattie had said, "I allow my first-line supervisors to select their employees."

Apparently, that didn't apply to me. I recommended a former colleague, Deanean Bullock, for the budget team lead position. Deanean had worked with me tirelessly in developing, formulating, and executing the Working Capital Fund (WCF) at the DHS. I believed that she was well qualified for the position.

Deanean was an exceptional budget analyst, one of the best I had ever known. I was confident that she would be an asset to ESA and an excellent candidate to fill the team lead position. She was invited to an interview with Georgia and me.

Shortly after the interview, Georgia requested that Deanean submit writing samples of her work and six references. Moreover, because I had referred Deanean for the job, Georgia told me that I had to make a case for why Hattie should hire her. This made it crystal clear to me that while I might have held the title related to my position, I had no decision-making authority on my own. It was also clear that they were making exceptions about the authority to hire in this position, another item that could be seen as part of their process.

I provided Hattie with a compelling case as to why I believed

Deanean would be an exceptional budget analyst team lead. Hattie's response to my recommendation was, "She doesn't have a degree, and I don't hire people without a degree."

I was livid because the comment was cold and calculated. First, the position did not call for the candidate to have a degree. Second, Deanean had been a budget analyst for more than twenty-one years. Finally, when I followed up with Georgia regarding the decision to hire Deanean, she stated, "We are not hiring her because we don't want any trouble here."

I took her comment to mean that simply because I had recommended someone, it denoted trouble if that person and I were to work together as a team. So, after they rejected Deanean, I made recommendations to Georgia to hire one of the analysts who was already on the team as the lead budget analyst. She objected and stormed out of my office saying, "You're on your own."

I was astonished at the remark because I believed one of the internal candidates was worthy of the position, particularly because she had been with the agency for years. Next, two other candidates were invited for an interview from the existing referral list; they interviewed with Hattie, Georgia, and me. After the interview and reference checks, Chad Everette was selected and offered the job as budget analyst team lead.

Chad and I worked well together, always strategizing on ways to improve the processes and procedures that were in place. He often reminded me that it was because I was on the interview panel and would be his supervisor that he had accepted the job in the first place. After Chad came on board, Georgia began preparing to leave. One week before her departure, as she was walking around the office, I heard Georgia approach my door and say while laughing, "Let me see how much more damage I can do before I leave." I believed she was referring to me.

Following Georgia 's departure, work conditions only worsened. As I sought to forge a better working relationship between the program offices and the OMAP budget team, I was accused of communicating with the program and not with Hattie.. For my short tenure at OMAP, I was damned if I did, and damned if I didn't. However, I was determined to stay positive despite my working conditions as I reminded myself each day that the size of the problem is not the issue; it is the size of the person that mattered.

Chapter 12

None of us alone can save the nation or the world.
But each of us can make a positive difference
if we commit ourselves to do so.

—Cornel West

In early August 2007, I had an appointment to meet with Miranda Hines, the DOL Civil Rights Center director. I had wanted to meet with her earlier, but when I called to schedule a meeting at the end of June, I was told she was serving jury duty and would not be back until August. During our meeting, I told her that since the second week of my tenure at ESA/OMAP, I had been experiencing an extremely hostile working environment and unprofessional treatment from Hattie, beginning with issues around my religious observances and compounded by racial microaggressions.

She quickly said, "No, no, I do not believe those are the reasons." She went on to say that she had known Hattie for some time, had been a good friend of hers, and had a good working relationship with her.

Hines tried to convince me that Hattie's conduct wasn't because of my religion or race, but because of past scrutiny on her leadership by the department. Because of that scrutiny, Hattie had to take precautions to make sure she covered all the bases of her leadership. She had to do this because of the departmental leadership's high standards for her. Hines told me to hang in there because things would get better, and she proceeded to give me her card with contact numbers just in case I needed to call her.

I left Hine's office considering what she had said and feeling dejected. *Is there any truth to what she was saying about Hattie's motivations?* I asked myself. If there was, it still didn't explain Hattie's coldness in our initial interview or her breaking the law by making such a fuss about a simple religious accommodation. Talk about shoddy leadership. Supposedly, she was genuinely concerned about scrutiny of her performance. *If that's true, then why didn't she ask me any questions at the interview to ensure that I had the skills to perform the duties under her leadership?* I thought.

Hattie had explicitly stated that I "was not the one" she wanted to hire. This speaks volumes and certainly had nothing to do with her performance concerns as the ESA director. In my view, it was a personal issue. I wrestled in my mind with what Hines had said, but I couldn't in good faith swallow her explanation.

A few days later, I met with Ethan Willis, the deputy assistant secretary of ESA to discuss the ESA object class realignment. The meeting went well, and after we had concluded, Ethan asked me how things were going in OMAP. Among other things, I told him that it appears that Hattie had been discriminating against me and subjecting me to a hostile work environment, making it difficult for me to perform my job. I mentioned that I was looking for a new job and had an upcoming interview with the Health and Human Services Department. He stated that he knew the person who I would be interviewing with.

After I told Ethan about my upcoming interview, he replied, "I am not going to tell you what to do, but I would hate to see you leave."

I sense the genuineness in his voice and in his demeanor. *How could I leave? I really like my job*, I thought. Ethan also said that he was tired of seeing good people leave the ESA and that he would rather see Hattie leave than see me leave the department. He finally asked me to let him handle the problem—that he was going to do something about my situation.

I agreed, thanked him, and left. Although I did not know what action he would take, he assured me that he would take care of the situation. I believed him and did not pursue any other activity.

Regarding the accountability actions Ethan had taken against Hattie, in his January 30, 2010, affidavit, he said: "Jean Francis did verbally notify me that she was subjected to unwelcome, offensive, and unprofessional behavior by Hattie Browne-Deville. I discussed

Hattie's management style and behavior in her annual and midyear performance review. As a result, I modified her performance standards to hold her accountable."

He further said, "I do not remember if an official management investigation was conducted."

The admission and narrative from Ethan were essential to my story. I believe they explained the actions launched against me in the days, weeks, and months that followed. After meeting with Ethan, I would occasionally pass Hattie in the hallway or run into her in the ladies' room. She would never engage in any meaningful conversation with me, except for a verbal reprimand. Despite poor working conditions, I fully engaged in my work and implemented new ideas and processes to create a better working relationship between the budget office and the programs. The irony was that I enjoyed the responsibilities of my job. For many years, I had been preparing myself educationally and professionally to get to where I was. I was finally there, and I felt accomplished, fulfilling my role with excellence. But my environment under the current leadership was not conducive to my success.

■　■　■

Although the team and I had encountered technical challenges with the new DEBS budget system, we were able to submit my first ESA budget on schedule under my supervision. The staff never had to stay past four thirty to get the budget done because I made sure that we started the process early. After the October 2007 OMB submission, the team and I received favorable comments from everyone except Hattie. These words of encouragement meant a lot to the budget team and me. And I received a signed postcard from the staff that read, "You are the best boss ever; thank you for being such a kind person and awesome boss."

Their words melted my heart. They were some of the best people whom I had worked with, and I greatly appreciated their exceptional work ethic and kind words. A few days later, one of the program managers stopped by my office to say hello and to see how I was doing. It was indeed a nice gesture, in my opinion. We chatted for a while, and as he proceeded to leave, he paused and said, "Thank you for being here; you are truly a breath of fresh air."

I smiled as he walked out the door. At that moment, I believed he understood what I was going through. He wanted to encourage me and let me know I was doing well in his own way. This was a moment of reflection for me.

After the OMB budget submission, the team and I began the planning and execution processes for the Congressional Budget Justification (CBJ) formulation. The OMB process had been seamless with only a few minor hiccups. So, based on lessons learned, the team and I developed a strategic plan to formulate the CBJ in a timely manner.

During this time, I was also planning for the Thanksgiving holiday. This is a time that means a lot to my family and me. It's a time when we feast together, celebrate the things we are thankful for, and share our memories of older generations who have passed on.

This would be my first Thanksgiving holiday in my position with the ESA. Our family get-together on Thanksgiving would be no different than in any from years past. I submitted a leave request in mid-August 2007, which was approved. Then, on November 9, 2007, Hattie forwarded an email threatening to cancel my leave. "If the updated narratives that include the performance data and all the new requirements are not submitted for my review by November 15, your leave will be cancelled."

Never in my eighteen-year career had I received such an aggressive threat. I felt like a kid in high-school rather than a GS-15 budget professional when she issued that unnecessary threat.

One month earlier, I had completed and submitted the OMB budget with no delay or incident. I displayed nothing but professionalism in completing my assigned duties. There were zero legitimate reasons for Hattie to threaten to cancel my leave request.

The thought of my Thanksgiving leave cancelled hung over my head. However, the team and I rose to the challenge. We developed a plan of action for updating the narratives and the performance data for all the new requirements. We involved each of the program office budget analyst to meet with us as we formulated their budget together in DEBS. The process was seamless, completed on time—as it would have been anyway—and we submitted all the documents by the due date. The next budget formulation phase would be in January, and I was confident that it would be just as seamless.

After my work was done, I walked out of my office and out of the Frances Perkins Building. I felt hopeful, ready, and eager to enjoy my Thanksgiving holiday with my family. Despite the challenges of my work life, I still had much to be thankful for!

Chapter 13

Exceptional leaders don't inflict pain, they share pain.

—Max De Pree

On November 11, 2007, Stormi Madison had been hired as my new first-line supervisor to replace Georgia. I looked forward to a great working relationship with her and, hopefully, a better working environment. The following week, I introduced myself and let her know that I was looking forward to working together. Unfortunately, she never shared the same outlook with me but, but I remained positive moving forward.

Stormi was not involved in the budget planning and preparation process in the weeks and months leading up to the upcoming CBJ submission in January. In preparation for the process, my team and I were busy developing the timeline and crafting the directives for the various stakeholders for a seamless, efficient, and effective budget process. On January 9, 2008, I worked with the budget team on completing and submitting the draft CBJ. Unfortunately, the process was such that we were at the mercy of each program submitting its budget on time. As fate would have it, by five thirty—when we were expected to finalize the entire process—the Office of Workers Compensation Programs (OWCP) submission was still outstanding.

I called the program manager who told me that she would get the information to us by close of business. At about six o'clock, we finally received the OWCP submission. Unfortunately, the program manager also indicated that she was leaving for the day. However, she gave me her phone number where she could be reached if there were any problems with the submission.

After the OWCP analyst reviewed the submission, there were discrepancies with some of the numbers for the mandatory accounts. I immediately tried to call the program manager to confirm those numbers and let her know there were discrepancies but could not reach her. This situation was a part of the budget formulation process, particularly when you had to receive numbers from other components. I left a message for the program manager to call us, and we were waiting for her call. At 6:45 p.m., Stormi emerged from her office and said that she had come to check the status of the draft.

The DEBS technician, who was with us during the process, told Stormi that the narrative was good, but they were waiting to verify a few numbers. Other members of the budget team also chimed in by explaining the nature of the dilemma. Stormi seemed unhappy, demanding a draft with no errors. "I don't care what you guys must do. I want a draft done tonight and a copy emailed to me right away!"

Following her outburst, Stormi called me to meet with her in my office and asked for an explanation. I sat in my chair and quietly reiterated what had happened.

Stormi bristled. "Well, I want a draft submitted to me tonight. I don't care what you guys must do to fix the errors! I want it done!"

I responded by inviting her to our next session. This was to educate her on the formulation process and some of the challenges. At this, she leaned over my desk and pointed her right index finger in my face.

"*You* come to *me*! I don't come to you! Do you understand that? And I want a budget done tonight!"

I felt as though I was a second-class citizen. Yelling and putting one's finger in someone else's face in the workplace is bullying behavior and totally unacceptable.

Stormi had been my supervisor for only eight weeks. Barely interacting with me during that time, I was getting everything appropriately done. She had yelled at me and pointed her finger in my face for a situation that was beyond my team's control. I could not help but think that Stormi had an ax to grind or perhaps had been instructed on how to deal with me. I felt as though she had been strategically hand-picked for the job. She had come ready for battle and to do damage.

As financial management director, instead of blowing her top when something went wrong, she should have sought to understand the problem. Furthermore, she should have gotten her hands dirty helping us to solve the problem. Those are the signs of an exceptional leader.

After the January 9 incident, I went to Stormi's office. I addressed her actions regarding yelling at my staff and me and putting her finger in my face. She listened expressionlessly. I continued by saying that I had left that night thinking that I needed to find a new job because my current job wasn't worth the stress and treatment I was experiencing.

Stormi replied, "I walked out of here thinking that you need to leave and find a new job, too." Her reply was not surprising to me, but the words hurt me to the core.

In the following weeks, Stormi persistently told me that she was going to write me up for what had transpired on the evening of January 9, 2008, and that I was "on probation." Finally, on February 7, 2008, ninety days after Stormi had been in the position as my supervisor, she called me to her office for a meeting.

Upon entering her office, she said, "I don't want to do this, but Hattie wants me to. So here we go." She presented me with a memorandum containing a laundry list of "concerns" that had nothing to do with what had occurred on the evening of January 9, 2008.

At the beginning of the meeting, Stormi stated that "Hattie" had wanted her to write me up, although she did not want to, but many of the allegations listed had occurred when Georgia was still my supervisor. Stormi identified her memorandum as a list of "supervisory concerns" that were previously communicated to me. These concerns "were previously communicated by Hattie Browne-Deville, director of the Office of Management, Administration, and Planning."

I concluded that Hattie was making good on her promise that my performance would never be "satisfactory." This was because I had told her that I wasn't willing to come in on my Sabbath, and I had rightfully brought up concerns about her behavior through the proper channels.

The memo listed every alleged and possible incompetence on my part, including my deficiencies in "managing multiple projects at one time, establishing priorities, developing realistic and meaningful plans, preparing detailed written guidance to supplement DBC guidance, making sure that program officials understood what they needed to do, and communication (needs to be automatic)"—just to name a few.

Stormi's laundry list of concerns had nothing to do with her unprofessional outburst in front of the team and disrespectful actions toward me on the evening of January 9, 2008. Moreover, the memorandum served as a reprimand over trivial matters, unwarranted criticism of my work, and issues that had existed before my tenure.

Despite the list of complaints aimed at me, I had not been written up, disciplined, or warned about their so-called poor performance issues at ESA. Instead, the lingering vendetta against me was clearly directed by Hattie who could not come to terms with my decision to hold my ground regarding my Sabbath and reporting her behavior to the proper departments.

After Stormi gave me the memorandum, I called a staff meeting with my team and shared the memo with them. They were shocked to see the allegations I was written up for. The team felt the impact because everyone had worked hard to resolve the issues stated in the memorandum. And this February 7, 2008, memorandum would not be the final memo.

■ ■ ■

My Federal career until this point had been exceptional. But at the DOL, and in less than a year, my career seemed to be moving south. In a hurry. Despite the professional turmoil, there were events that lifted my spirts and elicited smiles and laughter in my personal life. These events created a work-life balance that helped to reduce stress and kept me stable.

One of my favorite events is the annual US Dream Academy, Annual Power of a Dream Gala. The mission of the Academy is to educate, motivate, and encourage youths across America whose parents are incarcerated, to strive in fulfilling their dreams. The Gala is focused on celebrating the accomplishments of the students and faculties of the Dream Academy across the nation. It is also a magnificent opportunity to watch student performances and hear inspirational speeches from dignitaries, government officials, and celebrities who are committed to making a difference in the lives of the youths. And I too was committed in helping to make a difference.

I also had the esteemed opportunity to meet, greet, and take photos with my favorite celebrities and government officials. The Dream Academy Gala was an event that I looked forward to attending each year. It lifted my spirits and elicited smiles and laughter for that one moment in time.

At the end of my workday on May 8, 2008, I attended the 17th Annual Power of a Dream Gala. The theme that year was *Living the Dream—Rising Above the Clouds*. It was a fitting theme, one that helped motivated and inspired me to rise above the cloud of despair that seemed to hang over my head like thunderheads in a storm about to break. As a result, the atmosphere was breathtaking for me and the beam on my face was priceless. That smile did not mean my life was perfect. It meant that despite my workplace difficulties, there were people and events in my life that kept me smiling.

Still, with the exceptional and motivational environment of the Gala, time flew by quickly. Before I knew it, it was the next morning and I had to get back to work. I dreaded it.

Standing next Angela Bassett at the 19th Annual Power of a Dream Gala

Standing with Erica and Tina Campbell at the 8th Annual Dream Academy

Chapter 14

*Whether your workplace is a little toxic or a lot toxic,
you need to take steps to protect your physical, emotional,
and mental well-being. You deserve to be healthy.*

—Sarah Baker

A toxic working environment can affect your health and well-being and erode your self-esteem and confidence. This is because our work and personal lives are intertwined, and how can they not be? Toxic working environments are also linked to lower productivity, increased workplace dissatisfaction, low morale, and high turnover. Hundreds of studies have confirmed all of this. Yet rather than seeking to remedy the toxic environment at the DOL, the US government department set up to be a watchdog over such issues that had begun under Georgia and Hattie, Stormi seemed to be carrying the torch with her hostile and aggressive leadership style.

Less than sixty days into Stormi's tenure, many of the budget staff began the process of leaving ESA. One of them retired without notice, while a couple of others, including the budget team lead, departed by the end of April. But I refused to do the same. I didn't want to allow incompetent and discriminatory supervisors to force me out of my hard-won position and hard-earned career. I may have bent a little, but never would I break.

Under Stormi, the atmosphere in the office became even worse than it had been in the past. Team members were ready to leave because of the injustices that had been launched against me. As a result, my mental and emotional health was affected. I experienced frequent headaches, irritability, depression, and other symptoms of burnout. The stress began to take a toll on my body, and I often visited the employee health clinic at the DOL for migraines. In addition, my primary physician raised eyebrows concerning my elevated high blood pressure and cholesterol levels.

"What is going on in your life?" he asked.

I told him about the stress I was under at work. Then he referred me to an outpatient wellness program at the Walter Reed Medical Center. I attended it until I was no longer in the danger zone of having a stroke because of my high blood pressure and cholesterol levels. I felt like quitting my job, but I would never give Hattie or Stormi that satisfaction. No matter what they threw at me, I was determined not to give up.

My anxiety and depression weren't a sign of my lack of faith. Instead, they were signs of the traumatic events, pain, and anguish I was suffering for absolutely no reason but a petty vendetta. I employed an unrealistic faith posture of hope for Divine intervention each day. As much as I enjoyed performing the duties of my position, it became difficult for me to get out of bed on Monday mornings and report to work. The depression and anxiety had also morphed into episodes of insomnia.

As a result, I was experiencing long, sleepless nights of worry and stress where my mind would go on overdrive. When I was able to fall asleep, I would find myself rattled awake by nightmares and would jump up out of breath, sweating, and screaming. My husband would jump up behind me, hold me, and say, "It's okay, you're just having a nightmare."

With his help, I would get back in bed, hoping for better sleep the remainder of the night.

Throughout those experiences and accompanying emotions, Lionel had been my biggest supporter. We would decompress together on our way home after he picked me up from work. Often, he extended his professional advice to help me figure out how to best cope with what was happening. Our attendance at our church's weekly prayer meeting was an added blessing and it also helped with bolstering my coping mechanism at work. Finally, we also spent time at the gym working out together at least four days a week. What a difference our workouts made!

I was distraught. Mother's Day was approaching, but I barely noticed. On the Friday afternoon before Mother's Day 2018, Lionel picked me up from work. He brought numerous bouquets of roses to cheer me up after a tumultuous day. *What a surprise*! I thought. His smile as I left the building and approached the vehicle was priceless. I beamed back. My heart was filled with gratitude. My husband's caring ways and thoughtfulness not only put a smile on my face but filled my heart with gratitude to last a lifetime.

■ ■ ■

On May 28, 2008, six months after she had become my supervisor, I received a second memorandum from Stormi. She called me into her office for my midyear review. She told me that I was failing in my performance and harshly criticized my work. She said, "You have a lot of talent, but I don't think you are walking on the right career path."

Frankly, I didn't need the likes of Stormi to tell me if I had talent or not. She was unworthy, in my view, to give me or anyone, for that matter, any career advice. I knew my God had given me talents before meeting Stormi. And no one could have taken that knowledge away from me. I perceived that she was using the term *talent* as a backhanded kind of compliment that wasn't actually praise. She just meant, "You had nothing to do with the success here."

Stormi said further, "You plan and bring people together. I think you should pursue a career along those lines because you certainly are not the right fit to be in the budget arena."

What garbage, I thought. I was a better fit in the budget arena at ESA than she had ever been in her position as director of the Division of Financial Management. Here was a woman with poor leadership skills, very poor, who had never had a career meeting with me and who had known me for only six months—and believed that she should give me career advice after treating me like a second-class citizen.

Stormi created division, confusion, and low morale in her leadership role at ESA. She operated much like Hattie, but she was even more brazen. For example, her May 28 memorandum documenting my performance issues listed the same false allegations that had been included in her February 7 memo.

"This information is being provided to you so that you are clear on what the specific concerns are and can work toward correcting them if you are allowed to continue as branch chief of budget formulation and implementation," she said.

Stormi liked to remind me that I was on probation at regular intervals, as if to mock me, and our work relationship continued to deteriorate. She would frequently raise her voice at me to get her point across in our exchanges. While there were a few times when we sat and had a civilized conversation in her office, if Hattie were to stop by, her demeanor would change toward me instantaneously.

When Hattie was present, if I opened my mouth to make a statement on the issue discussed, Stormi would give a puzzled look as if I was speaking another language. She would ask, "What is she saying?" But of course, this was only if we were meeting with Hattie. If we were alone in her office, this was never the case.

Occasionally, she would work on her church program on her work computer in the evenings, struggling with using various components of Microsoft Word. She would often call me to render assistance while Lionel sat patiently in his car, waiting for me to finish helping her. Interestingly, when she needed my help, she always understood what I was saying.

Most of my original team members had moved on because of the caustic environment. There was only one budget analyst left on the team. To say that I was on the lookout for a new job would be an understatement. I had been looking for a new job since the second week of my tenure with DOL ESA. However, with only a "meets expectations" performance appraisal for my first year with ESA, it was challenging to compete with other GS-15s who were rated "highly effective" or "exceeds expectations."

On October 27, 2008, Stormi called me into her office and presented me with my performance appraisal. She had asked me to submit my performance assessment one week before the delivery. She had used the information to develop the appraisal. The only element I exceeded was about the departmental e-budget system, for which she had written me up several times throughout the year, even when we were no longer formulating the budget. She rated all the other elements as "meets expectations," which is like getting a C in school.

In the appraisal, she talked about my needing to become more engaged in the budget process to be "respected" as a branch chief. I was flabbergasted by the statement. But, coming from an individual who helped to create an environment that was always critical of my work, I brushed it off and kept moving. I didn't know who they thought I was, but I knew—and that mattered.

Stormi and Hattie were the only ones who didn't respect me as a person and branch chief. Their exaggerations and meritless criticisms showed their determination to drive me out. It was in this environment that I would perpetually remind myself that despite my unfortunate conditions, winter would always give way to spring!

It was a big surprise when Lionel greeted me with two bouquets of flowers. It was like springtime after leaving the office. Despite my struggles, I was truly blessed with a husband who loves and thinks about me

Chapter 15

People don't leave because of bad jobs.
They leave because of bad bosses and poor management
who doesn't appreciate their value.

—Bhola Das

By October 2008, with only one budget analyst left on the team, I worked with HR to fill the vacancies. I encouraged Tera Coleman, the only budget analyst left, to apply for the lead analyst position. I believed she was a good candidate and was knowledgeable of day-to-day operations and the budget process. After Stormi and I interviewed the other candidates, Claude Pierre was selected for the position. Stormi had met Claude before the interview, and she was adamant about him filling the position.

I was given no say in the matter. Only after I had done all the work to ensure that the recruitment process was on track, developed job analyst position descriptions, and scheduled the candidates for their interviews did Stormi even take an interest in who would fill the position.

As the branch chief, I had been robbed of the autonomy to make recommendations or decide who was the best fit for the position to work with me as team lead. When I made recommendations about a particular candidate, Stormi would say, "I don't like him because he talks too much," or "I don't think she is a good candidate because she didn't assert herself enough." She oversaw the selection process and had the final say about who was offered the position. Hence, Claude was selected as the best fit.

I was not content with the selection because I believed that Tera Coleman was the strongest candidate. Tera was devastated when she learned that she had not been chosen. During a discussion after the selection process, she said she had thought about filing an EEO complaint regarding the hiring process. However, she decided not to do so. I was empathetic because I wanted her to fill in the position, but Stormi had the last word.

Claude reported for duty as the new budget analyst team lead on October 14, 2008. Our working relationship was very strained for the first two and a half months. Claude should have been my closest ally in getting work done and managing the team. However, I got little support or cooperation from him. The previous lead budget analyst, Chad Everette, had been careful to meet with me and update me on ongoing issues. He ensured that I was kept abreast of every action and data-call to be completed or needed my attention. We had an exceptional working relationship.

This wasn't the case with Claude. Most of his time was spent in Stormi's office working with her and performing other assignments she had given him to do, as if she wanted to isolate him from me. When I confronted him on various tasks deserving of his attention, he would say, "I am working with Stormi." And my religion was still at the forefront of conversations. Stormi alluded to that in a meeting with Claude early in his tenure.

"Are you one of those who can't work on Friday evenings and Saturdays?" she asked him.

In response, he replied: "No."

■ ■ ■

During the period of October 14 through November 22, 2008, Claude and Tera were the only analysts on my team. The ESA and the program offices didn't have to formulate an OMB or CBJ budget submission because the department was on a continuing resolution during an election year. This extra time allowed me to update and develop ESA's standing operational procedures and continue working on filling the other vacant positions. I was still enrolled in my doctoral degree program. I was scheduled well in advance to be on leave for residency training during the week of the scheduled interviews. Stormi didn't want to schedule the interviews for when I returned, so she and Claude handled them all in my absence.

I returned from residency training and was notified that three new budget analysts had been selected. After receiving their names and contact information, I called each new hire to welcome them to the position. I also developed an orientation packet for each employee. The packet consisted of a welcome letter, a copy of the phone book, the internal training schedule, analyst assignment, and other information I thought might be useful to get them up to speed. Once they were officially on board, I met with each individual one-on-one to discuss expectations, among other things. Then I provided them with their individual performance plans.

The new team was getting acquainted as the days turned into weeks and weeks turned into months. President Obama was elected as the new president, and we were preparing to collaborate with the new administration. However, even with the new team of budget analysts in place and the new administration on the way, the working environment did not improve. Claude's account from his EEO Investigative Affidavit transcript of December 21, 2009, is as follows:

Investigator: "Did you spend most of your time working with Ms. Stormi Madison and/or did she give you your assignments? If so, did Ms. Madison tell you why she did this? If so, what did she tell you?"

Mr. Pierre: "I did spend some of my time working with Ms. Madison on certain issues such as the Working Capital Fund. Ms. Madison bypassed Mrs. Francis in assigning things for me to do. It was a challenging situation for me to be in."

Investigator: "Did you assist in interviewing and hiring?"

Mr. Pierre: "Yes, I did assist in interview and hiring . . . Mrs. Francis was not involved because she was on leave. Ms. Madison asked me to help with the hiring process. And I did. It was my first week of employment, and I did what I was told to do. It wasn't until much later that I realized and understood that I was being used by Ms. Madison. It was due to the friction between my supervisor, Mrs. Francis, and her supervisor, Ms. Madison."

The frictions were indeed intensifying. I was utterly demoralized by the situation. It caused severe disruptions in every aspect of my life, far beyond the workplace. Even when I was at home having conversations with my loved ones, I could not stop thinking about all the sundry problems at work. My insomnia and nightmares continued, and I even began sleepwalking. I experienced intense anxiety and increased high-blood pressure, and I felt emotionally distanced from Lionel. I also developed a binge-eating disorder, and on Sunday evenings, as I anticipated returning to work the next morning, I would have the desire to eat every hour on the hour. Not because I was hungry, but to deaden the thought of going back to work at the DOL ESA. Unsurprisingly, my cholesterol level skyrocketed.

My husband, meanwhile, had trouble finding stable employment after retiring from the military and a reorganization of his company. Hence, quitting abruptly wasn't an option because I had to support my family. I continued to hunt for and apply for new jobs, but I didn't see results fast enough. Due to changes that came with the new presidential administration, Ethan Willis was preparing to leave the department as deputy assistant secretary because he was a political appointee.

On his last day with the department in January 2009, he visited the ESA budget team and the leadership to say his goodbyes. He stopped by my office to wish me the best. It was sad to see him go, but I believe that having worked with him had been a gift, even for a short time. He was the best leader that I had met during my tenure with the DOL.

I had submitted my request to take leave for my next residency training during the first week of April, at the beginning of January 2009. My request for leave was approved. Therefore, the team and I should have engaged with the CBJ budget development process during the first week of January 2009. However, it was difficult to determine when that would be because of the new administration. So, we waited patiently for the budget office's news about when the CBJ was due. In the meantime, I was eagerly helping to prepare the new team for the challenges of formulating its first ESA budget. However, this was not a smooth process because of Stormi's constant interruptions.

■ ■ ■

There was confusion and division developing among the newly formed budget team during this time. At one point, Stormi called me into her office to say that the team members had complained that they were not getting proper guidance and training from me, implying that I was not doing my job. My first thought was, *Why are the team members complaining to Stormi without first approaching me directly with their concerns?*

At our staff meeting, I asked the team about this, and no one seemed to have any idea as to what I was referring. Before I came to DOL ESA, there was no internal training offered to budget analysts at all. This was discussed as a concern at the interview with the team, and I indicated that if I was hired, I would implement internal training, which I ultimately did. This would be a courtesy to the team and not to relieve the agency from its obligation to develop a budget for employee training and development.

During an election year, new staff came on board; hence, the team engaged in training on a host of topics because there was no budget formulation from November 2008 through January 2009. As the team completed the training, I developed the standard operating procedures for each topic. Each topic was either facilitated or presented by me, a budget analyst with expertise on the topic, or a subject-matter expert from another department.

The internal training provided the new analysts with the

necessary tools to be successful in their new roles. In addition, it helped them cement their knowledge on the topics and ESA business processes. Nothing like this had ever existed before I became branch chief for the ESA/OMAP. So, for Stormi to claim that I had not trained the staff was nothing short of ludicrous.

In my view, this was nothing more than a strategic attack against me, and it seemed as though I was a target for the enemy. The retaliation was now on full speed ahead no matter how much it veered from reality on the ground.

Chapter 16

In weak companies, politics win.
In strong companies, the best ideas do.

—Steve Jobs

On January 12, 2009, immediately after Ethan Willis left the department, Claude came to my office and told me that Stormi wanted him to keep her informed on my activities and bring her everything that I gave him to work on, daily. I wasn't surprised. I felt that Claude wasn't the only team member Stormi had asked to take back information about me to her. For example, after I had meetings with Tera Coleman, she would go directly to Stormi's office and brief her on the discussion. At first, I couldn't blame them. They wanted to avoid her wrath and keep their jobs. Claude had been very professional in coming to me. But that is not how you run a successful department.

During the following weeks and months, I noticed that Tera would prepare apportionments and leave out numbers or mistype the numbers. Finally, about the second week of February 2009, she prepared an apportionment for my signature. After reviewing the document, I pointed out some corrections that needed to be made. She returned the folder to me saying that she had made the corrections. When I checked the document, she had corrected the errors I had identified; however, there were other changes to the numbers in the document.

I questioned Tera as to why I was still getting a document with incorrect numbers. She took the folder from me and said, "Oh, here is the right one. I gave you the wrong one."

Apparently, Tera had the correct apportionment document on her desk. However, she gave me the wrong document to sign, perhaps knowing that the numbers were incorrect. I feared that the strategy was that if I wasn't careful in reviewing the documents, Stormi would catch the error or errors.

That would become another reason to say that I wasn't checking the work of my employees thoroughly. I questioned Tera as to why she would have two folders with the same document and just happened to give me the incorrect version and had the correct version on her desk in a folder. She could not explain it.

On February 25, 2009, I asked all the team members to provide updates relating to narrative and numbers for their respective programs. I requested the information at or around nine thirty with an expected response from all team members no later than two o'clock. I reminded the staff around noon. This information was necessary to complete and submit the monthly forecast. However, when I asked Tera for the information at or around two, she still had not updated and submitted the information that was necessary to complete the report.

When I asked why the information was incomplete and late, Tera told me it was because she had been working on a project with Stormi for most of the day. This is just one example of how Stormi would assign the staff to work on other projects without my knowledge.

Shortly after that, I conducted a staff meeting in the conference room and addressed specific items with each team member. When it was Tera's turn, I asked her about the status of the update that was due at two and why I had not received the information knowing that the forecast was due to be given to Stormi at the end of the day.

Tera began shouting at me in front of the other team members, saying, 'Don't talk to me like that, Jean. I was working all day with Stormi on a project, and I can only do one thing at a time!"

Tera had become very disrespectful during the meeting. At the end of the meeting, I asked her to stay to discuss the outburst. I had no idea that she was working on other assignments with Stormi. It had become clear that she had developed a close relationship with Stormi—ironic given that she had passed her up for a promotion.

I feared that Tera was working in concert with Stormi to develop a case against me to remove me from my position. She used Claude to report my daily activities to her, and I suspected that Tera fed damaging information about me to Stormi, who would turn around and use that information against me in closed-door meetings.

During some of my staff meetings, Stormi would open the door abruptly, interrupt the meeting and create unnecessary distractions. In addition, she would call on various team members to leave the meeting and perform other tasks without my approval. Her actions in front of the staff displayed utter disrespect and a lack of professionalism.

On one hand, Stormi would complain that the meetings were too long and that I needed to set up timeframes to end the meetings; on the other hand, she complained that I wasn't guiding the staff—a staff consisting of highly paid GS-12-13, and -14s. In addition, Stormi would raise her voice to me during the staff meetings on miniscule budgetary issues. In Claude's EEO Investigative Affidavit of December 21, 2009, he gave the following account of the interruptions and insults of Stormi toward me that were witnessed by him.

Investigator: "Did Ms. Madison ever interrupt or distract any of the complainant's staff meetings and/or did she ever tell staff to leave meetings and perform other tasks?"

Mr. Pierre: "I remember being pulled by Ms. Madison during staff meetings conducted by Mrs. Francis. I do not remember the exact date(s). However, I would say between January and March 2009."

Investigator: "Complainant claims that she was subjected to conduct or behavior that constitutes a hostile work environment. Other than as previously described, have you witnessed any incidents or actions or behavior directed toward the complainant that would constitute a hostile work environment?"

Mr. Pierre: "I witnessed Ms. Madison shout angrily at Mrs. Francis during one of our staff meetings in front of the staff concerning some budget issues. Mrs. Francis was hurt and humiliated. Mrs. Francis went to her office and shut the door."

■ ■ ■

Stormi's behavior made doing my job to the best of my ability impossible. The former and current teams weren't the only ones who noticed how I was being treated; I even hear from others who worked outside ESA that they had knowledge what was happening to me.

In addressing the conditions, Joy Rose from human resources stated in her March 16, 2009, email, "I've been thinking about you all day because of the unfair treatment you received. Hang in there and stay mentally positive. It will all work out. You need to start looking for a new job because this type of harassment will hurt/stop you from furthering your career." Yet another individual who served as a director for one of the program offices engaged me in a conversation with him one day and said, "I am aware of how you are being treated in ESA. But don't worry. Just remember that every dog has its day." He caught me by surprise. I had no idea that he was apprised of my situation. His words are still etched in my memory.

I tried to stay positive. However, no amount of positivity could change the fact that I was trapped in a completely dysfunctional working environment. I reminded myself each day that problems such as these never come to stay; they come to pass. And with each new day, I constantly hoped that this problem would come to pass soon.

Stormi immediately fired Claude when he told her that he would refrain from reporting my activities to her. I was Claude's first-line supervisor and had no idea Stormi was considering terminating Pierre's employment for alleged "poor performance." I was stunned when he told me that she had abruptly fired him. Claude had only been with the ESA/DOL for five months, and in my view didn't deserve to be fired.

At the DOL, these are the leadership behaviors that seemed acceptable and were protected. Yet, even more appallingly, these were people in government positions whose salaries were being funded by taxpayer dollars precisely to prevent such issues from occurring in other workplaces.

Indeed, as Peter Drucker declares, "a bad leader can take a good staff and destroy it, causing the best employees to flee and the remainder to lose all motivation." Unfortunately, this is precisely what I experienced at the DOL/ESA.

Chapter 17

Sometimes doing a good job at work is like wetting your pants in a dark suit—you get a warm feeling, but nobody else notices.

—Author unknown

On March 12, 2009, Stormi presented me with a notice of intent to place me on a Performance Improvement Plan (PIP). On one hand, I wasn't surprised, given that she constantly criticized my performance. On the other hand, in my previous performance review, from October 2008, Hattie and Stormi had rated my performance in all elements as "meets expectations." Since the last review, I had not received a cautionary notice about my performance, so there was no supporting evidence to justify a PIP in less than five months.

Stormi stated in the PIP that I was failing in leadership, problem-solving, and budget execution. However, her feedback was very vague and not supported by evidence. For example, she didn't explain in what areas of leadership I was ostensibly failing. Nor did she provide examples on the areas of problem-solving or budget execution in which I was failing. Moreover, since we had been operating under a continuing resolution (CR) during the period since my review and spending was at a minimum, there was no budget execution exercise to fail.

The memorandum also warned that Stormi would assess my performance after the PIP. That might result in my removal or a reduction in grade without further opportunity to demonstrate acceptable performance. It was extremely upsetting to read Stormi's claims in the PIP that I was "failing" in my role. However, I knew this had been a long time coming. Since Ethan Willis's departure, they had been preparing to go full throttle in removing me from my position as branch chief. As Stormi would tell Tera Coleman over the phone one day in April 2009, "Change is coming."

I believe that Hattie and Stormi, with Tera's help, were plotting to get rid of me. It had been set in motion at the very beginning of my tenure at the DOL. The glaring lack of evidence to support the allegations in the PIP was enough to make me feel justified that I had done absolutely nothing to deserve their actions against me.

I prepared a memorandum and attached supporting documentation to the proposed PIP in response. However, neither Stormi nor Hattie acknowledged my response or asked for a meeting to discuss the issues of concern to me. In my response, I stated that I believe the real reason for the "strategic" PIP was not because of alleged performance issues. Instead, it was retaliation against me and a precursor to withholding my within-grade increase, which was due on June 7, 2009.

■ ■ ■

On Friday, April 3, 2009, I organized a staff meeting with the team to discuss deadlines and assignments for the upcoming FY 2010 CBJ Budget Formulation. We had just received notice that the budget was due on April 15, and I was to be on leave the following week. The meeting was thoroughly comprehensive. Actions included assigning ownership of each budget section to an analyst, reviewing and completing the Budget in Brief (BIB), and developing a deadline schedule for the budget process. This information was sent to the ESA budget team and to Stormi.

The following week I was out of the office on leave. On April 13, 2009, I returned intending to review the comprehensive budget before submitting to the DBC on April 15. Unfortunately, despite the detailed timeline that I discussed with the team and forwarded to Stormi, many of the program offices had not submitted their requested data, to my astonishment. This was extremely problematic because a first draft was due in two days. Now the timeline would be impossible to meet.

Based on past experiences and the fact that I was now on "probation" per the PIP, I knew this meant trouble. And sure enough, I was blamed for not submitting the budget on time. Even though Stormi, the ESA financial manager, should have overseen the budget team and made sure they and the program offices adhered to the established deadlines in my absence.

In truth, the buck stopped with Stormi to ensure the deadlines were met in my absence. It seemed to be that those deadlines were being ignored to make it look like I had failed to submit my budget on time. I was convinced that I was being scapegoated, and felt further alienated by others in the department.

On the afternoon of May 7, 2009, around four thirty, Stormi stormed into my office as I was packing up to leave for the day. She had a piece of paper in her hand and said, "I know you are trying to get out of here, but I just wanted to give you this before you leave."

She threw the sheet of paper at me, and it landed on my desk as she left my office. Her conduct was incredibly offensive, but it didn't surprise me by now. I picked up the sheet of paper and read it—a memo from Hattie and Stormi stating that I would not be receiving the standard within-grade increase for my position that was due on June 8. Vague, as always, the reason for their denial was that it was "based on the fact my current level of performance at that time was unsatisfactory." I was not surprised. I had raised this issue as a concern in my response to the PIP.

However, I stood there in amazement. Instead of having a conversation with me as to why my wage increase was being withheld, she treated me with utter disrespect in how she delivered the memorandum. Moreover, I had never in my career been denied a wage-grade-increase.

It seemed incredibly unjust that I should be denied an increase six months after a performance appraisal. I was rated "meets expectations" in all areas. The PIP was presented to me on March 17, 2009, and lasted for ninety days. It had stated that "to be granted a within-grade increase, you must improve your performance to at least the 'effective' level." Still, I had not yet had another review since the October 2008 review. I was bewildered beyond words. Yet, this seemed to validate my fear that my tenure was threatened ever since the day I would not come in on my Sabbath.

Chapter 18

*Your value doesn't decrease based on someone's
inability to see your worth.*
—Author unknown

Stormi had indicated that we would meet every week while I was
on the PIP. I obliged. I also expected that, in these meetings, we would
discuss an individual development plan that identified the specific areas
I needed to work on and a system or scale for gauging my improvement
on those areas. Our first meeting was scheduled on May 25, 2009, at
noon. I told Stormi that noon was when I usually took lunch, and I
asked her if she would be willing to schedule the meeting at some other
time.

She became angry at my request and said, "Excuse me?" This was
an indication that she would not change the time of the meeting, and
she did not.

The meetings turned out to be meaningless at best. There was no
organization to these meetings or discussion of the elements outlined
in the PIP. Stormi would begin each meeting by saying, "I don't know
what we are going to do, Jean, because you are failing in the PIP."

She began to sound like a broken record, and it was hard to keep
a straight face. Puzzled with furrowed eyebrows of concern, I would
respond by asking her, "How does one fail a PIP and what measures will
you be using to help me to rise to the level you are expecting from me?"

Her response was always the same: "These meetings."

Then I would roll my eyes at the foolishness that I had just heard.

■ ■ ■

On May 29, 2009, Stormi came into my office holding the leave slip
for my upcoming leave, from June 8 through June 19. She placed it on

my desk and proceeded to say, "Your leave is through the nineteenth and that is when your PIP ends. We don't know what we are going to do because you are failing the PIP." She walked out of my office after making this statement.

There was no discussion of specific expectations for my improvement in our weekly PIP meeting, so it was unclear by what standards I was "failing" the PIP. Furthermore, there were no opportunities in these meetings for me to share my views or address any of the work-related issues that I believed were at stake. As far as I was concerned, the entire PIP was phony because of the vague and unclear statements about what I needed to do to improve and the lack of a tangible measure of my progress.

As the end date of my PIP approached, I was uncertain of my status, aside from Stormi's constant refrain that I was "failing the PIP." Finally, she told me that I was approved to attend some "training," however, there were no guidance on the training I should take. Hence, I enrolled and attended an introductory supervisory course that was available the first week of June. Then I headed off on my two-weeks of leave. This would be a time to intentionally search for new employment and get away from the chaos with my family on vacation.

■ ■ ■

Our vacations were positive and pleasant experiences for me and my family. They not only built memories for a lifetime, but they also helped us break away from the usual routine and open our minds to new cultures, foods, and experiences. At DOL, family vacation was one of the rays of sunshine that helped to lift my spirit and elicit smiles and laughter.

Orlando, Florida was our favorite family vacation spot since our kids were young. They were never tired of going to Disney. However, as they grew older, like all kids, our children outgrew things. As a result, the family decided to vacation in Las Vegas that year.

There were plenty of fun things to do with the kids even in a city built for adults, in planning our family-friendly vacation in Las Vegas. We visited the beautiful Bellagio Conservatory and Botanical Gardens, attended the tribute show *Michael Jackson One* by Cirque Du Soliel, and visited the Hoover Dam, just to name a few. Our children enjoyed their vacation to the fullest, and as a family, we had the time of our lives.

Our vacation was exceptional, and I did not want it to come to an end. The thought of returning to OMAP/ESA weighed heavily on my heart. But it was a two-week break in which I experienced pure joy and happiness with my family.

Before the training course and leave, sixty days of the ninety-day PIP had passed. I had hoped to get another job offer during the PIP period. I knew it would be impossible to dig myself out of a hole with Stormi and Hattie. However, an offer did not materialize. Following my leave time and a wonderful vacation with my family, I could barely bring myself to return to work. At this point, I hated to even see the building.

Our Vegas family Vacation

Chapter 19

No one should be singled out for unfair treatment or unkind words because of his or her ethnic background or religious faith.

—George W. Bush

On June 22, 2009, I returned to the office and spent the day responding to emails and catching up on other office duties. The office environment was quieter than usual, but I thought nothing of it. Stormi came to my office at four thirty and invited me to the conference room. When I walked into the conference room, Hattie was seated there already. I took a seat, and Stormi proceeded to tell me that I had failed in the PIP. Hattie interjected and said, "We're moving you out of your supervisory position. You'll be reassigned immediately to a non-supervisory position as a special assistant."

I was devastated, numb, and nauseated by this news. I watched Hattie across the table, and she looked gratified that she had succeeded in demoting me in a career that I had worked for years to build. Then, adding insult to injury, Hattie said that I should vacate my office and move into a cubicle that was already prepared for me and located in front of her office door. Imagine that! Words can never humanly describe what I felt when I heard those words. She also stated that she would consider including a door to the cubicle for my "privacy."

The reassignment to this position was significantly different, with little or no responsibilities. Hattie and Stormi's decision to demote me would have resounding effects on my career for years to come. But Stormi had no evidence to substantiate the claims of poor performance, and she would even admit this herself later. In her EEO response to the Investigative Affidavit of January 30, 2010, Stormi gave the following response.

Investigator: "Do you have any additional information or documents that are relevant to the issues of this EEO complaint and/or Complainant's claim of discrimination and hostile work environment? If so, provide a copy of those documents with an explanation of each."

Ms. Madison: "Unfortunately, I do not have access to many of the files or my emails since the abolishment of ESA. However, I believe that the following individuals can directly attest to the Complainant's performance deficiencies: Tera Coleman— formerly the senior budget analyst BBFI; Doreen Barker— formerly the Deputy Director of OMAP; George Hunter— Formerly ESA's DBC budget analyst. All three employees are still with the Department of Labor."

■ ■ ■

In my position as a special assistant, GS-15, my primary job was to check and print her calendar daily and do other assorted administrative tasks. This was not even a task that I'd been asked to do for my supervisor as a secretary, GS-5. I had never been so humiliated in my life. It was God's favor that followed me through my career. It was His favor that brought me to DOL/ESA. And I was confident that, despite of my current situation, His favor would follow me for the rest of my life. That day, they may have taken my job but not my favor.

Before the demotion and reassignment, I had already met with Maribel Foster with the DOL Civil Rights Office regarding filing an EEO complaint. After discussing the issues, Ms. Foster had told me that I needed to file a complaint immediately. In addition, she provided me with the necessary documents to start the process. But I still wasn't ready at that point. However, my demotion and removal from my office on June 22, 2009, gave me the motivation I needed to begin the EEO complaint process.

Before attempting to file the EEO complaint, I conferred with

Samantha White, Esq., and shared my story to get her perspective from an attorney's point of view. She listened carefully, reviewed my documents, and encouraged me to proceed with my EEO complaint. First, however, she said, "They'll say you had poor performance." Of course, they would, but they had little documentation to prove it. But they would find other means, I was warned.

She was correct in her assessment. But she also said subsequently, in a card she sent me for encouragement: "I can't wait to see what God is going to do for you." I never forgot that note from her, and I am still waiting for the opportunity to give her a good report.

In the following days and weeks, colleagues were shocked to see me working in a cubicle in front of Hattie's office. Hattie and Stormi, however, seemed pleased with their little accomplishment. They would often walk by my cubicle together joking and laughing, sometimes heading to midday religious services. As a GS-15, my workload had drastically decreased, and I was bored and unchallenged, but I refused to be defeated. Defeat is not how my story ends.

The prospect of no longer having to deal with Stormi seemed like a plus, and I was always professional in my daily dealings with Hattie. One of my favorite Bible verses is Mathew 5:44 that says, "But I say unto you, Love your enemies, bless them that curse you, do good to them that hate you, and pray for them which despitefully use you, and persecute you."

It was difficult, but God gave me the strength to do just that. I didn't know how He was going to fix my situation, but I was confident in my unrealistic faith that He would.

■ ■ ■

I began the process of filing my EEO complaint the first week of July 2009, which would start with an informal complaint before moving to a formal filing. One month later, the entire OMAP staff was asked to meet in the DOL auditorium for a meeting. Everyone was whispering as to what the meeting with the OMAP staff could be about. As the meeting convened, it seemed as though everyone was on pins and needles.

The facilitator greeted the crowd and proceeded to announce the decision to abolish ESA/OMAP. There were sounds of surprise and concerns that rose from the crowd. I sat in silence and heard Stormi asked vehemently, "Who made the decision?"

The department heads decided that all ESA/OMAP employees would be reassigned to new offices in the next ninety days. In addition, Hattie was to be reassigned to the Chicago office. God had moved quickly and in a phenomenal way, but this move would not end my fiery furnace experience at the DOL—not by a long shot.

As I waited for my new office assignment, my informal EEO complaint was in full swing. Johnathan Able, deputy assistant secretary for operations, ESA, met with me regularly. He was aware of the difficulties I had encountered with the managers of my former office. He was also interested in seeing if there could be a settlement to my informal complaint. There were three remedies I requested at a minimum.

The first was to change my job title and position back to budget analyst, a career path I had trained in and had many years of experience doing. The second was the removal of the PIP and records of poor performance from my personnel files. The third was overturning of the decision of withholding my within-grade increase. He said that he would see what he could do to get me back on the budget path.

A week later, Johnathan emailed me saying that "You are back in budget." Unfortunately, he also noted that he was unsure if he could retroactively provide me with my within-grade increase. Still, he would be able to give me a financial payout of $6,000 as a settlement for my within-grade increase.

However, despite the communication between me and Johnathan on behalf of ESA, an informal resolution to my complaint was not achieved. Therefore, I elected not to settle and to move forward with a formal EEO complaint for discrimination and retaliation. If I did not win my case, at least I would have the option of sharing my story with the world in the hopes of affecting change in other organizations. To this end, I was the author of my own story, and I was not finished writing yet!

Chapter 20

Everything in life happens for a reason, no matter how
hard or how unfair it may be.
Something better will always come out of it.

—Nishan Panwar

Next to your home, the workplace is where you spend most of your time. I had always taken an enormous amount of pride in my work. I was anything but an employee who clocked in and out every day just for the paycheck. My work was significant to me. As a result, my treatment at work was extremely painful, with effects that went far beyond a stalled career. I became depressed, unable to enjoy anything in my life, and this was hard on my family, especially Lionel. There were times I just did not want to participate in family activities. There was always so much to process in my mind.

The physical and mental health issues stemming from my stress at work were severe, and I sought professional help. I was prescribed medications for anxiety and sleep, and I was keeping my appointments with the Integrated Cardiac Health Program at Walter Reed Army Medical Center. They assisted me with stress reduction, exercise, and healthy eating. The Church was also a source of inspiration and solace in these difficult times—a welcome reprieve from the draining routine of my stressful lifestyle paired with the pressure to live up to responsibilities and success.

My grandmother had taught me early in life that one's church family can be a great support system for getting through difficult situations, a second family. In my adult life, I found this to be especially true. Whenever I experienced a tough week at work, the pastor's message on Saturday seemed to speak directly to my situation. It appeared that God knew just what I needed to get through each week, and I would leave church empowered and ready to tackle another work week.

There is a saying: "True friends aren't the ones who make your problems disappear. They're the ones who won't disappear when you're facing problems."

I met my friend Joy early in my tenure at the DOL, and she had proven to be that kind of friend to me. She was my sounding board when I wanted to share my work experiences, always taking the time to listen and always ready with invaluable advice. She was also my jogging partner during my morning exercise.

Joy had an effervescent personality, and she would invite me to attend Zumba class with her regularly. I could never keep up with her energy on the Zumba floor, but we had a blast. We would also schedule morning workouts together before work, which were true stress busters. I thank God I had a friend like Joy during this journey. She was indeed a blessing!

In addition to outside interests and friendship, my home was my sanctuary from the work environment. Lionel and my children helped me cope with stress and anxiety. They filled my life with joy, laughter, and love. Lionel regularly organized family activities such as kayaking, Mother's Day dining outs, birthday celebrations, and vacation trips—just to name a few. There was never a dull moment when we get together as a family. And it was with my family that I found comfort, belonging, solace, and understanding in my time of need.

Lionel loves to fish. "Fishing is a means of getting away from everything and enjoying uninterrupted conversation" he often says. Fishing was not my forte. "I don't have a single patient bone in me for fishing," I'd usually reply. One fine morning during this time, I ventured to accompany Lionel on a fishing trip with friends.

I wanted to experience the hype, and I also considered it a date. As a quintessential city girl who couldn't tell a rockfish from a croaker, I learned a lot about fishing that day, catching my first fish—it was a rock. Although Lionel caught a bigger fish, mine was the biggest fish that I had every caught. I must admit, after that experience, fishing is a fun filled activity. It was also a stress buster. I am a witness that with family in your life, in the difficult moments, you never imagine anything better.

■ ■ ■

In July 2009, I filed a formal EEO complaint with the DOL against Hattie Browne-Deville. It was for her violation of "Title VII of the Civil Rights Act of 1964, 42 USC. § 2000e, *et seq.* ("Title VII"). This title makes it unlawful for an employer to fire or discriminate against an employee because of the employee's race, gender, national origin, or religion. 2000e–2(a)(1)."

My complaint also addressed the personal vendettas of Georgia and Stormi. It seemed blatant to me that Stormi persistently wrote me up for alleged poor performance issues, threatening my position as a form of retribution.

These actions and behaviors had caused irreparable harm to my career and professional reputation. Individuals inside and outside of OMAP/ESA, including many of my subordinates, were empathetic to my situation and often provided words of encouragement and compliments that helped me get through this challenging period. There were days when I wanted more than anything to give up the fight, but my unrealistic faith in God—a faith that releases me from the power of life's limitations—kept me grounded. I strongly believed that nothing they did to me would keep me from my purpose. And I was comforted by this belief. A member of the HR staff stopped and talked with me briefly one day and said unequivocally, "Don't let them get away with this." I assured her that I wouldn't.

In my formal EEO complaint, as remedies to the specific actions against me, I requested the following:

1. Restoration of my job title as supervisory budget analyst and transfer out of the agency immediately.

2. Restoration of my step-increase retroactive to June 7, 2009, with interest.

3. Expunging of all performance appraisals and negative information related to ESA OMAP signed by Ms. Hattie Browne-Deville, Ms. Georgia Payne, or Ms. Stormi Madison.

4. An award of compensatory damages in the maximum reasonable amount for the humiliation, stress, emotional pain and suffering, loss of enjoyment of life, and damage to reputation endured during the discrimination, harassment, and hostile working environment.

■ ■ ■

Despite my situation, I continued to perform my job to the best of my abilities. Fearlessly. Because as someone once said, "You strike a woman, you strike a rock." In this regard, I am a warrior for justice to the end. I have a strong fighting spirit hardwired in my DNA. I gain strength from knowing that my ancestors struggled and survived against much worse atrocities that threatened to destroy them. But they never give up. In his book *Thou Who Hath Brought Us . . .*, Charles Edward Dudley, Sr. gives this account of various institutional struggles before Emancipation in the United States:

> The institution of slavery robbed the Black man of many things, to include a place to call home, dignity and self-worth, his health, the opportunity to learn, and his worship. His will was broken, and his sense of pride was taken. He suffered heart ailments, stroke, and affliction because of hours in the field under the scorching sun, learning to eat almost anything to survive. He was kept in ignorance by laws that denied him the right to learn to read, to

write, and to count. Finally, the religion of his homeland was characterized as heathen, demonic, and superstitious in nature; thus, it was outlawed. These practices were used to keep slaves subdued and subjugated, yet they survived.

Compared to my ancestors, I have lived a relatively easy and wonderful life before my tenure at the DOL. Although the details of their challenges are different from mine, there were common principles. At the DOL and in the twenty-first century, I was confronted with many of the same challenges. In some ways, the challenges were just as oppressive.

According to Dr. Edward Judson, "Suffering and success go together. If you succeed without suffering, it is because someone else had suffered before you. If you suffer without succeeding, it is so that someone else may succeed after you."

I didn't see any change in my fight for justice. However, like my ancestors, I believed that my workplace fight was not just for me. It was about making a difference and leaving a better place for the next generation. Change doesn't happen overnight, but change will come, with unrealistic faith, tenacity, and a fighting spirit. I truly believed that. Let me share with you one of my secrets for keeping hope alive in my situation.

I specifically remember one day in the office when the tension in the work environment had become increasingly pervasive and before I filed my informal EEO complaint, I thought that it was not worth the stress to continue working at DOL ESA another day. I had decided in my heart that I would leave for the day and never return. I sat at my desk in prayer and deep thoughts.

There was a knock at the door. Elaine, who was one of the budget analysts, had decided to stop by my office to visit. We talked. I shared my agony with her. Then she said, "I want you to go home. Get into your closet, close the door, and spend some time there meditating before you make any decisions." I told her that I would.

I don't remember getting into my closet and closing the door when I got home. Still, my family and I prayed for God's intervention in my work situation.

My family and I decided to attend one of the meetings in a series that was facilitated by the late Elder Walter Pearson at the Seabrook SDA Church, in Seabrook Maryland. That evening, the sermon title was "The Apple of God's Eye." Elder Pearson expounded on the fact that the apple of one's eye is a very sensitive place for which he or she is very protective. God holds his people as the apple of His eye, and He hates when someone plays with his eyes.

I left motivated and inspired after the sermon. I was equipped with the knowledge that God can hold me close no matter the situation. He can also protect me as easily as my eyelids protect my pupils. The sermon seemed specifically for me and was eye-opening and inspiring, to say the least.

The next day, I woke up with fresh insight and a new burst of energy. I went back to the office. Later in the afternoon, Ms. Brooks, FOIA specialist, told me that she had heard my laughter permeating the entire office earlier in the day. I smiled because I didn't notice, but she did. The secret to my difficult situation at the ESA was staying positive. Hence, I submit to you that no matter the difficult situations you may face in the workplace, optimism will help smooth the challenges over. Remember, as Roger Crawford stated, "Being challenged in life is inevitable, being defeated is optional." Stay focused. Stay positive. Trust God's timing.

■　■　■

I enjoyed the budget work I was doing and the meaningful work relationships I had forged with the program offices at the DOL/ESA. However, it felt like my career, my health, and my family were under attack. Yet throughout the struggles, my God never gave up on me. I never looked like what I had been going through.

Shortly after my demotion, and after ESA was totally abolished, I was reassigned to the DOL Departmental Budget Centers (DBC). My first-line supervisor was Osman Payne, who was the DBC director, and my second-line supervisor was Margaret Fletcher (both Caucasian and in their mid-forties, with no prior EEO activity). On October 4, 2009, Osman emailed me a description of the budget officer's position that I would be moving into. However, shortly after I rejected the $6,000 settlement, Osman emailed me on October 19, 2009, regarding a change in the position, which was downgraded from the original position of budget officer. The email reads as follows:

From: Payne, Osman—OASAM
Sent: Monday, October 19, 2009, 12:16 p.m.
To: Francis, Jean D—ESA
Subject: FW: DBC 0560-15 Team Leader Budget Analyst

Do you have some time this afternoon to discuss the current plan for joining DBC? This PD is a bit different than the initial one and I want to go over it with you.

Apparently, the original position had been withdrawn and changed. The new position was as a budget analyst team lead. My position description indicated that I was responsible for directing the work of analysts assigned to all budget accounts.

My primary duties included developing, planning, and implementing program strategies for the department's congressional and presidential budget justifications and reviewing the DBC's efficiency procedures and internal controls. With some trepidation, I looked forward to a new episode of my career with the DOL.

But this new episode would fall short of the change I had hoped for, and that would improve what was left of my once stellar career. In retrospect, it was the beginning of the end.

Me, Latisha & Jeanelle Laughing

Me and Lionel Kayaking

Catching my first fish

Chapter 21

Every single job is a challenge. You are walking into a new set,
a new character, creating a world and trying to get
comfortable to do your best work.

—Felicia Day

In November 2009, I stepped into my new role as a lead budget analyst for DOL Departmental Budget Center (DBC). Initially, I was optimistic that this would be an honest reset and a return to the career I had worked so intently for so long to develop. However, under different circumstances, the DBC would not have been my first choice of places to work at the DOL or even on my list. I had heard of discriminatory practices at the DBC from someone who once worked there, and it's the last thing I needed to deal with again.

On my visits to DBC before my reassignment, I noticed that it didn't seem like the agency wasn't concerned with diversity at the top. This is always a red flag. In my view, I didn't believe this agency was a good fit for me. The challenges in today's workplace are simply too complex and too massive to resolve without everyone at the table engaging and brainstorming in the decision-making processes.

This was tantamount to leaving bright individuals out of the discussions and leaving wisdom and innovations behind. That's a risk today's organizations cannot afford, particularly in the more enlightened new world of the new century. I didn't have a choice in the matter or any control of where I was reassigned. But I believed I had been strategically placed there for many reasons. Specifically, it was a career-ending assignment once I had filed my EEO complaint.

It quickly became apparent that things weren't going to go well at DBC. My first-line supervisor, Osman Payne, didn't assign me any work for the first nine months of my tenure, which was incredibly frustrating and troubling. I regularly asked my coworkers if I could help with their work.

On average, I completed approximately two hours of work a day. I was the only minority GS-15 employee in the DBC at the time. My coworkers noticed that I wasn't being assigned the work and responsibilities that other GS-15 employees were. They asked me why I wasn't getting any assignments or working on the budget like they were. I didn't respond to them as to why. I thought that perhaps Osman was working on a reorganization plan of the DBC personnel to place me correctly.

I didn't want to act or speak on feelings alone. I wanted to have solid information to prove that my DBC supervisor was acting unfairly toward me because of biases—my race, religion, creed, sexual preference, or gender. Or because he had been instructed to do so by administrators in other departments, i.e., Hattie. Such an act would be classic retaliatory behavior.

I may have been given the title of budget analyst team lead, but I had lost all job responsibilities in my transition to DBC. The few duties that Payne assigned to me were completely different from the original position description. These minimal duties included scheduling monthly budget meetings, booking a conference room, and subsequently, developing a training plan to build the agency capacity.

However, the agencies were never made aware that I was supposed to be helping them to build their capacity. I didn't even know that myself. So essentially, the only real work assigned to me was scheduling a monthly meeting and booking a room for that meeting once a month. I began to recognize Osman's MO.

In his deposition from March 19, 2015, with my attorney, Kate Canton Grant, he gave his account of my position and duties:

Ms. Grant: "So what position was Dr. Francis placed in?"

Mr. Payne: "It was a budget analyst team leader."

Ms. Grant: "And what are the duties of that position?"

Mr. Payne: "In general, it was to help the agencies build their capacity, to monitor and review items that were going through departmental clearance for budget issues. Eventually, we folded in improving customer service within—for DBC, interacting with external and internal customers, and then other projects as they came up."

Based on Osman Payne's description of my job, I was only a DBC gofer. Let's be real. I was present at his deposition and thought, *That was just a bunch of meaningless words.*

Traditionally, supervisors were to provide new employees with performance standards during the first month of employment. However, that didn't happen for the first seven months in my case.

Then on June 22, 2010, Osman called me into his office and told me that he had "forgotten" to put me on performance standards. He prepared my performance standards and asked me to backdate them to November 9, 2009. Osman's performance standards didn't reflect the complexity of work I was to perform as a GS-15 lead budget analyst. When I asked about my position as a lead budget analyst and why that wasn't reflected in the performance standards, he emphasized that my position "wasn't a job."

At that meeting, I asked Osman about my lack of assignments. He told me that I could assist Phil Anderson's group with one of his programs. Phill was the manager of the budget formulation and execution team and was also a GS-15. Hence, I worked with his team from June 2010 until September 2010 on budget formulation assignments and activities for the Office of Labor Management Standards (OLMS). However, as a GS-15 budget analyst team lead, I was never assigned a team.

At the end of the performance-rating period, Osman asked George

Hunter for input on my 2009–2010 performance review rather than asking me for my accomplishments and work completed. George was one of the individuals, Stormi Madison, my former ESA supervisor, had alleged in her affidavit statement from January 2010 would have information about my "poor performance." He was a GS-14 budget analyst team lead and the one assigned to accompany me on meetings with the OLMS analyst as he sat and took notes of the sessions. No sooner than I was assigned to DBC, George had been promoted to GS-15 budget analyst team lead.

■ ■ ■

On November 5, 2010, Osman forwarded a drafted performance evaluation for my review. Although he described the document as a draft, my second-line supervisor, Margaret Fletcher, had already signed it. As I reviewed the evaluation, I saw that many of my accomplishments were missing. Therefore, I provided Osman with additional documentation regarding the work I had completed that year with Phil Anderson's group. Osman refused to include the new information in the review stating that he didn't see any reason to change the document.

Hence, I didn't have the opportunity to provide any input into my performance evaluation. Moreover, in my performance evaluation, Osman characterized the budget work that I performed with Phil Anderson's team as a "special project" and "assisting the DBC team leader" George Hunter. This was incorrect; I never assisted Hunter. Instead, I was working with the program analyst on my own.

Healthy companies and organizations must foster an employee evaluation process conducive to employee growth. Asking an employee to participate in his or her own evaluation processes is customary and essential. Most importantly, when management and employee participate in the evaluation process together, this improves organizational effectiveness, stimulates communication, and provides clarity for future job performance. This is a no brainer.

During my eighteen years with various government agencies before working with the DOL, I have always had the opportunity to provide input into my performance evaluation, even at the ESA. My supervisors always made it a practice to ask for my accomplishments, making me think like I was a part of the process. Not so at the DBC.

I didn't sign the performance evaluation because it didn't comprehensively reflect my accomplishments. I also included a comprehensive memorandum regarding my feelings about the evaluation. This was for inclusion in my personnel files because I sense that the process was unfair and that I was being treated differently than the other White budget analyst team leads. In this regard, it also showed Osman's disrespectful attitude toward me early on. I assumed that he did not take to kindly of my action.

Shortly after my review, Osman invited his deputy and me to a meeting on November 30, 2010. He announced that I would no longer work with Phil Anderson's team. Unfortunately, he never provided an explanation for that decision. It seemed as though he was offended because of the memorandum I included with his performance appraisal to be included in my personnel files.

During the meeting, Osman looked my way, smiled mockingly, and said, "Well, no good deed goes unpunished. I've been developing the agenda for the monthly budget meeting, but I think you have the pizazz to do it better than I can."

I sat there in astonishment. Could he be referring to the EEO complaint I had filed? The memorandum? And what kind of "pizazz" did he think I could bring to developing a monthly meeting agenda? These and other questions permeated my mind, but I have learned along the way that you've got to be smart enough to play stupid. I shook my head with disgust and rolled my eyes at the foolishness I had just heard.

I had initially been hopeful about my new start at DBC. However, I had sat for nine months like an outcast. After witnessing the events of my first performance appraisal and this meeting, it was clear to me that the well at DBC had been poisoned by my ESA supervisors, among others. Although my title was budget analyst team lead and I had been assigned to the DOL budget office, I wasn't permitted to work on a single budget. Instead, Osman had decided to limit my role to administrative duties. It was like déjà vu after the experiences I'd had at ESA.

Osman would give the following account of his reasons why I wasn't performing the duties of a budget analyst team lead, at his March 16, 2017, deposition when I represented myself as *pro se*:

> **Mr. Payne:** "Dr. Francis wasn't [performing the duties of a budget analyst team lead] because there was a priority of a push by the assistant secretary for customer service and capacity building and clients for OASAM."

> **Me:** "So in essence, Dr. Francis was performing budget analyst duties that just include training of ABOs?"

> **Mr. Payne:** "She also had some policy review duties."

■ ■ ■

Osman's answers do not adequately explain why I had not been allowed to perform the duties I had been hired to do. However, in my view, my diminished role was a continuation of the discrimination and retaliation initiated by Stormi and Hattie, likely initiated by them through company communication. Stormi had once stated that I was "Not a good fit to be in the budget arena," and Osman was carrying her torch, from the looks of things.

In the coming months and years, Osman would assign me only lower-level administrative duties that should have been assigned to the administrative staff. I don't think he would have ever given one of these tasks to one of the White budget analyst team leads. Payne explained the discrepancy between the duties of my official position and my actual responsibilities as "a change in the president's management agenda." However, he couldn't provide any evidence regarding the president's management agenda that would cause him to change my responsibilities. My attorney wanted to get to the bottom of this. She deposed A. Wiley Thornton, Osman Payne's boss and my second-line supervisor, on the matter. On April 2, 2015, A. Wiley Thornton refuted Osman's claim. Here is his deposition account:

> **Ms. Grant:** "Have the offices that you supervise experienced any reorganization during your tenure?"
>
> **Mr. Thornton:** "We've reorganized HR."
>
> **Ms. Grant:** "Okay. Any other?"
>
> **Mr. Thornton:** "We've made changes to the small business office. We've changed what the RA's do. We've expanded the IT office. It's a dynamic organization."
>
> **Ms. Grant:** "Okay. Has Mr. Payne's office been reorganized during your tenure?"
>
> **Mr. Thornton:** "Not that I know of."

I was the only GS-15 none-administrative employee at DBC who was a racial minority. I was also the sole budget analyst team lead who wasn't assigned to lead a team or work on a budget. The other team leads— all Caucasian—were given supervisory duties or were responsible for leading a team of lower-level employees. They were invited to attend the budget meetings from which I was excluded. I was also given lesser assignments than the lower-level budget analysts who weren't team leads (all Caucasian). Yet, my title continued to be budget analyst team lead.

In the US Merit Systems Protection Board (MSPB) proceedings on May 1, 2015, which are discussed in a later chapter, I believe Osman revealed the true reason for this disparity. He gave the following account:

> **Ms. Grant:** "And how did the other analysts' positions differ from Dr. Francis' position, if at all?"
>
> **Mr. Payne:** "The other team leads belonged in—or belonged—or they are in the office of Agency budget programs. They have specific Agency assignments for what they do—and the folks they deal with. They do a lot more detailed work in terms of reviewing budget formulation submissions and starting apportionments. It's very technical-type work they do. Jean's position was to address all of what goes on in DBC in training the Agency budget officers. It was more along the lines of training and capacity building, rather than getting the technical work done."
>
> **Ms. Grant:** "During the time when Dr. Francis reported to you, did her job title ever change?"
>
> **Mr. Payne:** "No."
>
> **Ms. Grant:** "And did she ever receive a new written position description?"
>
> **Mr. Payne:** "No."

Osman chose to use the word *belonged*. When he stated that the other White team leads "belonged," whereas I did not, I understood this to mean that I didn't belong there as the only Black budget analyst team lead. I had felt this from him from day one and throughout my tenure at the DBC, but to hear him verbalize this in his choice of words in front of a judge was mortifying.

However simple those two words, "they belong," the idea behind them is so profound and deep-rooted that I could barely grasp their implications. Moreover, he described the work of my White colleagues as "very technical," and mine as more administrative. Furthermore, he revealed his belief that I wasn't capable of high-level work, but not based on my performance or ability. So what was it based on, then?

Moreover, despite Osman's belief at the MSBP that I wasn't capable of performing high-level work, he contradicted himself during his March 19, 2015 deposition with my attorney Ms. Grant when he stated that he believed I was competent to perform the work in my reassignment to the DBC. He answered her questions in the following manner:

> **Ms. Grant:** Did you feel that she was competent to perform the job in which she was being
> placed?
>
> **Mr. Payne:** Yes.
>
> **Ms. Grant:** Did you have any concerns about her being placed in that position?
>
> **Mr. Payne:** No
>
> **Ms. Grant:** Did you object at all to her being placed in the DBC?
>
> **Mr. Payne:** No.

Finally, Osman knew that I was a budget professional. There was no way he did not know this. As the chief for the ESA budget office, I attended the monthly budget officers' meetings that were facilitated by Osman. It was part of my job. Additionally, on regular intervals, I would receive messages and data-calls from Osman regarding budgetary updates and I always responded to his inquiries.

I also believe he knew that my ESA supervisors had demoted me from chief, budget formulation and implementation to special assistant. He apparently had no intention of undoing their action after I was assigned to DBC. During his March 19, 2015, deposition with my attorney Ms. Grant, my believe of this was confirmed (the Agency was represented by Ms. Lambert). And although he could not bring himself to address my position as chief for the ESA budget office, he would describe my position only as a "financial worker." And not only did he know that I was a "financial worker" as he described me, but he also knew that I was demoted to, as he would describe it, "Some sort of assistant to the administrative officer." Here are his responses to this line of questioning:

Ms. Grant: How did you come to supervise her?

Mr. Payne: When the current administration leadership took over, they disbanded the employment standards administration. And Jean was a financial worker in the office—Central Office for the Employment—ESA, Employment Standards Administration. When they broke that up, they then assigned people in that management group out to agencies, including former ESA agencies, CFO's office. And Jean was assigned to the Departmental Budget Center.

Ms. Grant: Did you know what her position had been at the ESA?

Mr. Payne: Not at the time of the dissolution.

Ms. Grant: Was there ever a point when you learned what her position had been at the ESA?

Mr. Payne: A Mostly, I know that she was some sort of assistant to the administrative officer. I don't remember when I gained that knowledge.

Ms. Grant: So she wasn't a budget analyst?

Mr. Payne: Apparently not, no.

Ms. Grant: And you said that you eventually became aware that she had filed EEO complaints during her time with ESA, correct?

Mr. Payne: Uh-huh.

Ms. Payne: When did you become aware of that?

Mr. Payne: I don't remember the exact date.

Ms. Grant: Was it early in her tenure at DBC?

Ms. Lambert: Objection, asked and answered.

Hattie had worked at the DBC for a short while, and Osman and my ESA supervisors were friends. Moreover, when Osman emailed me regarding a change in the position at DBC, Stormi Madison was placed in that position instead of me. It was the position that Osman had held before becoming the DBC director.

It appeared that Osman had just continued the same pattern as my ESA supervisors. In a conversation that ensued between him and my attorney, Kate Grant, on March 19, 2015, he described bringing Stormi Madison over to the office he had worked before becoming the DBC Director. Here is his account:

Ms. Grant: "Did any other Employment Standards Administration employees come to the DBC at that time?"

Mr. Payne: "Yes."

Ms. Grant: "How many?"

Mr. Payne: "One other."

Ms. Grant: "And who was that?"

Mr. Payne: "Stormi Madison."

Ms. Grant: "So what position was Dr. Francis placed in?"

Mr. Payne: "It was a budget analyst team leader."

Ms. Grant: "And what was Stormi's job?"

Mr. Payne: "She was the financial manager."

Ms. Grant: "Okay. How did Dr. Francis's job duties differ from those of her four colleagues?"

Mr. Payne: "They really had all different roles. The financial manager was the position I used to have where I was—it was managing specific appropriations."

I don't believe there was any happenstance in the erosion of my position at the DBC. The week that I was assigned to DBC, Osman had come walking down to ESA one day to see Hattie. I stopped him for a brief minute to engage him in conversation about the reassignment. A few minutes into our conversation, Hattie walked up as we were talking. As soon as she arrived, I excused myself while Osman and Hattie continued their discussion. Nothing just happens.

After I filed my EEO complaint, ESA was abolished. Hattie and all other ESA employees were reassigned. They were angry, and I believe that Osman wanted to vindicate his friends by demoting me and punishing me. He was the one who had declared the words "No good deed goes unpunished."

I was seeing this unfold right before my eyes.

Osman knew that I had been demoted to an administrative role. I wasn't working as a budget analyst immediately before transferring to DBC. But, in my view, he was determined to keep it that way. The following conversation ensued between Osman and my attorney at his deposition:

Ms. Grant: "Before Dr. Francis was assigned to the DBC, did you speak to her old supervisor?"

Mr. Payne: "Speak to?"

Ms. Grant: "Her old supervisor."

Mr. Payne: "I mean generally, yes, but not specifically about her."

■ ■ ■

It was difficult to believe that Osman didn't have specific conversations about me with my ESA supervisors. Based on what I had experienced at the DBC, I concluded that he had. Moreover, he was intentional about continuing the same pattern of behavior toward me, just like my ESA supervisors, only more subtle.

It would also emerge that during my time at DBC, there was a vacant budget analyst team lead position. I will never understand why Osman had me sit and do practically nothing all day rather than allowing me to fill this position. It was a waste of taxpayer dollars to not utilize my skills and experience. He later claimed in his 2015 deposition that he believed all the budget analyst team lead positions were filled. Following is his account:

> **Ms. Grant:** "Did you ever consider placing her in one of those positions?"
>
> **Mr. Payne:** "No."
>
> **Ms. Grant:** "Why not?"
>
> **Mr. Payne:** "I think they were all filled."
>
> **Ms. Grant:** "Did Dr. Francis work on any of the same projects as these other budget analyst team leaders?"
>
> **Mr. Payne:** "I can't really recall specifically."

However, a position was vacant after the budget analyst team lead for Employment Training Administration (ETA) had retired a year and a half after I was assigned to DBC. And in the spring of 2014, that individual was rehired as a contractor to perform the work of a budget analyst for the department. I was stunned as I pondered how I had sat in a cubicle at the DBC for four-and-a-half years and was never offered a job as a budget analyst but Osman able to approve a former employee—a retiree at that—to return to perform budgetary duties at the DBC.

When I had transitioned from DHS to DOL as chief, budget formulation and implementation, I wasn't there only for the paycheck. I took immense pride in my work, and I believed that I was there to make a difference. Now, at the DBC, I woke up each morning, got dressed, and showed up for work—however, there was no work for me to do.

Each morning, he would walk past my cubicle with his deputy, Cameron Bates, to get their morning coffee. He would glance in my cubicle to see if I was sitting there as if I were a misbehaving child ordered to sit in the corner. Of course, Osman was aware that I had no work to do. In my view, this was a waste of time, talent, and government resources.

I was born with a love for learning. So, during my time at the DBC, I pursued my PhD in organizational management with a concentration in leadership. This sustained me through my trials. Of course, I wasn't only becoming an expert in my field of research. Still, I learned valuable lessons that applied to navigating my ordeal at work and preparing myself for what would come next. I believe that organizations rise, and fall based on their leadership. Exceptional leadership is the backbone of an organization—I was clearly observing a counterexample of exceptional leadership at the DBC.

Although it felt like my federal career had gone south, I was determined to remain current in my field and to stay motivated. I knew that I would find a new job opportunity and that there would be a better day. So, I wanted to be prepared for when that day would come.

Under Osman's leadership, the DBC staff engaged in yearly March Madness activities surrounding the college basketball championship tournament, which had been prohibited by the DOL. This was the first time in my government career that I had seen any agency or department personnel engaging in March Madness while at work. However, these activities were popular at the DBC. Each participating staff member completed his or her bracket and submitted its content to one of the office managers, or Cameron Bates.

I wasn't a basketball fan myself, and the first time Phil Anderson placed the bracket on my chair to complete, I had no idea what to do with it. It probably goes without saying that I didn't participate. Once the brackets were completed, everyone's names were consolidated in an Excel spreadsheet. After that, emails would go back and forth, revealing who was winning and losing.

The winner was announced at the end of the games. DBC staff spent hours monitoring the tournament. They discussed the performance of various teams, watched games on the TV in the deputy's office, and yelled and cheered when their favorite team won.

■ ■ ■

Early in my tenure at the DBC, I had received an announcement for the Senior Executive Candidate Development Program for DOL employees. I spoke with Osman regarding the training and what needed to be done for approval. The program was intended for all DOL employees, and since I wasn't being kept busy by Osman, I thought this would be a good time to enroll. I approached him about the program announcement and what I needed to do to enroll. He told me that he would talk with my second-line supervisor, Margaret Fletcher, and get back to me.

Osman never got back to me. I approached him after a few weeks about the outcome of the training discussion. He stated that the request was denied because, "Those courses are not for you. They are for people who have been with the department for a long time. So, you just have to keep on asking." I couldn't believe the words that I had heard—*those courses are not for you*. I was horrified.

I knew that other employees had attended this training even after being employed with the DOL for less time than I had been. I was disappointed and embarrassed. My attorney later deposed Osman on whether I had ever requested training. He said that I had not.

On May 27, 2011, Osman invited me to a midyear performance review meeting. The midyear performance review is designed as a means for supervisors to discuss with employees their progress on goals and performance to date and develop action plans as necessary. The meeting was brief, and he told me that I was "excelling" in my work and that he had nothing negative to say about my performance. I shook my head in disbelief. There wasn't much for us to discuss in terms of the actual work I had been doing, since he had been assigning me so little. The meeting felt like more of a formality.

I asked him what was needed on my part to earn a performance rating higher than "meets expectations." Payne replied, "Oh, I didn't know you wanted to get above 'meets.' Then you need to go visit the agency budget officers."

He never stated why I needed to visit them. This was an inconvenient, and frankly irritating, recommendation. Many of them were in other offices outside the DOL Francis Perkins Building, which meant there would be a travel cost. Moreover, there was simply no reason for me to be visiting these individuals. I didn't understand why Osman would make such a recommendation. But Stormi was a budget officer. Perhaps he wanted me to go visit her. The meeting ended, and I quickly left his office.

Six months later, Osman and I met again to discuss my yearly performance review. Unfortunately, in developing the performance rating, he once again had not asked me for any input regarding the work that I had done.

At the beginning of the meeting, he handed me the performance appraisal and stated, "Your performance rating is 'meets,' because you have done nothing during the rating period that jumped out at me."

This was even though he had previously told me I was "excelling" in my duties at my midyear review. He made no suggestions for improvement, had taken no notes, nor did he discuss the possibility of performing work as a budget analyst team lead moving forward. If nothing had "jumped out" at him about my performance, it truly reflected negatively on him because he wasn't giving me any assignments to do. At this point, I was weary of the foolishness.

A few months after the performance review meeting, Osman asked me to develop a training plan based on the topic selections that had not been procured the previous year. I developed the plan, but he then told me there was no funding for contractors to facilitate the training because of sequestration. He recommended that DBC personnel facilitate the training instead. I engaged the team leads and managers regarding facilitating training on various budget topics. Karen Saxon selected a topic based on her expertise and was the first to deliver her training session.

I developed the announcement about the training, ensured there was a room available for it, and then developed a survey for providing feedback from the attendees on how the DBC could improve future internal training presentations. A survey is typically handed out to participants within the federal government agencies, from my experience. This process helps agencies to get feedback, ratings, and suggestions or recommendations at the conclusion of a training to make future improvements. The survey wasn't only for Karen Saxon, but it was to be used at the end of every course offered at the DBC. After forwarding the survey to Karen and explaining that the survey could be used after her training session, she angrily stormed over to my cubicle and said, "What is this? I'm not doing this. They don't pay me to do training!" She yelled and stormed off to Deputy Cameron Bates to lodge a complaint.

The fact that Karen scolded, "They don't pay me to do training" shows, or at least implies, that she was making it clear that unlike me, she was a budget professional. And I got the message.

Eventually, I left for the day. I returned the following morning to find a note taped to my computer monitor with the words *SEE ME* written in large letters and signed by Cameron Bates. I removed the letter-sized paper and began preparing for the day. Before I could go to Cameron's office to see what he wanted, he came to my cubicle and said in a stern voice, "Let me see what you want Karen to do."

I told him it was only a survey. It had nothing to do with training delivery. Still, it served as a feedback mechanism at the end of the training to help the DBC improve future course offerings. I gave him a copy of the survey, and he walked away. He approached me later in the day, returned the survey, and said, "She's not doing that." He walked off immediately, and I shook my head at the bizarre phenomenon. I was speechless.

Osman had been out of the office for a few days. When he returned the next day, I told him about Karen Saxon's outburst at me because of a simple end-of-training survey. He turned to me with a smile and said, "I heard." After that, there was no other DBC training planned. Osman stated that because there was a budget sequestration in place, employees could find and take free training when work was slow. I decided to do just that.

Osman's behavior toward me stuck out like a sore thumb. His actions suggested to me that diversity in leadership roles at the DBC was not a priority. Finally, one of the budget analysts noticed, stopped by my cubicle one day, and asked, "Why don't you do what we do?"

I shrugged and changed the topic because what was happening was beyond my control.

On November 8, 2011, I scheduled a meeting with my second-line supervisor, A. Wiley Thornton, assistant secretary for administration. The meeting addressed the lack of work consistent with my position description and to ask for his help in getting a reassignment or a detail somewhere other than the DBC. I also introduced a proposal that I had developed for improving customer service in the DOL and shared the proposal with him. He took the proposal and told me that he would "look into" my concerns when the performance issue with Osman was resolved. Unfortunately, although A. Wiley Thornton had finalized the performance issue by signing it, he had not communicated a resolution regarding the concerns I raised about it.

Thornton was my second-line supervisor; he signed off on my performance evaluations and would later declare that he never knew me. He also stated he didn't recall that I had shared concerns about my work in the DBC and had asked for a transfer. Not even the sparsely developed performance appraisal rating for me as a GS-15 raised his eyebrows. He just signed with no questions asked.

Thornton claimed he remembered nothing about the meeting discussions. I did not believe that he was being truthful. However, he quickly called Osman and alerted him about the meeting. Thornton said that Osman told him I was going to see him. Still, that conversation never happened between Osman and me. The following conversation ensued with Mr. Thornton and my attorney, Ms. Grant, at his deposition on April 2, 2015.

> **Ms. Grant:** "Did Mr. Payne give a reason that she was going to come and see you?"
>
> **Mr. Thornton:** "That she didn't like her performance rating."
>
> **Ms. Grant:** "And then, what, if anything, did you tell Mr. Payne about the meeting, afterward?"
>
> **Mr. Thornton:** "Nothing specific."
>
> **Ms. Grant:** "Just that the meeting had taken place?"
> The witness nodded his head.

■ ■ ■

After the meeting on the transfer, I never received a resolution from Thornton about a reassignment or a detail. He was silent about my concerns. Then, on December 12, 2011, a DOL announcement asked interested employees to respond to a Bureau of International Labor Affairs (ILAB) or Veterans' Employment and Training Service (VETS) detail because they needed the help. I was excited to see the announcement and didn't hesitate to submit my request to Osman, letting him know that I was interested. I specifically requested VETS. I always had a passion to serve our vets', considering Lionel was also a vet. So, I believed that would be a good fit. However, if a VET'S detail wasn't available, ILAB would be my second choice.

Since my duties were still limited to scheduling monthly budget meetings and no other substantive work, I assumed that Osman would have no problem with my request regarding the detail with one of these agencies. However, several months passed, and he didn't provide a response regarding my request. Instead, he stated multiple, contradictory reasons in his later depositions for why my request had been denied, including: "VETS, at the time was going through a lot of turmoil." Or "I didn't think it would be appropriate to send a detail," and "I didn't think we'd be able to learn very much going out there."

After telling my attorney that he had made the decision to deny my request, he told her that "I said I'd look out for other opportunities."

Imagine that! Osman was literally controlling my career path and making decisions for me when I asked for a transfer. In his view, my assignment under his leadership that consisted only of developing a monthly meeting agenda and finding a conference room for the meeting was enough for me as a Black professional woman in the workplace. My story is not uncommon in this regard.

According to the *Forbes* "The Women in The Workplace 2018" survey, "Women of color are significantly underrepresented. They are also far less likely than others to be promoted to manager, more likely to face everyday discrimination, and less likely to receive support from their managers." Unfortunately, I was one of those women who was experiencing such a trend. Still, I did not expect it in my idealistic days in a US government office, particularly the DOL.

Shortly after Osman denied my request to serve in ILAB or VETS, he stopped by my cubicle. He said he had found a detail for me to "get back into budget," smiling brilliantly as though he had done me a big favor.

"Really?" I replied, wondering what he might possibly suggest.

Rather than allowing me to work in my position as a budget analyst in the budget office where I had been reassigned or approving my request to work on a detail I was interested in, this was his course of action.

The detail that Payne had found for me was with the Women's Bureau. That would not have been my first choice, as the VETS was a better fit. I had, of course, requested his approval for two other details that I would have preferred, but Osman was throwing his weight around to control where I worked at the DOL. However, I agreed to the Women's Bureau detail because I thought it was better than sitting in a cubicle each day with nothing to do. I then reached out to the individual who was still in the position to discuss her daily workload and the date I would take over once she departed. She also supervised a team of six individuals, and we talked about their functions and how they would help me get the job done.

■ ■ ■

The day arrived when I was to report to my detail at the Women's Bureau. The director called a meeting in the conference room with everyone, and I attended. I introduced myself to the group, then I asked about the team that would be assigned to help me with completing the daily tasks. However, the director replied that the team had been assigned elsewhere and that if I needed help, I should ask if any of the team members were free to help. I sat puzzled. Her response wasn't making sense.

The following day, as I was sitting in the office developing a spreadsheet, the director walked into the office and said, "We don't need you here anymore. You can leave now."

I was shocked. "Now?" I replied.

She said, "Yes!" I packed my belongings and went back to the DBC cubicle, still puzzled about what had gone wrong. I told Osman about what had occurred, and he didn't have much of a reaction.

He just smiled and said, "Yeah. That's how she is," as if he had nothing to do with what had happened. However, he later stated in his April 2, 2015, deposition that my role in the detail he'd found for me "was more to help the Women's Bureau," rather than to serve in a budget role. Once I discovered this, I immediately understood what had happened. The deal with Osman was that I was only there as "the help."

Immediately after the Women's Bureau detail debacle, the DOL's Office of the Chief Financial Officer (OCFO), led by Jerry Bentley, was spearheading a three-hundred-thousand-dollar initiative for developing budget and financial management courses for the DOL workforce. Unfortunately, Osman submitted my name to the OCFO to be a part of the team of experts without my consent.

The meetings lasted several months, and the team and I identified a list of courses needed to aid the contractors in developing the course catalog and the online skills assessment tool. After participating in the assessment process, each employee would receive a report of the results. They would have the opportunity to see how they rated themselves and how the supervisor had rated them. Then the supervisor and employee would meet to discuss the rated results.

Finally, they would work together to develop an individual development plan of courses based on the course catalog and proficiency levels to help bridge the employee's skills gap. The survey and skills assessment results were confidential. It was a tool only used between the employee and his or her supervisor.

All budget analysts and financial management personnel were to complete the skills assessment survey, and so were the supervisors. On January 18, 2012, I received an email to complete it myself. It had been over two years since I had done budget work. However, based on the knowledge and skills that I had acquired from previous departments, I rated myself accordingly. As my supervisor, Osman had the opportunity to rate my skills set as a budget analyst team lead. When I received the results from his survey ratings, he applied a rating of one or two, sometimes zero out of a rating of five for each component. I wasn't surprised, but his low ratings were still infuriating to me, not to mention completely unjust. He never met with me to further discuss the rating.

Osman had never even allowed me to work on a budget. When he was asked by Ms. Grant at his April 2, 2015, deposition if he had completed a skills assessment survey on my behalf, he denied it. There was no way Osman did not receive an assessment to complete for all budget employees, to include me. I saw his rated results. But as my grandmother would say, "You can lock your door from a thief, but you can't from a liar."

Chapter 22

You have to be where you are to get to where you need to go.

—Amy Poehler

After the Women's Bureau Detail fiasco, I began searching in earnest for a transfer or detail position outside of the department. During this time, I was a member of the Executive Women in Government (EWG) organization and attended the annual EWG meeting. I inquired about a detail among the women seated at my table, and one mentioned that the Justice Department's Chief Financial Management Officer Willis Carter was looking for someone. She gave me his contact information. And I called Mr. Carter and we spoke about what the detail would entail before I decided to accept it with the Department of Justice (DOJ), Office of Justice Programs (OJP), Office of the Chief Financial Officer (OCFO). After my discussion with Mr. Carter, the assignments of the detail seemed impressive, and I accepted. My start date was to be June 18, 2012.

Before leaving for my detail, Osman scheduled a meeting to discuss my midyear review on May 31, 2012. During the meeting, he told me he had "no problem" with my performance. He also asked whether I had planned to return to the DOL after the detail and promised that if I returned, he would "assign me a position." I told him I wasn't certain, but the truth was that I hoped never to return. To say that I was happy to leave was an understatement.

During my tenure with the DOJ, I served as project manager responsible for researching, evaluating, and implementing an integrated budget environment (IBE), which would potentially replace the current processes with an automated, standardized process for budget formulation and execution. The system would have a consistent enterprise-wide look and would enable OJP OCFO bureaus and offices to manage budget data electronically through a centralized and secure database with a collaborative, user-friendly design. I was excited about working to develop and implement the system for the OJP OCFO, and I hit the ground running on the project.

Phase one of the project was initiated the last week of June 2012 and entailed developing a comprehensive action plan, which included the project approach, purpose and goals, scope definition, projected budget, risk assessment, and milestones, just to list a few. I spent countless hours researching and examining current systems to determine possible upgrades and improvements, surveying other agencies about their processes, and building a project team consisting of personnel from each division to discuss and brainstorm ideas. Phases two and three of the project were rolled out in August, and all went smoothly. For the first time in many years, I was feeling accomplished and truly enjoying my work.

Phase three of the project would be the implementation in mid-December 2012, and that was still to be determined. However, a project completion report and presentation were delivered to the deputy CFO and the CFO, and I received positive reviews. The project from beginning to end lasted approximately six months. Throughout this performance period, my supervisor, Willis Carter, praised my performance, describing me as having a "positive attitude," referring to me as a "hard worker," and saying that I was "persistent in getting internal and external staff to collaborate."

After the project, he even requested an additional sixty to ninety-day extension of my detail through March 9, 2013, so I could work on a new project. I was steadily seeking full-time budget analyst positions as well, and I also broadened my search by applying for training and development positions.

■ ■ ■

In November 2012, while still on the detail, Osman issued my 2011–2012 performance evaluation. Instead of asking me for my accomplishments, he emailed Willis Carter and asked for the information. Willis emailed me requesting my accomplishments, and he forwarded the information to Osman. As was his practice in past years, Osman rated my performance as "meets expectations."

Additionally, Osman failed to include any of the very positive and detailed feedback provided by Willis Carter and instead, stated on my performance evaluation that I "would be rated for my DOJ accomplishments when I return to DOL."

I objected to the exclusion and demanded that he included my DOJ accomplishments in the evaluation. Osman, in the end, reissued my 2011–2012 performance evaluation to include my DOJ accomplishments. However, the new evaluation also failed to address my performance rating based on the positive feedback from the Department of Justice. Osman continued to control my performance appraisal preparation by blatantly excluding me from the process or rating me as I deserved to be rated.

Osman scheduled a telephone call to discuss my revised 2011–2012 performance evaluation. I addressed the rating and asked him for his recommendations on what I could do to improve my performance. Instead of providing me with constructive feedback on how to improve, Osman cut me off midsentence, raised his voice, and said, "This is what I expect of *you*, as GS-15: *you* need to take the agency budget officers (ABOs) to lunch, develop relations with them, and then *you* can get to the next level."

Aside from being completely inappropriate, what did taking the ABOs out to lunch have to do with my performance rating? And developing "relations" with them to get to the next level? Payne was out of order, I thought.

I immediately ended the call and proceeded to address his outburst and comment in an email. Osman responded to my email by trying to minimize his suggestion, which I had found to be unprofessional and inappropriate:

From: Payne, Osman OASAM DBC
Sent: Tuesday, November 13, 2012, 6:03 p.m.
To: Francis, Jean
Subject: RE. Response to Performance Appraisal
Thanks. I'll include your comments, but I am not changing the appraisal at this point. My verbal comment during our discussion about taking the ABOs to lunch was never a specific performance expectation for the standard. Since you met expectations for that standard without taking them to lunch, it obviously wasn't a requirement for the standard.

It was an off-handed remark and a series of examples used to illustrate the need to build relationships with the ABOs. It is the building of relationships that was emphasized, as these are necessary to build trust with the ABOs so they see you as someone that can assist them, and they are comfortable providing you information; clarified that in our discussion when you questioned the remark.

I already had a professional relationships with the ABOs, which didn't require me taking them to lunch and developing "relations" to get to the next level. In my view, Payne would never have suggested this to one of my White colleagues. You may recall at our first meeting, he stated that he thought I had the "pizazz" to develop a monthly agenda. This was the man who had suggested that I had "pizazz" for administrative work only, which I interpreted as a not so-subtle racist comment. If meeting with the ABOs had been a legitimate and professional task that he had wanted me to undertake, in-office meetings between me and the ABOs should have been scheduled. This would have been a more appropriate suggestion.

In November 2012, I sent my second-line supervisor a comprehensive memorandum in which I raised concerns regarding my performance appraisal.

MEMORANDUM FOR: A. Wiley Thornton, Assistant Secretary

From: Dr. Jean D. Francis

Subject: Re: Performance Appraisal

Date: November 14, 2012

This memorandum is submitted to address concerns regarding the performance rating period 10/01/2011—09/30/2012, in Exhibit 1. As second-line supervisor, I believe that it is important to, once again, share concerns in an effort to keep you in the know. Mr. Payne has made some changes as noted in Exhibit 2, after discussion of the initial evaluation; however, the action is troubling regarding why the Department of Justice (DOJ) was asked to provide accomplishments and after submitting the accomplishments Mr. Payne failed to give proper rating for those accomplishments.

Instead, he annotated the DOJ accomplishments under other significant accomplishments with the statement "full evaluation will be provided once the detail assignment concludes." This concern was addressed during the November 5 discussion and verbal justification given to Mr. Payne for moving those accomplishments to the special projects section and a rating given because the work was done during the performance period. Further, this action begs the questions, why did he as for the information if the Department of Labor's (DOL) intent was to provide a future rating? Moreover, does it make sense to rate an employee after the rating period?

After discussing the work accomplished during the rating period for Result #3, Mr. Payne vehemently objected by stating, he "begged to differ." Instead, he provided an example of "visiting the Agency Budget Officers (ABOs) and taking them out to lunch," as what he considered as accomplishments for this element.

Mr. Payne's "off-handed" remark, as he describes it, is unacceptable malarkey at best and inappropriate. This comment begs the question, am I the only employee who is asked to visit the ABOs and take him or her out to lunch as a means to attain a better rating? Further, there were no series of examples as Mr. Payne stated in his response. Visiting the ABOs and taking them to lunch was the only example provided. I consider myself as a 'people-person' individual at DOL who believes in building working and professional relationships with colleagues, including the ABOs. I have not given anyone, including the ABOs, reasons to believe that I am an untrustworthy individual. Therefore, I take offense to Mr. Payne's comments insinuating a lack of trust that would make the ABOs uncomfortable with providing information should I ask.

In addition, at the Departmental Budget Center (DBC), the ABOs are assigned a budget analyst and a backup analyst. The analysts work as the liaison between DBC and the agencies on action items. A third party trying to build such an alliance would create confusion to some degree. Further, when someone other than the assigned analyst is requesting legitimate information from an ABO, it is my view that he or she has a responsibility to provide the information to get the work done. This action should not be contingent on a relationship but should be a part of the ABO's job. Therefore, the suggestion to visit him or her and take him or her to lunch so that a comfort level can be developed for providing requested information is unacceptable.

This is not the first time Mr. Payne refers to visiting the ABOs as a component for getting to the next level. The first occurrence was on December 9, 2011, when at the beginning of the rating period, I asked Mr. Payne what it would take to get beyond "meets expectations."

In Mr. Payne's own words, he replied, "Oh, I didn't know you wanted to get to the next level!" He further stated that I should be visiting the ABOs.

This statement is discriminatory and retaliatory at best because Mr. Payne does not assign any tasks that warrants visiting the ABOs to request information. Therefore, I am confused as to what the visits would accomplish and what information I am requesting.

It is appalling that for the hard work I have accomplished during the rating period and for the changes that I have affected, Mr. Payne has determined that my rating of "meets expectations" will suffice, in his view, because I didn't build relationship by meeting with the ABOs and taking them out to lunch. It begs the question what is the vision to be achieved and the goals and objectives the visits would accomplish other than building relationships?

Further, Mr. Payne didn't assign me day-to-day budget tasks during the rating period, except for the customer improvement project, to warrant these ABO visits for which he speaks of. Therefore, due to coming in every day and not having much of anything to do, I was happy to represent the DOL by accepting a detail with the Department of Justice working on a few important projects. My work consistently showed a high level of professionalism, competency, and timeliness. Because the detail is a reimbursable agreement, I thought it would be fitting to share completed projects during the rating period (Exhibits 4-7).

Finally, I am concerned that the DOL leadership pursues me as a target for bullying, discrimination, retaliation, and desperate treatment throughout my tenure. In Mr. Payne's own words on May 31, 2012, "I know you have been treated badly since you started at DOL."

I agree with this assessment; however, Mr. Payne has also helped to inflict some of the bad treatment; to that I say enough already. There may be no actions taken regarding my concerns; however, if I return after the detail as a DOL employee, once again, I request the possibility of no longer working with and for Mr. Payne.

Sincerely,

Jean D. Francis, Ph.D.

Mr. Thornton took no action to address my complaints. Additionally, he later denied that I had ever raised concerns regarding discrimination, harassment, or hostile working environments. I needed intervention. No one listened. When Thornton was later asked in his deposition about whether an investigation had been conducted into my complaint of harassment and a hostile working environment, he stated that he didn't know. He admitted to asking the human resources director, Sybil Frost, to "come up with a plan." However, he didn't know if the plan related to my complaint had ever been developed. Thornton's lack of concern and his unresponsive attitude to my troubles speaks volumes. The following is excerpted from his deposition on April 2, 2015:

Ms. Grant: Do you recall if you reviewed these materials that were attached to the email from Dr. Francis?"

Mr. Thornton: "I remember the email. I do not remember attachments."

Ms. Grant: "All right. So do you recall reviewing this memorandum prepared for you by Dr. Francis, dated November 14, 2012?"

Mr. Thornton: "Yes."

Ms. Grant: "Okay. Do you recall taking any action based on reviewing the memorandum?"

Mr. Thornton: "I sent it to the HR director."

Ms. Grant: "Okay. And that was Sybil Frost?"

Mr. Thornton: "That would be Sybil Frost."

Ms. Grant: "All right; any other action?"

Mr. Thornton: "No."

Ms. Grant: "Okay. And you didn't have a discussion with Dr. Francis about this memo, correct?"

Mr. Thornton: "No, I did not."

Ms. Grant: "Okay. Did you discuss the memo with Mr. Payne?"

Mr. Thornton: "No, I did not."

Ms. Grant: "Okay. Is there a reason that you didn't delegate to Carleen [an African American female on Thornton's leadership team] in this situation?"

Mr. Thornton: "Sybil is a very good HR director, has her own mind, and can give me better advice on this than Carleen can."

Ms. Grant: "Okay. Other than what we've already discussed, do you recall any other advice that Sybil gave you in this case?"

Mr. Thornton: "No. I do not."

Ms. Grant: "Do you know if there were any changes made to Dr. Francis's personnel evaluation as a result of this?"

Mr. Thornton: "No. I do not."

It's my belief that the leadership of the DBC objected to diversity in leadership roles in the department. I made multiple requests for reassignment to another agency, one that promotes an inclusive and diverse workplace where reprisal toward people is prohibited, and disputes are fairly and appropriately handled. My requests were always denied or ignored.

At the May 2015 MSPB hearing that will be discussed in a later chapter, Thornton said that I was "exaggerating" about Osman's "off-handed" comment that I should "take ABOs to lunch, [and] develop relations with them."

Imagine that! From this experience, I have gleaned that when it comes to the concerns of Black and Brown women in organizations—or at least in the DOL—our truths are described as "exaggerations" and falsehoods.

Appropriate action to prevent the recurrence of the discriminatory and retaliatory behaviors I was subjected to were never taken. Likewise, the department neglected to take the necessary steps to investigate the allegations against me. All of this occurred at the Department of Labor, no less, a government entity responsible for enforcing regulations regarding working conditions and employment issues.

The silence of the DOL leadership toward my concerns was heartbreaking. As Dr. Martin Luther King Jr., so eloquently stated, "There comes a time when silence is betrayal." I felt betrayed by the DOL.

Chapter 23

*Educating yourself does not mean that you were stupid in
the first place; it means that you are intelligent enough
to know that there is plenty left to learn.*

—Melanie Joy

Willis Carter had requested an additional sixty to ninety-day
extension of my detail. That rotation began on January 7, 2013, and
ended on April 7, 2013. The project was to develop a SharePoint
correspondence tracking system to ensure training was provided
to selected personnel for managing the system. The project entailed
significant research, planning, developing, and deploying of a system
that would control and track how correspondence moves from one team
member to another, as each participant collaborates in a document's life
cycle.

The new project included developing workflows for team tasks,
such as reviewing and approving correspondence. I agreed to the
extension with the hope that I would find a new position before the
extension ended. Although I would have liked to continue permanently
with the DOJ, there were no vacant positions available. I completed the
final project with a month to spare.

The thought of returning to the DOL weighed heavily on me, as
I wrestled with thoughts of resigning from government service and
pursuing academia. I have never known myself to be a quitter, so I
continued to pursue my fight for justice, taking it all one day at a time.

In the last week before leaving the DOJ, Willis Carter came to my
office, sat down, and spoke with me regarding my detail experience and
return to the DOL. He thanked me for helping to facilitate the various
projects and wished me the best moving forward. However, at the end
of our conversation, he said, "I'm sorry for you when you return to the
DOL. But just remember to choose your battles."

I wasn't sure what led Willis to say what he did, and I didn't understand what he was trying to convey, but his advice was chilling and worth thinking about.

During this time, I was also on the brink of completing my PhD, and I had embarked on developing my dissertation, entitled *Workplace Spirituality and Ethical Decision Making: A Case Study of Federal Government Executive Women.* The topic of my dissertation was driven by my personal experiences at the DOL with toxic leadership. However, through my interviews and data collection processes, I met and interviewed exceptional executive women leaders in various government agencies whose similar experiences helped to bring my research to life.

Before getting to the dissertation phase, I had to pass a seven-hour written exam. The preparation was grueling, but I was thrilled when I learned that I had passed with flying colors. Passing the exam was the beginning of my dissertation journey. I was assigned three mentors during the process. A mentor is extremely important in the process, but in my experience, this phase of the journey was the most complicated. I had to change mentors a few times and after asking the second mentor for clarification on a leadership theory, his response in all caps was FIGURE IT OUT! I dropped him like a hot potato. The next day, I requested a new mentor. In a few weeks, I was assigned my final mentor, Dr. Rubye Braye.

She drove all the way from North Carolina and met with me at a Kinkos in Laurel, Maryland. Dr. Braye spent hours with me reviewing, editing, and providing feedback on my draft dissertation. My draft was bleeding red, and I was at times overwhelmed by the work that was ahead of me. But Dr. Braye gave me hope when she said, "If you do exactly what I tell you to do and make all the changes to your draft, you will complete your dissertation in less than three months." She didn't have to tell me twice.

With Dr. Braye's guidance, I completed my dissertation in the time she stated. After five years of commitment and hard work, on July 27,

2012, I was preparing with enthusiasm to walk across the stage to be hooded and conferred with a Doctor of Philosophy in organization and management, with a concentration in leadership.

I couldn't have done it without Dr. Braye, one of the best mentors I have ever had. She was also present at graduation to provide support to those she had mentored in getting to results. Her presence with us was priceless. Truly, her exceptional mentoring was a brain to pick, an ear to listen, and a push in the right direction!

Me, feeling accomplished even in adversities.

Chapter 24

Often, intuition will direct you. If it feels right, it's probably right.

—Oprah Winfrey

In February 2013, I saw an announcement for an adjunct professor position with the American Public University System (APUS), and it caught my attention. I was interested in applying for the position because of its emphasis on educating the nation's military and public service communities; hence, I submitted my application.

In mid-March 2013, I was invited to an interview for the position. The interview went well, and a few weeks later, I was offered the position. I accepted the offer as adjunct professor in the School of Business. It was a part-time position; but I was excited about the prospect, nevertheless.

Although I accepted the position, I wasn't scheduled to facilitate a class until the end of August 2013. However, I was able to access professional development courses in all facets of training and development and course delivery in an online learning environment. I was happy for the opportunity. The courses offered certificates and would be helpful in developing my knowledge in a new career path and to teach some of the courses at the DOL as I had assured the financial competency development team of experts that I would.

My DOL/ESA EEO complaint was still ongoing during this time. In June 2012, after exhausting my administrative remedies with the EEO process, I had filed a civil complaint in federal district court regarding religious discrimination and retaliation from 2007 to 2009 during my employment at the ESA.

On or around March 8, 2013, I was invited to a deposition with a DOJ attorney representing the agency. It was difficult and painful sitting through the process and rehashing the actions that had led to the process. My faith didn't remove my pain, but it certainly got me through it.

After the deposition, a potential settlement offer emerged. The agency, through its DOJ attorney, offered a job, a clean record, and no more than ten thousand dollars. The agency's offer was simply not enough to compensate me for what I had been through, and I elected to go to trial. At this point, I had already spent over one hundred thousand dollars in attorney's fees from 2009–2013; I had also experienced stress, sadness, depression, loss of self-esteem, and developed an inability to sleep. I rejected the settlement for those reasons. I deserved more, and the DOL's leaders deserved to be held accountable.

The agency's desire to offer me a job when it was paying my salary for over four years as GS-15 was a simple disgrace. After being fooled once into accepting a "budget analyst team lead" position that had turned out to be an administrative job, I learned from my mistakes and avoided being tricked in the same way again.

The offer of a "clean record" also seemed misguided, and more like an easy way to shut me up while protecting the perpetrators and the agency, rather than holding people accountable. In my view, the term "clean record" seemed to be an oxymoron. After all, the DOL had not filed any charges against me. I was the one who filed charges against the agency. My stellar record before my employment with the DOL spoke for itself. It was because of that record I had been offered the job at the DOL ESA in the first place. And now after the department's leaders had discriminated and retaliated against me, it wanted to offer me a "clean record." I wasn't sold on the offer because, in my view, accountability matters. And that was missing from the equation.

Hence, to have taken the offer, considering the injustices, I would have chosen the side of the oppressor. Furthermore, accepting the settlement would have meant I could never tell my story.

When the agency declared that it would give me a job, I knew from experience that the job would never be a position I desired. Hence, I asked for my day in court to present my case before twelve jurors. In the meantime, I had no alternative but to return to my role at the DOL following the detail that I'd been on.

On March 9, 2013, I returned to the DOL DBC. Not surprisingly, Osman Payne assigned me no work once I returned. With nothing to do in my DOL position, I decided to take advantage of free training offered to faculty toward obtaining a teaching certification and regularly took courses offered at APUS. Payne had stated previously that there were no funds available for training because of sequestration and that employees must find free training when work was slow. Thus, I identified and registered for various APUS and other courses that piqued my interest.

On or around April 9, 2013, Osman emailed me about meeting with him to give me assignments—for the very first time of my tenure with the DBC. He proceeded to give me a list of administrative assignments with delivery deadlines, something he had never done before. He also began emailing me to check on the status of the assignments weekly, rather than stopping by my cubicle to talk to me about a specific task. There was no reason for him to monitor my performance of tasks so closely because I had always completed my assignments in a satisfactory and timely manner. I found Osman's micromanaging of my work to be demeaning and harassing.

However, I did as he asked, completing each assignment based on the due date and forwarding the completed work to him via email. When he was asked by the investigator in my EEO case against him on February 21, 2014 for the reason for the sudden assignment deadlines and weekly emails, his explanations were implausible. You may recall Osman had stated there was no funding for agency training because of sequestration. However, he stated one of the reasons for emailing me weekly was to "obligate funds for training."

■ ■ ■

Let me be clear. Osman didn't micromanage or monitor the performance of my younger, male, and female Caucasian GS-15 colleagues. These colleagues were allowed to regularly leave work in the afternoon for "coffee breaks" for multiple hours at a time and weren't questioned about their location or the status of their work. He treated me much differently than he treated my White colleagues, and more harshly, particularly after I returned from my DOJ detail.

I believe the micromanaging was punitive, mainly after my comprehensive memorandum of concerns to A. Wiley Thornton, while at the DOJ, about his behaviors. I came to find Osman to be very vindictive during my tenure at the DBC, and his actions toward me at this time were prime examples of this.

On or around June 6, 2013, I responded to one of his emails letting him know that I found his weekly emails harassing; but he ignored my concern and told me he would email me again the following week. After that response, I knew his actions were personal. But as Willis Carter had advised, I chose my battles carefully.

I ignored Osman's response because at that point, it wasn't worth my time and effort anymore.

Chapter 25

Strong people will automatically stop trying if they feel unwanted. They won't fix it or beg, they'll just walk away.

—Author unknown

One of the assignments from Osman was a training plan. Based on his brief April 9 conversation with me, I was to use the OCFO financial management and budgeting skills assessment catalogue of courses to develop a 2013 training plan. These were also the courses that I'd helped to develop with a team of experts for finance and budget professionals. I did exactly as he asked. He didn't provide any other guidance regarding developing the training plan, nor did he ever discuss the details of the completed training plan with me. However, he would state under oath in June and July 2013 in his depositions that he never received this plan from me.

I was the owner and developer of the plan, and the next step in the training plan process would be for the agency personnel to review it, confer with their supervisors, and identify the training components provided in the plan that would fill their skills gap. However, the OCFO was spearheading this exact process. It wasn't a task that I was to do because a contractor had been awarded three hundred thousand dollars to complete such work. What Payne had asked me to do was a duplication of effort instead of allowing me to perform my duties as a budget analyst team lead. He was intentional about making me a budget analyst team lead in name only. Even in my day-to-day duties, Osman was manipulating and controlling everything that I did.

I forwarded a draft of the plan I'd developed to him on June 4 after he requested a status update. It included all the components he had requested. He would later admit, "I didn't study it, really."

I was a trained budget analyst and not an employee skills

assessment specialist. Nevertheless, I completed the task based on the requirements. Osman expected me to develop a comprehensive training plan for the ABOs; yet, he had never suggested training for me to improve my knowledge of organizational training.

I was also confused that Payne only wanted ABOs to be trained. That did not make sense. And I perceived that his focus on ABOs, in this regard, was broached to minimize his inappropriate request for me to visit them, take them out to lunch, and develop relations with them to get to the next level. I wondered why he wanted a training plan for only ABOs. This would alienate the rest of the budget and financial management personnel if only ABOs were to be trained based on this plan. On the contrary, the OCFO's training plan encompassed all financial management and budget personnel, not only ABOs, and it also included me.

■ ■ ■

I had provided him with an exceptional and comprehensive training plan that included the courses and the free training components he had requested. On numerous occasions he claimed he never received it. After reviewing it in detail with him at his deposition, he reversed his claim, as he admits in the following conversation with me while I was representing myself at his deposition on March 16, 2017:

Me: "And you received the training plan on or around June 4, correct?"

Mr. Payne: "Right. But what I referred to as a training plan, it's the training plan that I was looking for, not the one that was provided."

Me: "So, we would have to submit the plan with the courses to the ABOs so they can have something to select, correct?"

Mr. Payne: "Right. But I think you have to understand my
statement that I really hadn't had a chance to look at what you
had submitted on June 4 in that great of detail. I was looking for
something else . . . I looked through the plan, but I didn't study
it, really."

Payne admitted that he had received the plan I had provided to him but
didn't review it in "great" detail. He began describing a training plan
that was in his "head." I was totally confused by his response.

After he failed to review the comprehensive training plan I had
provided, he forwarded a message and it reads as follows:

From: Payne, Osman OASAM DBC
Sent: Thursday, June 06, 2013, 1:38 p.m.
To: Francis, Jean OASAM DBC Subject:
RE: Follow-Up

Thanks. Stopped by to discuss, but you were away. This is helpful,
but not what I was looking for or what we discussed back in April.
We discussed developing a training plan of courses that DBC would
provide for the department as we did in FY 2011. As a reminder, it
has to heavily rely on topics that can be delivered using internal
resources since we don't have funding for contracted training
because of sequestration. The plan is to reflect those areas that were
identified as needing improvement in the OCFO skills assessment
and your discussions with the Agency Budget Officers. If you haven't
already, please get the agency specific skills assessments from the
OCFO.

You need to meet with each Agency Budget Officer to discuss that
assessment and have them identify those areas where they would
like DBC to assist in developing capacity. You should also provide
them the document you sent me as they may find it helpful.

Please schedule your meetings by COB Tuesday and provide me
a copy of the schedule. All meetings should be completed by June
19. I also want a summary of each meeting, including the areas the
agency identified where they would like to build capacity. I should get
these meeting summaries by COB the day following each meeting.
After you have met with each agency budget officer, you should be
able to develop the training plan that we originally discussed and
that outlined below. Since we are now later into the fiscal year, the
training plan should cover both the remainder of FY 2013 and FY
2014. I want a draft of that plan one week after your last meeting with
the Agency Budget Officers.

In his email above, Osman changed the scope of the assignment and
began assigning me new tasks and deadlines relating to scheduling
individual meetings with twenty-three agency budget officers to present
the new training plan beginning on June 7, 2013, and providing him
detailed summaries of all meetings each day. This assignment was to be
completed on June 19, 2013.

Osman was laying this heavy task on my shoulder that wasn't
even my job. Additionally, he didn't even notify the supervisors or
the employees that I had been assigned the task. If I had done what
he was asking, I'm certain the supervisors and the employees would
have complained. Additionally, human resources would have gotten
involved because this would have been performing a function that
only a supervisor was allowed to do. It was confidential and privileged
information that I wasn't authorized to review with an employee.

When I told Osman at the midyear review meeting on June 27,
2013, that he had erred in assigning me the task of going to the ABOs
to "discuss their assessment," which is a task only their supervisors can
do, he stated that it was a "miscommunication." I was dismayed when
he uttered that word because, in my view, he knew exactly what he was
saying.

■ ■ ■

I had also indicated on April 29, 2013, that I would be on leave from June 10 through June 28, 2013. All the DBC staff, including Osman, received the leave calendar on May 1, 2013. At the time when he wanted me to accomplish that ridiculous task, many of the ABOs were on summer vacation in June 2013. Therefore, it was impossible for me to complete the summaries and meetings with everyone by June 19, 2013, even if this was a task that I could have performed and if my leave hadn't been scheduled for June10. I do not believe that the "miscommunication" wasn't that he found out I was to be on leave as he wanted others to believe.

The following conversation ensued with Osman and Ms. Grant at his deposition on March 19, 2015:

Ms. Grant: "What were the miscommunications that occurred in June regarding her work assignments?"

Mr. Payne: "Yeah. I had asked her to do a series of things, not realizing she had planned to be out on leave. And then once I realized that, I backed off and then decided to regroup and attack it again, the issues, at this meeting."

Osman knew I had requested vacation time on the calendar, but he was scheduling work on my vacation time. He was demanding that I complete that detailed task in less than a week, nonetheless. He claimed that this action was the result of a "miscommunication." However, the miscommunication I saw was when he requested that I go to the ABOs regarding their assessment in the first place, not because he was denying my leave.

He claimed in his deposition that once he realized I was going on leave he "changed" the deadlines. There were no deadlines to change. He didn't have any discussions with me regarding any deadline changes. He was assigning me to perform a task that wasn't my job responsibility. There is no deadline to change about that.

Additionally, when he was asked about the normal process for taking leave within the DBC, he said that each manager has his or her own methods. However, when he was asked about his specific method, he basically said that he would take a leave slip, an email, or a verbal request. What blew me away regarding Osman's response was when he was asked how his employees were aware of his preferences for leave requests. He stated, "I don't know." If his employees do not know his preference for taking leave, who was going to tell them, if not him?

I attended Osman's deposition and based on his responses regarding his involvement with his employees, I shook my head and thought, *What a waste of taxpayers' dollars*. Here is his response following a conversation that ensued between Osman and my attorney during his deposition on March 19, 2015:

Ms. Grant: "Did you send around an email saying this is how you should make a leave request to me?"

Mr. Payne: "No, I did not."

Ms. Grant: "Do you have that conversation with employees when they're new?"

Mr. Payne: "No."

Ms. Grant: "Does your office maintain a leave calendar, so you know when people have scheduled leave?"

Mr. Payne: "We have a leave calendar, but it's a general plan. It's not an approved scheduled leave."

Ms. Grant: "What does that mean?"

Mr. Payne: "It means that people are thinking about taking those

times off, but until they have communication with a supervisor,
it's not approved and it's not definite."

I was duly confused regarding his explanation about the leave calendar
and struggled to fully comprehend the process as he tried to explain
it, particularly after being assigned to the DBC for almost five years.
Because if there was one thing Osman was intentional about, it was
ensuring the administrative officer developed and disseminated the
quarterly leave calendar for the office. By doing so, not only would he
know when everyone was scheduled to be on leave, but everyone in the
office was also privy to this information. When Osman was asked if I
had documented my leave, he stated on one hand that, "She did."

However, he also testified that he had no knowledge of my leave. His
testimony was all over the place. My leave request was submitted at the
end of April 2013, and the leave calendar was forwarded to everyone,
including him on May 1. Osman's assignment with its unrealistic
deadlines was forwarded to me by email on June 6, 2013. Furthermore,
there is no way he couldn't have known that I had documented my
intention to take leave beginning on June 9.

There was never any meaningful discussion between him and me
regarding work projects or how I could be effective in the sparse work
projects he assigned once a year. His communication with me regarding
the budget meetings was through email, which was to inquire if the
agenda was developed for the meeting. Additionally, Osman would
pass by my cubicle every morning and afternoon and he would never
offer even the slightest greeting.

However, I wasn't offended by his actions because on many
occasions in the past he had shown me the type of character he was.
His actions spoke louder than his words.

After receiving the training plan, extensive DOJ detail report, and
internal and external customer service reports, Osman did nothing with
any of the assignments. He didn't even share them with anyone. It was
as though he threw them all in the trash. I asked him what he had done

with the extensive report he had requested regarding my detail with the DOJ, when I represented myself in my case. I had spent an enormous amount of time developing the report and showing how many of the processes that I had learned and developed could be implemented at the DOL. When I asked Osman if he had looked at the report and forwarded it to anyone, he said, "No."

I followed up by asking him what he had done with the report. He contradicted himself by saying he had "read it" and saw it might be applicable at the DBC.

But I didn't stop there, I also wanted to know what Osman had done with the exceptional training plan I had worked so hard to develop and submitted to him. He stated that I had never completed the plan or submitted it to him. Like the DOJ detail report, I wanted to know what he had done with the training plan and whom he had shared it with. After all, he had provided strict due dates for each assignment. To my chagrin, Osman had received the training plan but never shared it with anyone. He didn't even review the document. I was totally beside myself at this point. *What an abuse of power*, I thought. In my view, it wasn't just his abuse of power that was the problem, but it was the power he had been given by the department in the first place.

Chapter 26

Discrimination has a lot of layers that make it tough
for minorities to get a leg up.
—Bill Gates

Research has shown that retaliation is the most common form of workplace discrimination. In her 2019 article review on workplace retaliation, employment law attorney, Sapphire Legal says, "This explains why employees are so often reluctant to complain about mistreatment . . . to include lack of promotion, disparity, unpleasant working environment, bullying, and harassment. When an employee raises concerns and files a complaint regarding those concerns, unethical leaders will retaliate against the employee in most cases." Based on my DOL experiences after complaining about mistreatment, I can relate. You may also recognize yourself in my story and could also relate to the quandary presented by an employer's adverse action.

Moreover, it would turn out that I was far from being the only DOL employee who had faced this kind of treatment. The Equal Employment Opportunity Commission (EEOC) confirms this phenomenon in its statistical report from 2019. "Retaliation charges experienced the largest gain in percentage of all filed charges in FY 2019, which was an increase of 2.2 percent from the prior year," the report said. "Consequently, retaliation charges continue to represent most charges with 53.8 percent of all filed charges in FY 2019."

Hence, my two lawsuits both named *Francis v. US Department of Labor*, and others such as *Sewell v. US Department of Labor, Thompson v. US Department of Labor, Weingarten vs. US Department of Labor, and Edwards vs. US Department of Labor*, represent even only a fraction of the discrimination and retaliation-related lawsuits that employees have filed against the Department of Labor since 2009.

One of these DOL employees said in his lawsuit testimony: "I swear before God that I personally witnessed eight highly competent African American federal employees be denied promotions and assignments that would enhance their careers. I was ordered to remain silent while a Black woman was treated like a wild animal and herded into subservient jobs for many years because of the color of her skin."

But the discriminatory and retaliatory pandemic is not exclusive to the DOL—it permeates all industry. Journalist Emily Flitter comprehensively reported the pandemic of systemic racism inside American Financial Services industry in her book *The White Wall*. Flitter stated in her book that in the financial industry there are extreme power imbalances. Among other egregious acts against people of color, she further stated that:

"They were without power were kept isolated and apart. Starting out in disadvantaged position meant being kept in that position by virtue of being powerless. Speak out and risk losing everything. The same is true for people trying to advance their careers in banking and finance. Because the industry is still dominated by White men, minorities and women learn that if they manage to get ahead, the best thing to do is to count their blessings, keep their heads down, and try not to make trouble . . . .When they experience discrimination in the office and tried to speak out, only to be told that their employer saw no evidence of discrimination." These testimonies remind me of my own experience at the DOL.

When I share my story with others, some describe what had happened to me as discriminatory, sad, and unfortunate. Others empathize with me in a meaningful way. However, I consider what has happened to me as nothing less than an intentional and public lynching in the workplace, an example of twenty-first century Jim Crow. The Jim Crow laws were overruled by the Civil Rights Act of 1964 and the Voting Rights Act of 1965. However, in the end of my pursuit for justice in my cases, I see little difference between what happened to

Black people during the Jim Crow era and what happened to me in my litigation against the Department of Labor nearly five decades after the Civil Rights Act became law.

■ ■ ■

Regarding my vacations, they have been one of the most pleasant and cheerful events in my life, especially, while working at the DOL. Each year, I looked forward to the great escape from the workplace. It was a time to refresh, revive, and restore my mind, body, and soul with my family and friends. You may recall that when our children were younger, Orlando Florida was our favorite vacation spot. Specifically, Walt Disney World—our destination stop. Our vacations at Disney were marked by Mickey Waffles, colorful parades, princess hugs, and touring Cinderella Castle, just to name a few. However, my kids came of age and decided that they had outgrown Disney. And cruising seemed like a much better vacation and the best way to travel.

I was first introduced to cruising in the summer of 1993 by my Pentagon colleagues. I was a bit hesitant to go not knowing what to expect. I surrendered to the invitation and took the plunge. My colleagues and I went on a three-day cruise to the Bahamas. I had never been on a cruise, so this was a new experience for me. I must admit that I would have been one of those people who previously would have turned up her nose at the thought of being stuck on the ocean somewhere on a ship for any length of time. But at the same time, the idea of cruising fascinated me. After our vacation, I came back a convert. Today, I just succumb to the cruising life and keep the vacation moving. As a result, my family and I have been cruising ever since that day. Where else can you join hundreds or thousands of people on a ship in the middle of the ocean, somewhere in the world, having fun?

Moreover, the great appeal of cruising vacations provides an escape from the hassles and chores of your real life to include, leaving your worries at the shoreline, disconnecting from the rest of the world, and living your best life. It is a place where you are pampered, entertained, and experience the opportunity to visit many different destinations in one trip.

If "living my best life" was a triple decker chocolate cake, on my cruise vacation, I had eaten the whole thing—every time. A suite is always my cabin of choice. Because lounging on the deck each night brings me closer to the sounds and sights of the deep blue sea, the rhythmic ebbs and flows of the waves, and experiencing the most beautiful sunset and sunrises, among other things. It's always therapeutic. And for that one moment in time, my problems cease to exist.

In the summer of 2018, my high school bestie Eudora Eudovique accompanied me on a cruise during my tumultuous time at the DOL. Eudora and I know each other since seventh grade. Time and distance had separated us after high school, but we telephonically stayed connected at regular interval. We looked forward to seeing each other again and enjoying our vacation. As we spend time together in our cabin talking about our past and present life situations, I shared my work experiences with her. Eudora sat and listened intently and provided hope and encouragement for me to continue my journey. I was fortunate to have my friend to confide in again. We decided to tour the city of San Juan among other historic sites together and we had an exceptional time. While at the market square, I worked up the nerve to take a picture with an iguana on the top of my head. Like the kid I was at my grandmother's house, I trembled in my walking shoes. But I did it anyway, and the experience is lasting memory.

The following year while on a Southern Caribbean escapade with Lionel, still confident from having an iguana on my head, I decided to stage a photoshoot with not one but two capuchin monkey at the St. Kitts market square. The experience was tense, but the feeling of excitement was grand.

We woke up the next morning in Barbados to blue skies, crystal clear waters, and a fresh burst of energy. Lionel and I decided to spend the day at one of the exhilarating beaches. We hurriedly prepared ourselves for the day and with glee disembarked the ship. We walked from the port to the marketplace, purchased local fruits of our liking, and hired a cab to the nearest beach. The body of water was breathtaking. And the beaming sun felt comfortable—like a warm blanket enveloping our bodies. After spending hours frolicking in the water and enjoying the scenery, by three o'clock, we were lying lazily in a quiet, secluded, ultra-romantic part of the beach—wishing the moment could last forever.

It was time to return to the ship. We had less than an hour to get there. We'd asked the cab driver to pick us up at four o'clock. He agreed. But it was apparent he was running late at half past the hour. He arrived frantically at 4:35 p.m. Lionel erupted, "You're late!" The driver replied, "I got held up in the traffic, but I'll get you back in time." We hurriedly got into the cab as the driver headed toward our destination. "Have you visited Rihanna's childhood home?" he stated as he swerved in and out of traffic. "No!" Lionel responded. "You don't want to come to Barbados and not visit her childhood home" he replied. "I'll take you there with enough time to board the ship," he said with jubilation. Although time was not on our side, we decided to take him up on his offer. We had visited Barbados on many occasions but had never thought of visiting Rihanna's childhood home.

Hastily, he drove to the destination as we frantically and persistently checked our watches knowing that we were teetering on borrowed time to return and board the ship. When we arrived, he said, "This is it! Hurry, stand in front of the house so I can take your picture." Anxiously and with excitement, we did. We rushed to stand in front of Rihanna's childhood home, stole a kiss, as our cab driver watched with a smile, and took our picture. The excitement was surreal.

"Get back into the car," he said with urgency, after taking the photos. "I have ten minutes to get you back to the ship. He didn't have to tell us twice. We were able to get back and say our goodbyes with five minutes to spear. We smiled as we walked the gangway to our cabin because our day was stupendous.

Nothing last forever. Even vacations come to an end. It was time to get back to the real world and the DOL. But, without a doubt, my first day back in that environment inspired me to book my next vacation immediately.

■ ■ ■

On June 24, 2013, after returning from another cruise vacation, I filed an informal complaint against Osman for harassment and discrimination based on race, and retaliation for prior EEO activities. It would be another attempt to address my concerns to the leadership and for motivating a change. The mediation for my informal complaint was scheduled on August 21, 2013, and the DOL leadership consisting of A. Wiley Thornton and George Fox, Thornton's deputy director, once again declined to address my concerns regarding Osman or accept any offer my attorney recommended for settling my claims. It was as though they were the face of the DOL. I was disappointed.

The leadership also ignored my physician's request to provide me with a less stressful work environment and, again, denied my request to transfer to another agency. In Fox's own words at the MSPB hearing regarding a transfer, he stated, "Now, we're not—and I'm personally not going to do this, and none of my managers are going to do this. We're not going to pass a problem around."

The most nauseating thought was that I was considered a "problem" for raising legitimate concerns regarding employment issues. That thought rested heavily on my heart. This situation was affecting my health and total well-being. I took the following directly from the memorandum my physician Dr. Joan Johnson, Walter Reed National Medical Center Bethesda, written on June 7, 2013:

To Whom It May Concern,

Dr. Francis has been a patient in the General Internal Medicine Clinic at Walter Reed National Medical Center, Bethesda. She has had several primary care providers over the past several years and was most recently assigned to me as her new PCM. I met Dr. Francis on March 13, 2013. She has been diagnosed with adjustment disorder with anxiety in 2009, after frequent complaints of excessive worry, headaches, sleep disruptions, decreased energy, emotional eating, and weight gain, elevated blood pressure, frequent crying, heart palpitations, and sadness.

    Her problems with stress began approximately seven years ago related to a legal battle regarding workplace discrimination and retaliation. She was referred to behavioral health, psychiatry, and psychology and was given medications for anxiety and sleep. She entered the Integrated Cardiac Health Program at Walter Reed for eighteen months to assist in behavior modification, stress reduction, exercise, and healthy eating. She is still receiving psychotherapy.

    I recommend that she continue with behavioral health, and if possible, seek a less stressful work environment.

    Please contact me with any questions regarding this matter.

Sincerely,

Joan M. Johnson, MD

Much like my memorandum of concerns to Thornton regarding Osman's egregious behaviors against me, the DOL leadership ignored my physician's letter as well as my psychologist's letter. Instead, Thornton, my first-line supervisor and his deputy, Mr. Fox, were resolved to protect Osman. In my psychologist's memorandum on June 1, 2013, she said the following:

Dr. Francis has a number of symptoms that are consistent with individuals who have experienced trauma. These include nightmares, flashbacks, rethinking over and over of the events, depression, anxiety, sleep disturbance, appetite disturbance, and panic attacks. These issues can be directly related to her ongoing difficulties at her place of employment. In fact, Dr. Francis did tell her agency she was having these difficulties. She related this in the form of a memo sent on March 18, 2009.

Dr. Francis is continuing to see me on a weekly basis in order to continue to help her with these anxiety and depressive symptoms. These symptoms appear to be a direct result of her difficulties at work. None of these symptoms are pre-morbid, that is, Dr. Francis didn't have any of these anxiety or depressive symptoms prior to her ongoing difficulties at her place of employment (Department of Labor).

I hope this letter is helpful. Please let me know if I can be of further assistance.

Sincerely,

Sonia Peters, PhD

Finally, no intervention on my behalf was of any concern to the DOL leadership. I had an opportunity to speak with one of the DBC administrative employees about my problems with Osman and expressed that I wasn't being assigned any work relating to my position description. She told me that she noticed that the DBC had a culture where African Americans of a higher grade are treated differently than their White counterparts. She told me about a male African American team lead who wasn't given any work, filed a complaint, and was moved to another department. I don't know the male employee's name or any other details about him.

She also told me that she had been asking to transition to an assistant budget analyst at DBC. She said that the leadership ignored her request and brought in a White person as an analyst instead. Another African-American female who worked with the DBC told me that she too experienced discrimination and had to leave immediately. She stated that the DBC is not a good place for people of color to work. A walk through at the DBC would reveal this fact based on how and where people of color were assigned.

Cruising with my friend Eudora

In Barbados with my husband

Chapter 27

Good leadership requires you to surround yourself
with people of diverse perspectives who can disagree
with you without fear of retaliation.
—Doris Kearns Goodwin

My midyear performance review with Osman was scheduled for June 27, 2013. Payne seemed visibly upset at the meeting. I saw his face flushed red as he glanced at me. Then, he simply handed me a red pen and said almost inaudibly, "Sign here," pointing to the review. I thought this was strange because there were numerous black and blue ink pens on his desk. "Why do you want me to sign in red?" I asked. He said, "Because I can see it better." I could sense the anger in his voice. I had just filed an EEO complaint against him, and I perceived that his request at this meeting was vindictive and retaliatory at best. I believe that Payne's action of wanting me to sign an official document with a red ink pen (which is not standard practice) was intentional and intended to send me a passive-aggressive signal.

The midyear review should have been completed once I returned from the DOJ in March 2013. However, Osman failed to do this supervisory obligation and instead had only scheduled the meeting immediately after I had filed my EEO complaint. Payne had nothing to say about my performance at the meeting. I signed the form to show that he had met with me, no matter how brief the exchange.

We had no conversation regarding my assignments or performance issues at the time. Yet, he would later claim that he was concerned about not receiving the training plan. Why not use the performance review session to discuss these concerns? I wanted to get a good understanding for why he did not discuss any performance issues or take notes at the meeting. I questioned him about it when I represented myself at his deposition on March 16, 2017. Here is his account:

Me: "Did you take notes of the [midyear review] discussions?"

Mr. Payne: "No, not of that meeting,"

Me: "Why didn't you take notes of the discussions?"

Mr. Payne: "I thought it went very well. I didn't think there was a need to take notes."

Me: "Have you ever taken notes of any midyear reviews discussion with you and Dr. Francis?"

Mr. Payne: "Not that I can recall."

Me: "Did you have concerns about the training plan, as you stated? And don't you believe that would be a good time to annotate the meeting, and annotate what your concerns were?"

Mr. Payne: "Well, Dr. Francis had just told me how she found my style harassing, and we had a good meeting and came to an agreement on how we would move forward on getting the training plan. So, I decided to treat her the way she had asked to be treated and let her take responsibility for completing the tasks that she agreed to take on, and I would take the ones that I agreed to take on."

Me: "Wouldn't it be beneficial to have that in writing to show that you discussed the plan and moving forward, how the tasks were going to be handled?"

Mr. Payne: "Given the way it turned out, yes, it would have been beneficial."

This was a direct contradiction to the testimony he had given at his

March 2015 deposition, however. The following conversation had previously occurred between Osman and Kate Grant at his deposition on March 19, 2015:

Ms. Grant: "What was the tone of the meeting that took place on June 27 [2013]?" she asked.

Mr. Payne: "I thought it was very productive," he said.

Ms. Grant: "Did you give her any constructive criticism?"

Mr. Payne: "No."

Ms. Grant: "Did you tell her there were any areas in her work that needed improvement?"

Mr. Payne: "No."

Ms. Grant: "This is an email. It's been marked as Exhibit 3. And it's from you dated June 28th. So, this would be the day after the midyear review, correct?"

Mr. Payne: "Yes."

Ms. Grant: "All right. And it looks like you sent this to yourself. Is that correct?"

Mr. Payne: "Correct."

Ms. Grant: "And is that something that you regularly do?"

Mr. Payne: "Sometimes; yes."

Ms. Grant: "Why did you do it in this case?"

Mr. Payne: "I just wanted to maintain a record of what we discussed at this meeting."

Ms. Grant: "Why?"

Mr. Payne: "Primarily, because of the miscommunication that happened before, I wanted to make sure I was keeping track of communications, make sure I didn't—we didn't have miscommunications again."

Ms. Grant: "Is this a way that you document your midyear conversations with all of your direct reports?"

Mr. Payne: "No."

Ms. Grant: "Just Dr. Francis?"

Mr. Payne: "I don't recall if I did any with any others."

Ms. Grant: "I'd like to go back to the email that's marked Exhibit 3. Did you send a similar email to Jean summarizing your meeting?"

Mr. Payne: "I don't recall."

Ms. Grant: "But you definitely didn't send her this email, correct?"

Mr. Payne: "No."

Ms. Grant: "Why not?"

Mr. Payne: "I don't know."

In Osman's note to himself on June 28, 2013, he had annotated an entire page of interactions that never happened. Among other things he included: "Had a good meeting with Jean yesterday on her midyear appraisal. We worked through miscommunications and developed plans to accomplish for the remainder of the year. I thanked Jean for creating the tracking template and asked her to send it to me. I indicated that it's a good opportunity to get into the details of other DBC operations, which should help her in her customer service and ABO competency assignments. Jean asked how I would treat the completion of her DOJ detail in her final appraisal, and I indicated that I would get feedback from Willis Carter and put it in special projects."

He then added the following: "She also noted that the date of the midyear was after the May 31 date required for other appraisals and I indicated that I had been talking to HR about other issues and they noted that I should wait ninety days after her return from her DOJ detail to have my midyear review discussion with her."

He never had a single conversation with me regarding any of the statements that he later annotated to himself. Perhaps he spoke with HR, but I certainly don't know which Jean he was referring to. It certainly wasn't me.

■ ■ ■

The midyear performance review allows supervisors a formal occasion to talk with employees about past performance to date. It's an opportunity to provide positive feedback on their accomplishments. It's also a time to give constructive feedback on areas where performance may be lacking and discuss goals for the future.

Osman had done no such thing at the June 27, 2013, midyear review. Instead, he simply asked me to sign the document with a red ink pen followed by no discussion. Nothing about the meeting was "productive" as he had claimed. He didn't share any concerns regarding poor performance in any areas, not even alleged poor performance relating to the training plan. Instead, he wrote a note and sent it to himself. What a laugh!

The following interaction occurred between Osman and Ms. Grant, at his deposition on March 19, 2015:

Ms. Grant: "What were the miscommunications that occurred in June regarding her work assignments?"

Mr. Payne: "Yeah. I had asked her to do a series of things, not realizing she had planned to be out on leave. And then once I realized that I backed off and then decided to regroup and attack it again, the issues at this meeting."

Ms. Grant: "And what were those goals?"

Mr. Payne: "We wanted to complete the—I wanted to complete putting together a training plan and hopefully deliver most of that plan before the end of the performance period. But I wanted to do it in combination with what the CFO was doing."

Ms. Grant: "And what was the CFO doing?"

Mr. Payne: "They were following up on their skills"

Ms. Grant: "Were there any deadlines associated with that assignment?"

Mr. Payne: "Yes. I wanted to roll out how we would approach this with the agency budget officers. And I wanted to do it at the next agency budget-officer meeting."

The DOL was already paying a contractor to put a training plan together for budget and financial management professionals. The CFO was spearheading that initiative. Hence, neither Osman nor the DBC were required to complete any other training plan to combine with the CFO.

That would have been a duplication of effort and a waste of government resources and man hours. As a matter of fact, the OCFO representative was invited at the DBC budget meetings to provide regular updates on the OCFO training initiative. Finally, neither Osman nor any one at the DBC supervised the ABOs. They were assigned to other agencies led by leaders who should have been the ones to address training and development concerns.

Osman was laying the burden of training ABOs on my shoulders as though that was my job. Yet he failed to identify even one training course to help me perform this ridiculous job he was imposing on me. The ABOs had supervisors who I'm sure could identify training for them to do their jobs, if necessary. I wasn't their supervisor; I was a budget analyst whom Osman was denying the opportunity of performing her job.

However, I stayed motivated with knowing that a breakthrough in my situation may have been delayed but that the struggle for it must go on. I am unwilling to take falsehood lying down. I'm committed to scoring a win for the naked truth.

Chapter 28

Before you are a leader, success is all about growing yourself.
When you become a leader, success is all about growing others.

—Jack Welch

The mark of a good leader is not that you can convince other people to follow you, but that you can empower others to lead. I had clearly never been empowered to lead at the Department of Labor. Instead, I had experienced the exact opposite style of leadership. I had been made powerless and helpless in that environment, and I had wasted seven years of my career. But I've learned that no experience in life is wasted if you have the right mindset; it's always a lesson learned.

After the midyear review, Osman didn't assign any additional work to me, though I continued to complete the earlier tasks he had assigned by the dates that he had outlined. Still, this wasn't enough to keep me busy, and weeks, and then months, passed without having enough work to do. So, I decided to use my unoccupied time at work to improve myself and learn. I continued to take the professional development courses from APUS and other educational platforms to stay current in my field of study.

But Osman wasn't through with me yet. In early August 2013, Rob Briar, the DBC DEBS and IT administrator, had a conversation with me that started with a discussion on what I was doing with my PhD. When I told him I had just started as a part-time adjunct professor with APUS, Rob seemed surprised. He told me that his wife was also in academia and that she developed courses at her place of employment. But he would later deny that he had said this.

He also said that he was preparing to launch a DEBS certification training initiative and that my training and experience at APUS would be exponentially helpful in launching it. Rob said it would require an online course delivery platform, and it would entail course development, syllabi, and a certification program. He asked if I would be interested in leading the initiative.

As I considered the proposition, I wondered whether I was up to the task, given that I was just beginning to learn the tricks of the trade of facilitating an online course delivery platform at APUS. However, Rob said that if I developed the program, I would have a team to work with me and to help develop the course material. I told him that I would give it some thought and get back to him. Rob immediately spoke with Osman about our discussion and the initiative, and within a week of our initial discussion, Osman invited us to a meeting to discuss the DEBS training initiative and next steps.

I was surprised he wanted to meet so quickly. I hadn't even decided on whether I would facilitate the initiative. The meeting lasted an hour, and the conversation was very comprehensive. Osman called the meeting, but he would later say in his deposition with my attorney that he remembered nothing of our discussion. On the contrary, he seemed to have had a very good understanding of what was discussed when he was deposed March 16, 2017, while I represented myself. Here is his account of the meeting:

> **Me:** "Is that the email you sent out regarding the DEBS certification program meeting or discussions?"
>
> **Mr. Payne:** "Yes. I organized the meeting."
>
> **Me:** "Can you state exactly what the discussions were at the meeting?"
>
> **Mr. Payne:** "No, I can't. I don't recall much of that meeting actually. As I said before, I know Rob wanted to establish a certification program and that is about the gist of the meeting that I remember."

Me: "So, you remember nothing of this meeting?"

Mr. Payne: "Not really. No."

Me: "What was your takeaway from the meeting?"

Mr. Payne: "That you and Rob had agreed to work on certain things to move forward on the certification programs."

Me: "What was that end result to be?"

Mr. Payne: "A program—training program that if you took—if a user took the classes that they would be a certified DEBS user."

Me: "And if they were to be certified as a DEBS user, what would be the process to make them certified?"

Mr. Payne: "They would have taken the identified training."

■ ■ ■

During the meeting with Osman, Rob spoke about the initiative in detail. The process entails developing a multitude of courses to be accessed through DEBS. I was reluctant to spearhead the initiative for the reasons I've mentioned, but was happy to pursue it, particularly when Rob said that I would have a team to help with the process. It also gave me a project on which I could focus and which I would bring benefit to the department.

I shared some of what I was doing at APUS and how it may help me provide a proposal and presentation for the DEBS initiative. This was well-received by Osman and Rob. I also talked about the courses I had been taking and certification I had earned at APUS in preparation to teach some of the courses through the OCFO at DOL.

Rob also said that he was experiencing low participation in the DEBS courses he was facilitating, and he asked me for my suggestions on improving the learning process and attracting more participants. I provided a few suggestions and recommended that he implement a survey for the learners to complete at the end of each class.

This would provide feedback for improving future course offerings. My recommendation seemed well received. Rob reiterated that the DEBS initiative would require online and classroom training, developing syllabi and course material, and that it would require certification because participants would be given a certificate upon completing the courses.

Osman wanted me to research online platforms based on my experience with APUS. At some point, I would have to deliver a presentation on the research, the level of effort it would take, and a suitable platform for the new initiative. After the meeting ended, I left Osman and Rob in the conference room as they continued their discussion. My mind was in overdrive after the meeting.

I spent the rest of August 2013 putting together a research and development plan for the program. I was cautiously optimistic and excited. I had been tasked with researching and developing an online course delivery platform, and this was a big deal. At least, that's what I thought.

I was to be the "champion and overseer of the new initiative," in Rob's words, and I took the challenge seriously. Although I had no expertise or training in developing such a platform, I was excited about the undertaking, and I believed that I could see it through. It would be much like the budget formulation and execution system initiative that I had researched and made a presentation on to the DOJ OCFO. I was an excellent project manager, and this was a worthy challenge. However, in this case, I had access to online learning platforms from various universities that would be helpful with developing a presentation and making recommendations to Osman and Rob.

I approached the project from a comprehensive perspective. I pride myself on having an eye for detail, and I brought this detail-oriented approach to the DEBS initiative. I tried to consider every potential detail of course development and tools implementation for helping a learner to succeed in an online learning environment. Osman had not recommended any specific education websites to use in my research; hence, I used the educational sites I had access to. After all, he had indicated that the project was mine to develop, and I was preparing to do so.

I thought it would be a good idea to introduce the tool and its capability as part of the DEBS training initiative project presentation. During the research process, I reviewed the online course delivery platform of APUS, Capella, and University of Phoenix to make recommendations for rolling out the DEBS initiative.

To understand the APUS Saki course platform from a faculty perspective, I had to access the courses to become familiar with the various components that make up the courses. Additionally, I would not have been able to give a presentation to Osman and Rob if I had no experience with the Saki course platform. Then, once I had a comprehensive grasp of how the Saki platform worked, I decided that, of all the others I had researched, it was the best platform for the DEBS training online course delivery initiative. In my research and development, I saved various course modules, rubrics, and syllabi on my work computer for future presentations and to help develop the DOL platform. Why reinvent the wheel when you can attach what already exists to a new wagon?

I also saved APUS student work I had graded using the Grammarly writing tool because I thought the tool would be beneficial, especially in helping with writing during the budget formulation process and beyond. The tool was also excellent for enhancing vocabulary and improving one's writing skills.

It turns out, none of the hard work I had done mattered. Osman would later deny even knowing about the DEBS initiative that he had assigned.

Osman had the following conversation with my attorney at his deposition on March 19, 2015. Here is his account:

Ms. Grant: "Are you familiar with the DEBS user certification and training program?"

Mr. Payne: "Doesn't ring a bell, no."

Ms. Grant: "Do you recall a time when Dr. Francis worked with the DEBS team in developing an online training program?"

Mr. Payne: "Yes."

Ms. Grant: "And who requested that she work with the DEBS team?"

Mr. Payne: "It started with a conversation between her and Rob Briar, who is the manager of the DEBS unit. And when they told me about it, I thought it was a good idea as well."

Ms. Grant: "How much time did she spend on this project?"

Mr. Payne: "I don't know."

Ms. Grant: "Do you know if she was successful in completing her assignments related to this project?"

Mr. Payne: "I don't know."

Ms. Grant: "Did you ever review any of her assignments related to the project?"

Mr. Payne: "No."

■ ■ ■

After the informal complaint process and mediation failed, On September 12, 2013, I filed a formal EEO complaint, which included employment discrimination based on race, sex, and reprisal for prior EEO complaints. I was also furloughed on September 15, 2013, because of a government shutdown.

Suddenly, Osman and Rob were no longer interested in the DEBS initiative. Based on his response, they didn't ask how much time had been spent on the project or reviewed any of the assignments. Interestingly, Osman didn't seem to have had any problem with my performance during the meeting with Rob. This was not a project that you would have assigned to a poor performer.

I had the following conversation with Osman while representing myself at his deposition on March 16, 2017. Here is his account:

Me: "When you met with Dr. Francis regarding the DEBS training initiative, did you have any concerns about her poor performance?"

Mr. Payne: "Well, at that point I was getting a little worried about whether I would get a training plan. I was also worried about the—I think it was because the internal focus group discussion was due by the end of September. And I hadn't really seen those, so I was a little concerned about those two items, yes."

Me: "Did you talk to Dr. Francis about those issues and concerns?"

Mr. Payne: "No."

Me: "So, you didn't have any problems with declining performance?"

Mr. Payne: "No."

Me: "And you didn't counsel her on any performance issues?"

Mr. Payne: "No. I did not."

On May 14, 2013, at 5:56 p.m., I had forwarded an email to Osman to let him know that the DBC internal focus group meeting was scheduled for the afternoon of May 23 from two thirty to three thirty. On May 20, 2013, I forwarded another email regarding the meeting, to which Osman responded. At no time did he communicate to me that he was "worried about the internal focus group." This is further supported by the following set of emails between the two of us about the internal focus group on May 20, 2013:

> **From:** Payne, Osman —OASAM DBC
> **Sent:** Monday, May 20, 2013, 10:48 a.m.
> **To:** Francis, Jean—OASAM DBC.
> **Subject:** RE: Follow-Up
>
> Thanks. Is Traci facilitating? Also, what level of participation from me
> do you think is appropriate?

■ ■ ■

> **From:** Francis, Jean—OASAM DBC
> **Sent:** Monday, May 20, 2013, 12:02 p.m.
> **To:** Payne, Osman—OASAM DBC
> **Subject:** RE: Follow-Up
>
> I will facilitate. You are welcome to participate if you are available,
> but if you are not available, that's okay. It would be a nice gesture to

stop by at the beginning of the meeting letting the group know the importance of good customer service at the DBC, thank them for agreeing to participate in the focus group, and letting them know their ideas will be greatly appreciated for improving internal and external communication. Also, let them know you are on board with the initiative and are motivated to make improvements in internal and external processes. This will potentially motivate them to be more forthcoming in sharing their ideas. Hope this helps.

■ ■ ■

From: Payne, Osman—OASAM DBC
Sent: Monday, May 20, 2013, 12:37 p.m.
To: Francis, Jean—OASAM DBC
Subject: RE: Follow-Up

It does. I'll help kick it off and turn it over to you. Has the invite gone out yet?

■ ■ ■

From: Francis, Jean—OASAM DBC
Sent: Monday, May 20, 2013, 12:40 p.m.
To: Payne, Osman—OASAM DBC
Subject: RE: Follow-Up

Yes, I am also planning on getting cupcakes; you are welcome to share the cost.

■ ■ ■

From: Payne, Osman—OASAM DBC
Sent: Monday, May 20, 2013, 12:42 p.m.

To: Francis, Jean—OASAM DBC

Subject: RE: Follow-Up

Certainly. It will help me in resisting the urge to bring in donuts. Let me know how much you need.

The email trail above would refute Osman's claim about not having any knowledge regarding the internal customer service focus group assignment. Similarly, the external focus group meeting was also completed on September 23, 2013, and a memorandum of the interview results was developed and forwarded to Osman. Yet, he said he was concerned about these assignments because he supposedly had no knowledge that I had completed them.

After Osman received the result of the internal and external focus group meetings, he testified that he had done nothing with the information, particularly after he had been emailing me weekly asking for status updates. Although he stopped by and spoke with the group, Osman said that he "didn't know the specific people."

Moreover, he said he didn't get the summary. However, that was one of the assignments for which he rated me "meets expectations," because I had met the "OASAM milestone."

The following was taking directly from Osman's deposition by my attorney, Kate Grant, on March 19, 2015:

Ms. Grant: "And then you said Jean will provide a summary of the internal discussion session. Do you know when the internal discussion session took place?"

Mr. Payne: "I don't remember the specific date."

Ms. Grant: "Who participated in that?"

Mr. Payne: "It would have been DBC staff. I don't remember the specific—I don't know the specific people."

Ms. Grant: "Do you remember if she provided you with that summary?"

Mr. Payne: "No, I don't remember."

■ ■ ■

Although I had been offered an adjunct professor's position with APUS in March 2013, I didn't begin facilitating a course with APUS until September 2013. However, I was provided a mentor in June 2013 and was an academic observer to her classroom. As a mentee, I was able to observe the APUS online platform from a faculty point of view. This experience helped me with understanding the APUS course-delivery platform and to begin gathering information for making recommendations to implement the DEBS training initiative based on the meeting with Osman and Rob. As indicated earlier, I also had experience with two other universities as a student, and I was able to gather information on those platforms.

Also, I was furloughed on September 15, 2013, because of a government shutdown. During this time, I took three weeks of leave to stay at the Wildwood Lifestyle Center in Georgia to de-stress and focus on my health. I didn't return to work until the last week of October 2013.

When I returned, I noticed that my computer had been moved. I initially assumed it had been moved by the cleaning staff as they cleaned my workspace, so I ignored it. I also noticed that my password no longer worked when I tried to log in, and I had to contact IT to change my password. In the coming months, I would come to understand what had happened. In my absence, Osman had ordered an investigation into my computer usage based on alleged "declining performance" after my midyear review.

I would later learn that Osman had initially ordered the computer audit immediately following our August 13 meeting about the DEBS online learning initiative, and that it was carried out while I was on vacation. He used the guise of "declining" performance and "poor productivity" to justify the audit of my computer. However, I know of no DOL policy that states supervisors are permitted to audit an employee's computer for poor performance issues. He continued to use the "training plan" he specifically stated that he had received, but that he didn't review, as an excuse for his actions.

His action was concerning to me and while representing myself pro se during Osman's deposition on March 16, 2017, I had the opportunity to confront him about it. Osman admitted, in his own words, that there was no such policy. I asked Osman if he had requested the audit into my computer and the following conversation ensued:

Me: "Did you request an Audit of Dr. Francis' computer?"

Mr. Payne: "In discussing with George (Fox) performance issues, I made the statement to him that I wasn't sure what Dr. Francis was working on since she didn't produce this element, but she always seems to be busy. And he told me that he—there are people that can look into that. And I asked him if he could have people look into that. So, I asked George and then George asked the OCIO folks to look into it."

Me: "So, is it the DOL policy that if an employee has performance issues, to audit his or her computer?"

Mr. Payne: "No."

Me: "And have you ever requested an audit into another employee's computer?"

Mr. Payne: "I have not. My reason was she seemed very busy, but, yet the work didn't seem to be coming and the government-assigned work didn't seem to be coming. I wanted to know what she was working on."

Me: "What is the government's assigned work that she wasn't producing?"

Mr. Payne: "The training plan."

Me: "And when you requested the audit, what did you want to see?"

Mr. Payne: "If there were things outside of government work being conducted on that computer."

Me: "And what were—what sites did you want to see?"

Mr. Payne: "I was specifically interested in educational sites."

Me: "And why were you specifically interested in educational sites?"

Mr. Payne: "Because I had known you had gotten your PhD the year before and that perhaps you were doing something similar using the government computer."

Me: So, how did you come to that conclusion because of the PhD?

Mr. Payne: "Well, I—from the first day we met you've been

interested in education and training. And since you pursued one degree, I thought it's fairly logical to think that you were doing something similar."

Me: "Well, that's an assumption, isn't it?"
Mr. Payne: "Yes, it is."

On December 5, 2013, I received a letter from the DOL Civil Rights Center stating that my EEO complaint had been transferred to the DOL Administrative Review Board (ARB) for continued processing, due to a potential conflict of interest. I understood that to mean the conflict of interest was because Mr. Thornton was my second-line supervisor, who was also Osman's first-line supervisor. The complaint included Osman as well. All OSAM employees' EEO complaints were processed through Thornton's office; therefore, my complaint was transferred to prevent a conflict of interest.

■ ■ ■

On December 5, 2013, Osman invited me to a meeting to discuss my performance review, which should have been completed on September 30, 2013, at the end of the fiscal year. The performance review was ninety-days late. For the first ninety-days during the performance year, I had worked at the DOJ on additional assignments. Osman never asked me for my input into the appraisal for the work that was done at the DOJ. I walked into his office and sat down. He passed the review to me and said, "Your performance evaluation is 'minimally satisfactory;' you need to sign here."

I sat there appalled. I couldn't believe he would wait until three months after my performance evaluation to claim that my performance was "minimally satisfactory."

When Osman was asked the reason for the delay, he said that "it was because the shutdown pushed deadlines back." However, the shutdown was less than two weeks in September. He was also asked if he had requested my input into my performance appraisal. Osman declared that he had asked for my input "at the performance appraisal meeting." In truth, the performance appraisal was already completed and ready for me to sign before the meeting, with no input whatsoever. The document wasn't a draft; it was in its final stage because he asked for my signature.

The time that a supervisor would typically address performance-evaluation issues is at the midyear review. I asked Osman why he didn't ask for my input into the appraisal or share the draft with me for review. He didn't answer my question. I asked him if that was the way he treated other employees.

He raised his voice and shouted, "YES!" I knew that wasn't accurate. I told him things had to change because what he was doing wasn't right. He replied with a smile, "Yes. Things are going to change." I sensed something sinister about his attitude and response. And I wanted to know what he meant by it.

I asked him about it while representing myself pro se at his deposition on March 16, 2017. He gave the following account:

Me: "Did you remember Dr. Francis mentioned after the discussion that 'there's got to be a change?'"

Mr. Payne: "Yes."

Me: "And do you remember you said to Dr. Francis, 'Yes, there will be a change.'

Mr. Payne: I agreed with her that, yes, there needed to be a change."

Me: "When you stated something is going to change, what did you mean by that?"

Mr. Payne: "I just meant that whatever relationship we had wasn't working and something needed to change to make sure that it was going to work in the future."

Me: "And what was that something?"

Mr. Payne: "I didn't know at that moment."

He didn't raise any performance issues at the midyear review, nor did he assign any other tasks except for the DEBS initiative. Osman also stated at his deposition that, as far as he was concerned, at the end of September 2013, my performance was fine. If that was the case and the rating period ended on September 30, 2013, my performance review should not have been minimally satisfactory.

I felt that Osman's low rating wasn't about my work performance; it was about retaliating against me. He knew that I was preparing to teach a course at APUS because we had talked extensively about developing an online learning platform analogous to APUS in our DEBS initiative meeting with Rob. He was chock-full with information, and he knew exactly what he was going to do with it. I had the following conversation with Osman while representing myself pro se at his deposition on March 16, 2017:

Me: "Did Dr. Francis performance deteriorate between March and June? Did she have performance issues?"

Mr. Payne: "I would say no."

Me: "Did she have performance issues in July?"

Mr. Payne: "No."

Me: "At the end of September 2013, did you state that you didn't have performance issues with her, correct?"

Mr. Payne: "As far as I was concerned, yes, her performance was fine."

■ ■ ■

I believe Mr. Payne's rating of my performance as "minimally satisfactory" was retaliatory. He said at the deposition that his other direct reports, for this rating period, received "exemplary" ratings. Osman also stated that he had never given a "minimally satisfactory" performance evaluation to any employee. Although Osman stated on the performance evaluation that I "successfully assisted the DBC Director in meeting all OASAM milestones on time," he rated me as "minimally satisfactory."

Osman admitted, in his own words, that my work wasn't lacking during the midyear performance evaluation nor did my performance deteriorate between the midyear performance conversation in June and the final evaluation in December. My second-line supervisor deemed employee performance issues should be raised "continually." Other than the August 13, 2013, meeting on the DEBS initiative, Osman didn't assign any other work products after April 2013.

I was present at Osman's deposition and was dismayed to hear his responses to the questions. And I was confident that his attack against me, in every action, was personal. The following conversation convened with Osman and my attorney on March 19, 2015:

Ms. Grant: "In your tenure at DOL, have you ever given another employee a 'minimally satisfactory' performance evaluation?"

Mr. Payne: "No."

Ms. Grant: "Have you ever given an unsatisfactory performance evaluation that would be the lowest possible level?"

Mr. Payne: "No. I have not."

Ms. Grant: "Do you know for how many years you have been issuing performance appraisals?"

Mr. Payne: "About ten, I think"

Ms. Grant: "Did you give Dr. Francis any guidance on how she could improve and get a better rating during the next cycle?"

Mr. Payne: "No."

Ms. Grant: "At a later date, did you give her any guidance on how she could improve?"

Mr. Payne: "No."

Ms. Grant: "Did her performance deteriorate between your midyear performance conversation in June and the final evaluation in December?"

Mr. Payne: "I would say no."

Yet, although I had developed the training plan and submitted it to him, Osman continued to deny receipt of such document. Finally, Osman stated in his performance appraisal that I had successfully met all the milestones that year. Yet, he rated my performance "minimally satisfactory." Still, I wanted to understand the reason Osman had rated me that way.

The following conversation that ensued with Osman while I represented myself pro se at his deposition on March 16, 2017:

> **Me:** "You stated that, 'Based on the FY 2013 OASAM operating plan, Dr. Francis successfully assisted the DBC director in meeting all OASAM milestones on time' and you included all the components that were met. When you stated that Dr. Francis met all OASAM milestones on time, can you explain what you were referring to?"

> **Mr. Payne:** "Well, the standard lists specific events and products that were to be done by certain dates and in going back and checking my records for the year, I had something from Dr. Francis on each one of these items. So, I marked this as met expectations."

And yet I was still rated as "minimally satisfactory."

Moreover, after meeting with Osman to review my 2012–2013 performance, he never gave me new performance standards for 2013–2014. I had always received new performance standards for the next year after my yearly performance review. When I asked Osman's administrative officer about my performance standards, she told me that she had not seen any performance standards for me. The DOL had to produce the performance standard during the documentation collection phase of my case; it responded, through the DOJ, by saying the performance standard would be provided at a "later date."

The document never materialized. It appears that Osman didn't develop the 2013–2014 performance standards, perhaps because he knew something was about to "change." I had the following conversation with Osman during his deposition on March 16, 2017:

Me: "Is it your testimony that you prepared a performance standard for Dr. Francis?"

Mr. Payne: "Yes."

Me: "You have no evidence of that, correct?"

Mr. Payne: "I have the standard. I have no evidence that she received it."

Me: "And you stated this was in December 2013?"

Mr. Payne: "That's when I believe the meeting took place, yes."

Me: "Do you have any notes of the meeting?"

Mr. Payne: "No."

Osman didn't prepare or provide me with performance standards for 2013–2014. Perhaps his plans were likely already in place to terminate my employment. I believe that after I filed my EEO complaint he asked his friend to audit my computer to find some kind of evidence he could use to justify my removal. And I felt that his attitude toward me was hostile at the performance appraisal meeting.

When I walked out of his office after my performance review of December 2013, I was convinced that he was intentional about ending my career.

■ ■ ■

On December 24, 2013, through my attorney, Joseph D. Gebhardt, LLP, I amended my formal EEO complaint. Mr. Gebhardt suggested that the amendment specifically include erosion of my duties, which would be the foundation of the EEO case. The amended EEO complaint not only addressed the erosion of my duties, but it also comprehensively addressed retaliatory performance issues to include: (1) erosion of my duties in such a way that I had been denied the opportunity to work fulltime in my position as a budget analyst team leader; (2) that I had complained to my second-line supervisor, A. Wiley Thornton, regarding my employment concerns and my complaints and concerns had been ignored to date; and, (3) I addressed the minimal performance rating, which I'm confident Osman had issued in retaliation against me because of my EEO complaint.

The amended complaint was based on retaliation for my prior EEO activities, sex, race, religion, and age discrimination in violation of Title VII of Civil Rights Act of 1964 and Age Discrimination in Employment Act. It was hand-carried to the ARB office on December 24, 2013. I waited, hopeful for a positive resolution.

The response to my concerns was a long time coming. I thought that surely, I had provided enough evidence to see and experience much needed results.

But even if I did not get justice, I was reminded that "Whosoever sows injustice will reap calamity, and the rod of his fury will fail." Proverbs 22:8. With those words in mind, I was comforted because God had assured me that He was in control of my situation no matter how long the process took.

Chapter 29

You can't comfort the afflicted without afflicting the comfortable.
—Princess Diana

In addition to dealing with the workplace issues, my beloved mother was grappling with health challenges during this time. However, her heart and mind were filled with God's Spirit and truth. Even when her health was deteriorating, she would call me each day inquiring how I was doing at work. She would always conclude by saying, "Momma is praying for you."

Approximately two weeks before Thanksgiving 2013, my mother was rushed to the Southern Maryland Hospital, in Clinton, Maryland. Her health had begun to fail fast. Mom had lost consciousness and was placed on life support by the time I got to the hospital to see her. This sudden turn in her health took us by surprise. Even though we knew she was sick, we had not realized how serious things were. Thanksgiving was a blur that year as we hoped and prayed that Mom would recover and be home soon; however, the days turned to weeks, and she was still on life support.

My siblings and I had a meeting with her doctor. We asked him to be brutally honest with us. "Her condition is deteriorating," he told us. "Her organs will shut down one by one, and she will only remain alive through life support." I felt as helpless as a tiny child as I tried to digest what he had said. The decision to take her off life support was imminent.

With one last-ditch effort, my sister Arlette reached out to MedStar Washington Hospital Center, and they agreed to have Mom transferred to their hospital to see if they could intervene and administer another procedure that might help with strengthening her heart and minimize the swelling to her body.

Although at MedStar the doctors did all they could to improve her situation, her health was failing by the day. We began praying for a miracle. Mom was the bedrock of our family and the one who prayed for us through difficult life situations. On January 4, 2014, I visited Mom with my children. We walked into her room as she lay motionless on her bed. I sat by Mom's bedside in the ICU; her body was in an induced comatose state. The two monitors attached to her body were showing number counts that indicated her unstable condition had not improved since I had last visited.

■ ■ ■

I began to reminisce about the past as I watched her. I was her first child and a gift to her from God when she was just twenty years of age. She named me Daphnie Jean, which meant an *evergreen laurel tree, to whom God is gracious.* I remember vividly how Mom would dress me up when I was a little girl, with beautiful bows in my hair, a hat on my head, and pearls around my neck. She was a proud and doting mother for all the world to see.

My mother was there to celebrate with me during all my accomplishments; she would always tell me, "Mama's proud of you." And I knew very well she was. Her last celebration with me was on October 13, 2012, when I celebrated obtaining my PhD. Mom's health was already deteriorating, but she was there. Of all the gifts I received that evening, I was most touched by the envelope Mom gave me with a $400 gift certificate. She had been too ill to work, and I do not know how she amassed the gift. It was an example of how she loved and had always sacrificed for me.

■ ■ ■

Mom had always been so full of life and a truly spiritual woman. However, on the evening of January 4, 2014, I could see that she was losing her battle to hang on. I remember saying, "Don't go Mom; please don't go. Who's going to pray for me?" As I lay there crying, one tear escaped her eyelid and trickled down the side of her face. I moved my hand off her chest and tried to wipe the tears. She slightly turned her head as though she didn't want me to move my hand off her chest. She had a ventilator to help get the oxygen into her lungs. She couldn't speak with me. I prayed that she would improve gradually with time.

The nurses came into Mom's room and got ready to clean her up for the night. Visiting hours were almost over; once the nurses came to take care of her, my children and I prepared to leave. I looked back at Mom one last time. She was looking at me. I told her that I loved her, and I would be back tomorrow to visit the next day. She kept looking at me. I didn't want to leave her. On Sunday, January 5, 2014, at 9:30 a.m., my sister called and said the doctor had called and told her Mom had passed. It was as though my heart fell to the ground on getting the news. That day, I lost someone dearest to me who I didn't even get to say goodbye to. That's painful! Oftentimes, I wish I had stayed with Mom instead of leaving the hospital. Life has never been the same. Nine years have passed since that day when Mom took her last breath, but still, the memories of her still rest within my heart.

Mom died at age seventy-five years old. I was fifty-five when she died, a difference of twenty years between us. The number twenty in the Bible symbolizes the cycles of completeness and is often connected to a perfect period of waiting, labor, or suffering. In my hours of grief, God showed me that, even in my mom's death, His ways are perfect. My mom was a blessing to me and to my siblings, and I feel very fortunate to have been raised by such a phenomenal woman, one who loved God and made many sacrifices to provide for her children.

On January 19, 2014, we memorialized my mother. Family and friends came from near and far. And amid the pain and grief over losing my mother, I still had to deal with the hell going on at work. I was physically exhausted and emotionally spent. As the investigation and legal case was ramping up, I wasn't sure how I would get through it without her support.

But Mom had taught me throughout the years to be strong despite adversity. She always reminded me that my hardest times would lead to the greatest moments of my life; hence, giving up is never an option. And, as the saying goes: "Tough times never last but tough people do." I believed it!

Mom and me at our first mother-daughter photoshoot.

Mom celebrating me at my graduation celebration.

Family members who gathered to memorialize my mom.

Chapter 30

It is during our darkest moments that we must focus to see the light.

—Aristotle

February 21, 2014 was a frigid day. I sat at my desk in the Francis Perkins Building at the DOL, where I had worked as a budget-analyst team lead, in name only, at the Departmental Budget Center (DBC) for almost five years. Just a month earlier, my family and I had memorialized my mother's passing, and I was still missing my mother dearly and trying to cope with the loss. My mom had been a staunch supporter of my career and a great inspiration to me throughout my life. Her daily calls had kept me going, and now the silence of my phone was deafening. I had never known silence like this. I had lost a partner personally and professionally.

You may recall that almost four and a half years earlier, I had been reassigned to the DBC from a position in a different agency at the DOL, after filing an Equal Employment Opportunity (EEO) complaint with the department for religious discrimination and retaliation by my supervisors.

I had hoped that my reassignment to the DBC would be a chance to start fresh in a new agency. And I was eager and ready to put my past struggles and the abominable treatment I had experienced at the hands of my previous supervisors behind me and begin a new phase of my career. However, that had not been the case. What I had experienced in my previous position continued during my tenure at the DBC.

To this point, my duties were still merely limited to performing administrative tasks, developing the agenda for our monthly budget meeting, and booking a conference room for that meeting. I attempted to push back against what seemed like a workplace inequality pandemic against me. But the responses just seemed to mutate into new and more brazen forms of retaliation.

You may recall that in June 2013, I filed a second EEO complaint against Osman for retaliation and erosion of duties. You may also recall that in December 2013, during my performance review meeting, Osman had declared that "Something has to change." Interestingly, on or around February 14, 2014, I completed the questions for the department's EEO investigation proceedings in my case and submitted them to the investigator.

One week later, as I sat at my desk, a DBC administrative employee came to my cubicle and told me that she had just received a call from Osman. He and HR were waiting to speak with me in the fifth-floor conference room.

"Really?" I asked in surprise. I had no idea why Osman would want to meet with me. What was going on?

Since my reassignment to the DBC in November 2009, Osman had rarely spoken to me, keeping our interactions to a minimum and aggressively keeping me out of the loop of the budget process. Moreover, he only assigned work to me once each month, and any dialogue between us was predominantly via email. At the end of the performance year, he haphazardly threw together my performance evaluation without asking me for input and called me into his office to ask me to sign it without discussion. Now, suddenly, he wanted to meet with me in a conference room—and with someone from HR. I wasn't sure what was going on, but it couldn't be good.

I began the long walk to the conference room. Osman and Fachnan Ellis, a young human resources specialist, were sitting at the large boardroom table. I pulled up a chair and sat down across from Osman. He barely looked at me. I noticed his hands were shaking, as though my presence unnerved him. He shuffled a stack of paper in front of him, and his voice quavered like an autumn leaf as he began to speak. "I am proposing to remove you from your position," he stated. Osman continued with his reasons for the proposed removal: (1) excessive use of government equipment for personal, unofficial purposes on APUS (American Public University System) website and (2) improper use of official work hours for personal, unofficial purposes.

I was shocked when he listed the reasons. With a puzzled look and furrowed brow, I immediately asked:

"And you're telling me this now?"

As I sat waiting for an answer from Osman, Fachnan interjected:

"It's just a proposal. It doesn't mean you're going to be removed. George Fox is the deciding official. He has the final say. I recommend you get an attorney who can help to develop a response to the proposal by the due date. The response must be sent to me. If you have any other questions, please feel free to contact me."

I looked at Osman with disgust. He nervously handed me a printed copy of the proposal, which was intended to remove me from my twenty-five years of government service, his hands still shaking like Jell-O in an earthquake. I wanted to ask if he needed a doctor. My path at the DOL had been far from smooth, but the extreme disciplinary action that I was now facing seemed to come with little warning and the allegations completely unfounded. I felt that the allegations were meant to attack my character.

None of this arose in a vacuum, however. As I have mentioned throughout my story, I believe there was a history of harbored animus against me among upper-level management in the organization leading up to this event. This had begun almost six and a half years earlier, and two weeks into my tenure with the DOL because of my need to observe my Sabbath.

At this February 21, 2014 meeting, however, I was particularly surprised that Osman would propose removing me considering a meeting we'd had six months earlier with DBC Departmental E-Budget System (DEBS) and the IT Administrator, Rob Briar. You may recall that in early September 2013, Rob had approached me about developing an online course delivery platform for DBC staff, saying that I would be "the champion" for the initiative. I was very interested in the opportunity, and as a follow-up, Osman, Rob, and I met to discuss plans for it.

You may also recall that Rob and Osman had approached me about developing the online course platform ostensibly because they knew that I had just accepted a position as an adjunct professor at the American Public University System (APUS), a private online learning institution. At our scheduled meeting on August 13, 2013, they explained that they wanted me to share my APUS experience with them and help them to develop a similar online learning platform for this new training initiative. During our meeting, I spoke in detail about the APUS online course delivery platform, the courses I had taken, and how I might be of help with developing a similar platform for the DBC.

Afterward Osman approved the initiative. He said the details of building the project were mine to work out, and I began strategizing for it immediately. Now, after having worked on the initiative for four months before it was unceremoniously shelved, Osman was proposing to fire me for doing the work necessary to complete the project he had approved. He was accusing me of accessing the APUS site during working hours and teaching from my cubicle located in a busy thruway. Osman must have understood that I would need to access the APUS site at work to develop an online learning platform for the DBC, though he had never asked me about the details of the project after our meeting, as he rarely asked me about anything pertaining to my duties.

During his deposition on March 19, 2015 related to my EEO case against him, Osman was questioned about the project. He stated under oath that he thought the initiative was "a good idea," and that he had approved the research required to obtain the result, expecting me to work on the details of the project and prepare to give a presentation. The paper trail was there, so there was nothing else he could say.

From his 2015 deposition:

My attorney: "Did you ever review any of her assignments related to the project?"

Mr. Payne: "No."

On March 16, 2017, I represented myself pro se during Osman's deposition related to my removal case. I wanted to again confirm with clarity that I had correctly heard and understood Osman's expectations about the project. I asked if he had indicated at the meeting wanting a presentation based on my research. From his 2017 deposition:

Me: "But you were expecting a presentation for the initiative, correct?"

Mr. Payne: "Yes."

However, once Fachnan Ellis testified at his deposition, it became clear that Osman had told him just the opposite, falsely claiming that he had not approved the project. Fachnan was puzzled, because I had indicated that Osman had assigned me the task of developing an online learning platform modeled after the APUS platform. After the removal oral reply meeting with George Fox, Fachnan had called Osman and asked if he knew whether I was teaching for APUS, and if he had asked me to develop an online learning platform. Osman denied everything.

The following conversation ensued at Mr. Ellis' deposition as I represented myself pro se on March 15, 2017:

Me: "You stated in your response that, 'After the meeting, I called him (Payne) and asked him, you know, this came up in the oral reply. What truth is there to that?' What did you want to know from Mr. Payne that was true?"

Mr. Ellis: "Mr. Payne—pardon me. Dr. Francis had expressed that Mr. Payne had known about the APUS instruction while it was going on; and that surprised me, because I had spoken to Mr. Payne, and I had not heard that. So, I called him to see if there

was any truth to the assertion that he had known all along that
Dr. Francis was doing the APUS instruction, and he said that he
had not known."

I had shared with Osman and Rob at our meeting what I was preparing
to do at APUS, the courses I had taken, and how the experience would
help with developing the online training initiative that he thought was
a "good idea." Osman said under oath that I had "hidden this" from
him. Hence, based on his testimony, he had no other option but to
propose removing me from government service.

The US Merit Systems Protection Board (MSPB) is an independent
judicial agency that was established to protect the Merit System
Principles while promoting an effective Federal workforce free of
prohibited personnel practices. I had filed an appeal to the removal with
the MSPB on or around January 13, 2015, based on discrimination,
retaliation, and removal from my position.

The proceeding was held on Friday, May 1, 2015. At the MSPB
hearing, in response to my second EEOC claim, Osman was asked
what else he considered in making the decision to fire me. He stated
under oath that "there were a lot of things considered." One of the
things he stated he considered in the removal process was my alleged
"declining performance." This allegation was never substantiated nor
had he provided any evidence to support his claims, yet he used it as a
means for requesting an audit into my computer usage and to remove
me from my position.

Osman never provided any evidence of my "declining performance."
Apparently, he was not required to provide any evidence of his claims
to the agency or the courts. He simply had to say it was so, and that
was enough.

Osman also alleged that I had hidden my work on this project
from him and that fact had "pushed" him to propose my removal, as if
he were doing it because he had to and not because he wanted to. As
I sat in the hearing and listened to his testimony, I was confused and

disturbed. He knew full well about the project because he had approved it. He also knew that I would need to access the APUS site during work hours to do research for the project.

Under the guise of my "poor performance," he had ordered an audit of my work computer, which meant he could see exactly what I was using my computer for, and he would have known that I was going into the APUS system, among others, to do research on it. None of these allegations had been brought up in our last performance review meeting.

Finally, Osman stated the following: "When I sat down with her in April, and her initial performance standards, discussion for the year, and in our midyear, one of the questions I asked her is what else did she want to work on in DBC?"

But we had never met in April for a midyear review. Moreover, there had been no progressive discipline or supporting evidence to corroborate his allegation. Osman had never asked me any questions regarding what I wanted to work on in DBC in April or June 2013.

In pursuit of his proposal to remove me after I had completed and submitted the investigative questions to my formal EEO complaint in mid-February 2014, the following conversation ensued with Osman and my attorney at the MSPB:

Ms. Grant: "So from then, what happened?"

Mr. Payne: "Well, then I worked with HRC, Fachnan Ellis, mainly. He took the first shot at looking at what was in the report and how to make that into a proposal for removal. I worked with the Chief Information Officer (OCIO) on how to take what was in this report and the details behind it. He came up with the first draft and then sent it to me. I made some comments, edits, questions, and that went back and forth for a few months, and we finally came to an approach for proposed removal and sat down in late February."

I believe that Osman's proposal to remove me from my position was vindictive. He launched his proposal to remove me from government service one week after I had submitted my EEO complaint for investigation against him for discrimination, retaliation, and eroding of my duties as a budget analyst team lead. His actions toward me from the start, by excluding me out of the team loop, were also suspicious, and likely retaliatory because of my previous EEOC complaints prior to my reassignment to DBC. This was not the only adverse personnel action that I had experienced in my seven-year tenure with the DOL— they were countless. However, this would prove to be the final act in actions targeted against me for speaking truth to power. Mind you, this is the government branch that is supposed to protect all American employees against such actions.

Osman treated me as though I did not belong in the DBC from the start. Was he instructed to do this? I don't know. But to add insult to injury, based on the work he had assigned (or lack of work), I believe Osman intentionally segregated me, the only Black GS-15 budget analyst team lead, from my White colleagues who were also budget analyst team leads. The reason he gave for not including me as part of the budget analyst team leads was that my job was "administrative" while the jobs of my White colleagues were "technical" because they worked on the budget process.

Soon after I filed my EEO complaint regarding his actions in this regard and the erosion of my duties, I think Osman wanted to fire me. I wasn't sure how he had justified his action, but I eventually learned his intentions soon after the meeting on the DEBS online learning initiative. Telling his associates that my performance was declining and that he was not getting the completed work assignments, he requested an audit into my computer usage, specifically asking for "education sites." Perhaps the meeting on the DEBS online learning initiative on August 13, 2013, had given him an idea of how he could use my research and research materials to remove me from my position. Based on his response regarding the project, he had no interest in the project or what had been done.

Osman went further than the act of auditing my computer. During the time he was making his case for auditing my computer, you may recall that I had taken four weeks sick leave from my position to stay at the Wildwood Lifestyle Center in Georgia, from October 6, 2013, to October 31, 2013, to reconstitute my mental health and recover from the toxic work environment at the DOL. When I returned to the office on November 4, 2013, I noticed my computer had been moved and my password disabled. I eventually discovered that not only had Osman had my computer audited, but that he'd also had the OCIO, as well as himself, mapped into my computer. In this way, they were able to see every online activity that I had done daily. He also had all the documents on my computer copied and placed in an empty Xerox box, and the agency displayed the box on a shopping cart as if it were a trophy it had just won.

Additionally, I noticed when I logged unto my computer that my profile had been changed, with two lowercase t's added at the beginning of my username. Osman called me at my desk phone one day to ask, "Do you know what those two t's mean?" Puzzled, I replied, "No!" He responded, in a soft, mocking tone, "I will call IT and see what that means." He then hung up. I sat there, still completely puzzled at what had just transpired.

In court depositions, I had the opportunity to ask Mr. Hue Hoang, one of the IT personnel who was asked to audit my computer, about circumstances surrounding the profile change.

Mr. Hoang stated that my profile "was changed at that particular time and it meant that it was done because the account was going to be purged, disabled, put on hold, or litigated, and that request had to come from a manager."

It's now clear to me that immediately following our conversation about the DEBS online initiative, my employment became tenuous.

That fear was cemented when I overheard a deputy to Osman say, "Well, I hope it works," as I saw Osman standing in front of Cameron Bate's office door engaging in a cagey conversation with him. That image is forever etched in my memory.

Osman claimed that I was not doing "the work." He would later contradict himself by testifying that there was no specific work assigned to me during this time. He also claimed that my "performance was declining," but would also contradict himself by testifying that there were no performance issues. Finally, Osman requested that his friend and accomplice, George Fox, audit my computer in search of "educational websites" because of my alleged "poor performance." These are the exact sites we had discussed at the meeting on August 13, 2013, and this is documented.

The conference room meeting with Osman and Fachnan Ellis was traumatic, but it was not the worst situation I had faced in my tumultuous stint at DOL or in my life. I knew I had done nothing wrong, and I believed that I would survive the obstacles. Still, as I returned to my desk, I felt that I was at a crossroads, in jeopardy of unjustly losing the career that I had worked so diligently for eighteen years to build.

I had consciously worked twice as hard as my counterparts to propel my way up from a GS-5 secretary to a GS-15 chief for budget formulation and implementation. That had been no small feat. Until now, I had never been disciplined for poor performance, and charges had never been brought against me for misconduct. Moreover, it was because of my work ethics, exceptional performance, and a good report from my DHS supervisor that I had been hired at the DOL in the first place.

■ ■ ■

After I returned from my DOJ detail, as the custom was before I left for the detail, I had no work assignment. When Osman was asked at the MSPB hearing what he had assigned me upon my return from the DOJ, he said nothing for "two to three weeks." Hence, I kept my mind busy by registering for courses offered at APUS. Osman was never asked the reason for not assigning any work. It appears that information was not important to the DOL or the MSPB tribunal.

I never stopped working on myself in this environment. Osman stated that individuals can take classes when the work is slow. My White colleagues were taking classes at this time, as well. I specifically heard Beth say, "I have two classes to take." The work wasn't slow in my case. Although I showed up every day to work for four and a half years at the DBC, I had no job. He was confident in testifying that he didn't "recall" assigning any work for an entire year and the agency protected his actions.

The sad part about coming to work daily with nothing to do, is that Osman was being paid and compensated with a five-thousand-dollar bonus in 2011, a six-thousand-dollar bonus in 2012, and a promotion from the DBC. Moreover, immediately after he instigated my termination in 2014, his salary increased from $164,761 to $182,885 annually. The increase in Osman's salary was very unusual for any government employee.

In my view, Osman and his accomplices should be required to repay the funds back to the taxpayers. Additionally, the department owed me a brand-new career path because they had robbed me of the budget-analyst training for which I came to the department. Every site on the report from March to August would reveal a free course I was taking and the certificate that I had earned. Moreover, based on an APUS memorandum, I wasn't offered a class to facilitate until August 2013.

The following is from a letter dated March 12, 2014, from the HR department at APUS, regarding the date when I began teaching online courses for the university.

To Whom It May Concern:

This letter is to clarify the employment status of Jean Francis who is currently employed with American Public University System (APUS) as a part-time instructor, in the School of Business.

Dr. Francis's hire date was April 23, 2013. However, she didn't actively begin teaching for or receive compensation from APUS until August 2013.

All APUS faculty members work remotely. Residency does not affect eligibility to work remotely and therefore faculty members are free to work from anywhere within the United States. If you need any additional information or assistance in this matter, please feel free to contact us.

Sincerely,

Ryan Jordan, Faculty Human Resources Assistant

This memorandum refutes Osman's claim that I was teaching on the job beginning April 2013.

When I presented the evidence in my response to George Fox, he said, "Although you weren't teaching, the classes have nothing to do with budget analyst duties." When I heard this, I almost choked on my saliva. I couldn't believe what I was hearing. The problem was that I wasn't serving or given the opportunity to serve in my position as a budget analyst team lead. And now they wanted to use the "budget analyst" trump card to bolster their claims.

There was simply no evidence that I was teaching on the job. According to Osman's testimony at the MSPB Hearing the audit report didn't show whether I was taking a course or teaching. I had been completing training courses to keep my skills current, but never was I teaching. The report they generated didn't provide any evidence of teaching. I had proof that I did not even begin teaching until after this date, but such facts did not seem to matter to the department.

The courses I began facilitating in August 2013 at APUS were attended by working adult learners who are predominantly military personnel. These were students who had elected to take online courses so that they could complete the material at their own pace, located in time zones across the world, including Hawaii, Asia, and Europe. There's no way these learners are going to leave their jobs during the day or come to a class at ungodly hours for which I was allegedly teaching on the job for lectures.

Additionally, my cubicle was in a busy thoroughfare. There were budget analysts sitting all around me. No one ever heard or saw me teaching. Yet, Osman was terminating my employment for an alleged forty hours of "teaching for APUS" at work, in a cubicle, for eight months. According to Fachnan Ellis, the report from the audit couldn't identify whether I was taking a course or teaching. The following was taking directly from his deposition on May 15, 2017:

> **Me:** "Is it your testimony that the report does not differentiate whether Dr. Francis was taking courses or whether she was allegedly teaching during work hours?"
>
> **Mr. Ellis:** "The report does not draw that distinction, to my recollection."

Finally, during his testimony under oath at the MSPB, Osman was also asked by my attorney if the agency's audit report shows when I was teaching and when I was taking classes. Osman said, "It did not." Yet, Osman would claim I was teaching for profit during work hours. This was a claim he could never substantiate. I took the following directly from the MSPB transcript of Osman's testimony at the MSPB Hearing on May 1, 2015:

> **Ms. Grant:** "Do you still have the Agency's audit report in front of you?"

Mr. Payne: "Yes, I do."

Ms. Grant: "Does this report differentiate between times when she was teaching classes and taking classes?"

Mr. Payne: "No, it does not."

■ ■ ■

On March 21, 2014, I submitted a written reply to the Notice of Proposed Removal to George Fox, who had requested the audit. Osman and George acted as the judge, jury, and executioner in my removal case. There was no outside investigation done on my removal charges. No one else came to ask for my side of the story. It appears there was a conflict of interest, and that the decision was biased. The evidence I submitted to refute each of the claims had been ignored.

They fabricated the plan in such a way that the removal claims took precedent over my discrimination and retaliation case. And they were all protected in every sense of the word and at every level of my search for justice. When Osman was asked if there was any other investigation to their teaching claims, he said an investigation was "not applicable." I took the following directly from Osman's February 21, 2014, responses to the investigator's questions on my EEO claims:

Investigator: "Are you aware of Complainant (or anyone acting on behalf of Complainant) bringing to the attention of any other management official concerns about harassment/hostile work environment? If so, to whom did he/she inform of his/her concerns and when, to the best of your knowledge."

Mr. Payne: "No, I'm not aware of any hostile work environment concerns raised by the Complainant."

Investigator: "Was an investigation conducted into the Complainant's allegations of harassment/hostile work environment? If so, by whom and when?"

Mr. Payne: "Not applicable."

Investigator: "To your knowledge, what was the outcome of the investigation? Please provide a copy of the report."

Mr. Payne: "Not applicable."

Investigator: "Was Complainant informed of the outcome? If yes, how?"

Mr. Payne: "Not applicable."

Investigator: "Was any corrective or preventive action necessary? If so, what action was taken?"

Mr. Payne: "Not applicable."
Investigator: "If no investigation was conducted, please explain why."

Mr. Payne: "Not applicable."
Investigator: "Have you received training on anti-harassment/ hostile work environment while employed by the agency? If so, when?"

Mr. Payne: "Yes, we have training every two years. My certificates for completing this training in 2010 and 2012 are attached."

I provided evidence that I didn't violate the DOL's "Appropriate Use of

IT" policy, which allows limited personal use of DOL office equipment. I showed that I conducted relevant training and development in the tasks Osman had assigned me, both during my lunchtime and when I had no work assigned.

The allegations should not have been substantiated because signing up to take a course at APUS didn't cause harm to the agency or the public. White employees were signing up for outside training elsewhere and taking these courses during the time I was taking courses. In fact, the behavior was encouraged by the administration regarding "self-investment to better serve the public." This has also been my experience in all government agencies that I have worked in the past.

During the time George and Osman were proposing to remove me from my position for taking a course from APUS, the secretary of labor forwarded an advisory notice authorizing professional development. Based on the Policy Advisory 14OHRPAA02, if the DOL fired me because I was engaging in professional growth to change my position in helping the organization, then it discriminated against me in this regard. I know of no other employee in the DBC who was fired for taking courses, although there were many employees taking courses at their desks.

Finally, I showed that I wasn't teaching courses at APUS for commercial purposes or to support any for-profit activities, other outside employment, or business activities as Osman claimed. I showed I did the online research based on a meeting with Osman, who approved researching and presenting a proposal for a DEBS online training initiative. I basically followed his instructions. He recommended no specific resources for the initiative. He said that he had left that decision to Rob and me. George Fox's response was that if I wanted "to do something like this I should have asked." I was stunned when he made that statement. Osman had approved the initiative for me to do "something like this."

■ ■ ■

On May 6, 2014, George Fox decided on the proposal to remove. He upheld my removal. I was surprised by his action because I had provided enough evidence for him to reverse the decision. I believe he was protecting his friend.

The concerns of conflict of interest existed, which was confirmed by the agency's reassigning of my EEO case. Yet the agency was able to implement my removal with no such conflict being raised.

Chapter 31

Getting fired is nature's way of telling you that
you had the wrong job in the first place.

—Hall Lancaster

My position was terminated on May 9, 2014, after twenty-five years of service to the US government. I walked out of the Frances Perkins Building with mixed emotions. I had recently lost my mother. Now I was losing my livelihood. In addition, the DOL leadership had tarnished my reputation by terminating me based on "poor performance" and "misconduct" charges. They had upended my career and assassinated my character; however, I knew who was in control despite the outward outcomes and events. The truth is that I had been through the worst season in my life during my tenure with the DOL. I would never wish the abuse I experienced on anyone else. However, I was comforted in knowing that before God formed me in my mother's womb, He knew me, sanctified me, and ordained me. Therefore, that season of my life was not a surprise to Him. I was born for this—predestined by God for such a time as this. It was my assignment and I had to complete it. I begin preparing to file my termination appeal to the MSPB through my attorney.

On September 9, 2014, my counsel inquired about agreeable dates for deposing Osman and Thornton. However, the DOL counsel responded on September 10, 2014, declining the depositions. The agency counsel wrote:

> [W]e respectfully decline your request to depose Mr. Payne and Mr. Thornton. The June 13, 2014, Acknowledgment and Order (Order) issued in this case specifically required you, if you wished to engage in discovery, to file your initial requests within 30 days of the date of

the Order. As you failed to do so, you are not entitled to commence discovery now.

The decision for the DOL counsel to deny me the opportunity to engage in the process of discovery and gathering evidence in my removal case was devastating. The sworn testimony from the witnesses would be crucial evidence to contradict or discredit their evidence against me. Effective depositions may have had a dramatic impact on the outcome of my case; however, I was denied this opportunity prior to having my case heard by the administrative judge at the MSPB.

On October 20, 2014, the DOL and my attorney agreed on a thirty-day suspension moving forward with filing my case with the MSPB. During this time, they began the discussions on a possible settlement agreement.

On November 12, 2014, the agency wanted to offer a settlement in my removal case. However, it didn't want to settle unless I agreed to settle my discrimination case. The individual to sign the settlement was George Fox. My lawyers at the time thought he was offering a good settlement, that they had too much information on me, that it would be an uphill battle to win my case, and that I would be able to move on with the removal of the charges from my record.

Much like my first case with the DOL, the agency wanted me to accept a settlement of no more than ten thousand dollars for clearing my record as though I had committed a crime. I wasn't sold on the offer; however, I told my attorney that I would think about it. I also raised concerns that the entire process was a conflict of interest, reiterating that George Fox was the one who had audited my computer, decided on my firing, and was the one signing off on the terms of a settlement he was imposing on me—which didn't make sense. They were operating as though the DOL was a company that they owned.

I thought and prayed about it, but I couldn't agree to sign a settlement document when I knew that the claims against me were false and that the entire process was biased. To settle, and suppress my story for a pittance, when I knew without a shadow of a doubt that the allegations were false, would be comparable to saying that the leaders of the DOL had done nothing wrong. I was going to keep the process moving and expose the systemic racism, the good ol' boy system, and how unethical leaders can use their position to disenfranchise those who are powerless. As stated earlier, I was born for this.

The settlement terms and conditions that I refused to accept included: ten thousand dollars in a lump sum payable to my attorney, rescinding my removal SF-50 and issuing a new SF-50 indicating that I had "resigned for personal reasons" from my position at the agency effective May 9, 2014, expunging all information and references related to the Notice of Proposed Removal and Decision on Proposal to Remove from my personnel file including my Official Personnel File (OPF) and any other system of records, and to withdraw with prejudice the appeal identified as Merit Systems Protection Board appeal and Equal Employment Opportunity complaint, and any and all existing grievances, and administrative or judicial appeals or complaints, which may have been brought against the Agency, including—but not limited to—to Merit Systems Protection Board appeals and Equal Employment Opportunity complaints relating to the appellant, with no right to raise these issues again. The lists of waivers in the proposed settlement document were quite extensive; however, the one that caught my attention the most was the one that stated the following:

> Appellant agrees not to apply for, or otherwise seek, a position with any part of the Department of Labor, including all units, sub-agencies, and components throughout the United States for a period of ten years from the date of execution of this Agreement. Appellant agrees that if she does apply for, or otherwise seek, a position with

> the Department of Labor within that time period, she will be deemed
> ineligible, and that the Agency may disclose this Agreement, and the
> facts behind it, to the part, unit, sub-agency, or component to which
> Appellant applied.

After reading the waiver above, I laughed out loud, literally. If they believed I would ever again want to apply to DOL and its agencies for a job, they were totally mistaken. I had been treated like a common criminal because of my Sabbath. My good name had been sullied and my position and career path stripped from me. Why would I ever want to work for this toxic organization again? Moreover, why would I want to settle with people who had treated me this way?

On December 8, 2014, my former counsel filed a motion to withdraw from my case based on my request, and on December 10, 2014, my new counsel, through The Employment Law Group, P.C., entered her appearance in my MSPB case. In addition to entering her appearance, I met with Mr. Oswald, who advised me not to accept the monetary settlement. After we discussed the case, he provided a comprehensive advisory opinion. I took the following conclusion from the letter that was dated on May 12, 2014:

> We believe that you have a strong retaliation claim and that your
> removal was motivated by Payne's retaliatory animus toward you.
> I believe that you have viable claims under Title VII of the Civil Rights
> Act of 1964, 42 USC. § 2000e, et seq. ("Title VII"). Accordingly, I
> agree to represent you on an hourly basis.

I retained The Employment Law Group; P.C., and I was required to make a twenty-five-thousand-dollar advance payment toward the company representing me in my case. This amount was a part of the retainer fee and to begin the work of representation. Moreover, I was further required to keep a ten-thousand-dollar positive balance in an escrow account throughout the course of my representation. This was a challenging obligation to meet, because not only was I unemployed, but I was also still paying attorney fees in my first case with the DOL ESA office. Pursuing my case was challenging both financially and emotionally.

In mid-June 2014, I began receiving unemployment benefits because the DOL didn't respond to the unemployment letter that was sent to the department by the District of Columbia Unemployment Office on my behalf. The biweekly amount significantly differed from the annual salary I received before my termination. To say that the difference stung tremendously is an understatement. To meet the financial burden of pursuing my case, I almost exhausted my TSP retirement savings, as well as additional savings from Lionel's 401K. I also applied for nearly four dozen budget and teaching positions from various companies to include USAJOBS, for which I was neither hired nor contacted for a single interview.

Throughout the remainder of 2014, I submitted hundreds of resumés to federal, state, and local government entities, as well as various school districts, universities, and other organizations for positions in budget, finance, teaching, and training and development since those were the fields in which I had credentials and experience. I rarely received responses, and when I did, they didn't result in any job opportunities for me. I couldn't help but to become suspicious that the DOL was blackballing me because I had filed a lawsuit against the agency.

I happened to call one of the employment agencies one day to inquire about the status of my application. The recruiter asked me about the various positions I had held in the past and then said, "And what about what you did at the Department of Labor?"

I was flabbergasted before he hung up the phone. From this exchange, I was confident that the DOL was still retaliating against me. But I was comforted in knowing that my heart was saturated with the truth despite the falsehood lobbed at me.

■ ■ ■

The year was 2014. And it was nearing the holidays. My home was filled with gloom. I'd been out of a job for seven months and was also preparing to fight the legal battle of my life. I was going to do it scared in my own strength but, I was also reminded that God promised to be with me. My mom was no longer with us. It would be our first Christmas without her—her presence was greatly missed.

The loss of my mom exacerbated my sense that there was no time to sit around and ponder what the holiday would be like without her. I was determined to embrace every opportunity to bring light and hope to my family for the Thanksgiving and Christmas holidays and beyond. I began planning for the Christmas family get-together immediately after Thanksgiving. I was intentional that we would have an exceptional holiday. The plan included a family talent show after dinner. Additionally, I decided to invite a special guest—myself, performing as Mariah Carey.

I dressed the part and my bodyguards—my son-in-law and grandson—were there to protect me from the cheering crowd. When I made my grand entrance, everyone was astonished. Smiles, shouts, and laughter permeated the room. I introduced myself and began my performance—"All I want for Christmas is You." Truly, all I wanted for Christmas was my family.

The performance was enjoyed by everyone. We had had an exceptional Christmas that year despite of all the troubles we had seen. And the tradition continued beyond 2014. The presence of my family has brought me an immense amount of joy, love, and laughter in my tough times and that will last a lifetime. Truly family is everything and everything is family.

I never allowed my situation to break my spirit. Someone once said, "Sometimes people try to destroy you, precisely because they recognize your power—not because they don't see it, but because they see it and they don't want it to exist." I concur!

In the coming weeks and months after hiring The Employment Law Group P.C., the pursuit of my MSPB case was in full swing and I hoped and prayed for the best.

Part IV

· · ·

Speak Truth to Power

Chapter 32

Injustice anywhere isa threat to justice everywhere.
—Martin Luther King, Jr.

The MSPB hearing was scheduled for May 1, 2015. The DOL had developed a plan for separating my discrimination complaint from Osman's removal allegations, which meant that my attorney wasn't allowed to speak one word about my discrimination case. So in essence the department and the justice system kicked my discrimination complaint to the wayside. Judge Mason was overseeing the proceedings and he made it clear that my discrimination case wasn't before him.

In my view, it was futile to address my removal case without incorporating my discrimination complaint, because I felt that discrimination and retaliation had brought me to this juncture. However, I believe that the administrative judge had also erred by denying me, through my attorney, an opportunity to engage in discovery on the removal. By disallowing me to do so, I was unable to present evidence in support of my affirmative defenses. My attorney was limited in what she could address at the hearing.

The judge allowed me, through my attorney, to amend my June 6, 2014, two-paragraph appeal with a fifteen-page detailed appeal on February 24, 2015. However, he arbitrarily didn't allow me to engage in discovery regarding my affirmative defenses, which were put forth in my amended appeal. Such a decision was arbitrary, which ultimately disadvantaged me for several reasons: first, I couldn't issue discovery requests; second, I couldn't depose George Fox, the decision maker, at all; and third, I couldn't depose Osman on my removal. Such a decision was contrary to the judge's own ruling on my motion to amend my complaint, in which he wrote, "The Board's jurisdiction is limited to the adverse action, in this instance, the appellant's removal."

Despite recognizing the removal as the issue to be adjudicated before the MSPB, the judge denied me the opportunity to engage in discovery on the very same topic. Had I been able to engage in discovery about my affirmative defenses and additional facts identified in my amended appeal, I would have had more documents and testimony to help me meet my burden at the MSPB hearing. Additionally, I would have had documents and testimony to prove that the agency didn't meet its burden to show, by a preponderance of the evidence, that I was engaged in improper use of official work hours for personal and unofficial purposes. I believe that Judge Mason's decision to not restrict but to deny me complete discovery was erroneous and an abuse of discretion.

I sat in the hearing with my attorney. I was the only Black person in the courtroom. My accusers were all White men who I felt had abused their power and the power of their offices against me at the DOL, namely Osman, Thornton, Fox, and Rob. Even in the courtroom, it appeared that they were given special treatment because of their color. I sensed it when the judge excused their misdeed of auditing my computer because of alleged poor performance.

To this allegation he said, "They don't have to prove any of that. That's irrelevant to me. I mean, they're simply showing a chain of events that preceded the discovery of the misconduct." I sat in disgust, and I thought, *How can the judge say, "They don't have to prove that? It was the reason they gave for auditing my computer."* That was the beginning of the chain of events. Moreover, there are no DOL polices that give supervisors the authority to audit an employee's computer based on poor performance even if that was true. I knew then that there was no hope for me with this judge at the helm. I told my attorney I wasn't hopeful based on the direction of the proceedings. I was distraught.

I felt upfront and early that there would be no justice for me. The judge seemed to defend their actions against me. It was all about what Osman said. The judge stated that my performance wasn't an issue, while it was in fact this alleged 'declining performance as means for auditing my computer' that was the reason we were there.

The agency's stated reason for initiating an investigation into my computer use was Osman's allegation that my performance had declined. However, the judge didn't allow any inquiry as to the agency's motive for the December 2013 "minimally satisfactory" performance evaluation. In doing so, Judge Mason didn't give me, through my attorney, an opportunity to present evidence in support of my affirmative defenses that the basis for the audit was pre-textual and discriminatory. In essence, the judge said, "I don't need to go there. I don't have authority to go there." I shook my head in the courtroom and I thought, *Is there any justice for Black and Brown people like me whose lives matters?* Then suddenly, I remembered that my God said, "Vengeance is mine, I will repay." I didn't know when He would repay, but I was confident that He would keep His promise.

Throughout the MSPB proceedings, the judge repeatedly expressed that the only issue before him was "whether the removal is discriminatory," and didn't accept the minimally satisfactory performance evaluation as evidence of discriminatory and retaliatory animus. Nothing was said about the assignment Osman had tasked regarding researching and presenting information on a suitable platform for the DEBS online training initiative. The training initiative and the training plan were two different assignments.

I took the following directly from the MSPB transcript on May 1, 2015:

Judge Mason: "Yeah. The performance is not an issue. I mean her performance. They didn't charge her with inadequate performance."

Ms. Grant: "Well, they initiated the audit because of inadequate performance."

Judge Mason: "Okay."

Ms. Grant: "And misuse of official time indicates that she is ignoring duties that have been assigned to her in order to do something personal."

Judge Mason: "Okay. Neither I nor you can create a charge and then require the agency to prove it. I mean, the agency has specified the misconduct they view as improper, and they have to prove the thing that they have alleged."

Ms. Grant: "So, the motivation for the audit is irrelevant?"
Judge Mason: "The agency's explanation is that there was a question about what Ms. Francis was doing."

Ms. Grant: "Right. And it's our position that that question is pre-textual and invented in order to build a case to allow them to terminate her."

■ ■ ■

The judge refused to hear any discussion about declining performance allegations from my attorney. The problem was that my alleged poor performance was the premise for the auditing. Yet, the judge was refusing to hear arguments about the issue. Moreover, Osman threw everything including the kitchen sink at me. I believe he was creating a distraction and a smoke screen to divert the attention from my discrimination and retaliation complaint to the alleged misconduct for accessing APUS website. He requested that every file and every document on my computer be copied and filed in a Xerox box. If this was a scare tactic, it didn't scare me.

I looked through the box after my attorney received copies of the documents. In the box were the files that I had saved for the DEBS initiative presentation, files I had saved from all the training I had taken, a copy of my completed dissertation that I had promised to share with all the executive women in government who had participated in the research, and a copy of the manuscript for a book. The dissertation was completed in 2012. I received the final and published copy in early 2013 and I shared copies with the executive women who worked at the DOL once I returned from my detail.

Regarding the manuscript, I had begun writing the book in 2011 and had completed it before my DOJ detail in 2012. The manuscript was on my computer because the DOL OASAM, under Thornton's leadership, was requesting proposals for a customer service call center, and I had decided to develop a proposal for submission. Instead of reinventing the process, I referred to my manuscript to use a similar graph presentation for the customer service call center, and various excerpts from the book in developing my proposal. I gave Mr. Thornton the proposal on the day I spoke to him about a detail or transfer from DBC. My proposal was accepted by the OASAM leadership, and the graph and charts were also used to roll out the new customer service call center. Although my proposal was accepted and used, I didn't receive any recognition for my submission. That didn't bother me. I was happy to help with the development of the new call center.

The book that I had written was titled *The Seven Characteristics of Exceptional Leadership*. The toxic leadership I had experienced under leaders such as Osman, Thornton, George, Stormi, Georgia, and Hattie had prompted me to write it. Osman had seen the draft manuscript after he audited my computer, and he would testify at the MSPB that the book was about my "activities with American Public University."

There was no evidence of that, but I'm certain his claim was well accepted. Moreover, as a new adjunct faculty member, why would APUS entrust me to write a book on leadership for its students? I don't believe this would ever happen. Yet, Osman was speaking as though he was an APUS representative regarding my book.

Osman also claimed that every document he had downloaded from my computer was evidence that I had been teaching during work hours. However, the files were from various university websites for use in my presentation on the DEBS project. In this regard, let me share with you the following conversation between Osman and the agency's counsel, Ms. Lambert, at the MSPB hearing on May 1, 2015:

> **Mr. Payne:** "Well, on her profile for American Public University System, it says that she was working on a book entitled Seven Characteristics of Effective Leadership, and that's the title of this file here."
>
> **Ms. Lambert:** "And that's not related to her job?"
>
> **Mr. Payne:** "No."
>
> **Ms. Lambert:** "And let's turn to the last item in specification, that specification, on the page. What is that?"
>
> **Mr. Payne:** "It's a file on her DOL hard drive having to do with her activities with the American Public University System."
>
> **Ms. Lambert:** "You see, it says 'manuscript final'?"
>
> **Mr. Payne:** "Yeah; it was, you know, having to do with, again, her public university manuscript that she had needed for those activities."

I sat shaking my head and couldn't believe what I was hearing. But I know the truth. Today, I am a proud author of my book The Seven

Characteristics of Exceptional Leadership and APUS had nothing to do with it.

My attorney was able to ask Osman a few questions regarding the audit. The judge seemed quite protective regarding what questions could be. As the hearing proceeded, I was hopeful. I needed an attorney to speak authoritatively at the hearing, but I don't believe that happened. I directly took the following from the MSPB hearing as Ms. Grant questioned Osman on the audit and my performance evaluation on May 1, 2015:

Ms. Grant: "Did you ever counsel her on her Internet use?"

Mr. Payne: "No, I did not."

Ms. Grant: "Did you ever ask her what she was doing with her time?"

Mr. Payne: "No, I did not."

Ms. Grant: "So, when specifically, did you learn that she was spending her time on these APUS activities?"

Mr. Payne: "When I received the report on December 12 of 2013."

Ms. Grant: "Did you revoke her Internet use at that time?"

Mr. Payne: "No, I did not."

Ms. Grant: "Did you instruct her to cease these activities?"

Mr. Payne: "Not at that time, no."

Ms. Grant: "When did you tell her to stop these activities?"

Mr. Payne: "When I met with her for her proposal for removal in February."

Additionally, I believe that the report had been altered to reflect only APUS to support his narrative of me using my work hours to teach. There was no evidence of the University of Phoenix (UOP) or Capella University online platforms that I had researched for the DEBS initiative, particularly since Grammarly was only on the UOP website. After I reviewed the report and noticed the discrepancies, I concluded that it had been changed to reflect Osman's narrative.

I think Osman had no interest and no expectations regarding the project because his goal was to use the information against me. The following was taken from Osman's deposition while representing myself pro se on March 16, 2017:

Me: "When were you expecting the presentation for the DEBS initiative?" I asked him.

Mr. Payne: "I don't recall ever setting a deadline mainly because we were in discussions of the shutdown of the federal government. Two weeks after we had this meeting, we were shut down for days and a lot of things got pushed to the side. And I never focused my attention back on this specific project."

Me: "But even though you didn't focus on it, were you expecting Dr. Francis and Mr. Briar to continue doing work as it relates to the project?"

Mr. Payne: "At that point I didn't have any expectation because of what had happened during the government shutdown."

■ ■ ■

During my research for the DEBS online and face-to-face training initiative, not only did I research the APUS course-delivery platform, but I also researched Capella University and the UOP platforms. However, as stated, they had not included these universities in the report. Osman provided me a copy of the report with the proposal to remove. They only included APUS in the report. Immediately, I knew it was incorrect. I had used Grammarly, an editing tool UOP website for editing and submitting all the memorandums I had developed from April to September 2013. Yet, they didn't include those activities in the report.

If the "forensic" auditing report was correct, those activities should have displayed in the report as well. I can't say why or who altered the report, but the result seemed to confirm Osman's claims of excessive time spent on the APUS site without mention of any other sites.

Regarding the courses I had taken Osman said, "[The] content of the courses didn't appear to be related to the work of a budget analyst." He did not acknowledge that he had eroded my duties and had taken away my budgetary responsibility for the four years that I had been assigned to DBC. He did not report to HR representative Fachnan Ellis that the only task I was assigned was to develop training plans and schedule monthly ABO meetings. Fachnan only knew what Osman had conveyed to him. Fachnan was questioned about this at the MSPB Hearing in 2015:

Ms. Grant: And what did you think about this claim that Mr. Payne knew?

Mr. Ellis: Honestly, I thought that was a little strange because I didn't think Mr. Payne knew. If he had known about it; he didn't react the way I would expect someone who had known about it to react. And I, after this meeting, called him and asked him, you know, this came up in the oral reply. What, you know, what truth is there to that? And he said he had no knowledge that she had worked at APUS, as indicated in the report and the proposal.

He was asked the same question at his deposition on March 17, 2017:

Ms. Grant: What did you think about the claim that Payne knew?

Mr. Ellis: If I recall correctly there, she was saying that, I don't know if it was at this point or a later point, but she said that Mr. Payne had asked her to develop some kind of training, and that her work at APUS was to develop that.

Ms. Grant: Okay. And did you find that credible?

Mr. Ellis: No.

Ms. Grant: Why not?

Mr. Ellis: So I had actually reviewed as part of the process, at the proposal or decision stage, some of the summaries and content of the courses, and they did not appear to be related to the work of a budget analyst."

I sat in awe as I listened to this and wondered if it was because I'm a Black woman that he thought that my truth wasn't credible.

Were Osman and George Fox so desperate to terminate me that they used Fachnan Ellis to do so? He was an HR specialist who had never removed a GS-15 before. He stated that it was something he always did but couldn't name anyone else but me. I took the following from his testimony at his deposition on March 17, 2017:

Me: "Is your involvement in the removal of a GS-15 something that you would normally do in your capacity at that time?"

Mr. Ellis: "Yes."

Me: "How many GS-15s have you worked on removing or the removal process?"

Mr. Ellis: "One."

Me: "Just one? And who is that one?"

Mr. Ellis: "Dr. Francis."

Me: "And how long have you been in HR-related positions?"

Mr. Ellis: "I have been in HR with the federal government for approximately five years."

Me: "Five years? And do you believe that a removal of a GS-15 is something that a GS-12 should be involved with?"

Mr. Ellis: "Yes."

Me: "In what way?"

Mr. Ellis: "As a GS-12 in the Office of Employee Relations, at the time, that was the journey level position, meaning it was the highest grade that you could achieve as a nonsupervisory employee in the office. So, the removal of any employee that was handled by the office could be handled by a GS-12."

I have worked in many government agencies and have never heard of a GS-12 handling the removal of a higher-level employee. That was always an action for upper management to do.

Osman was asked during the MSBP by my attorney to briefly describe my performance for the first year he supervised me. He responded by saying, "I rated her highly effective that first year."

She followed up by asking about the subsequent years for which he stated, "In the second and third year, she was rated as, I rated her as meets expectations or satisfactory; in 2013, I rated her as needs improvement."

As the conversation continued, my attorney wanted to know what had happened to cause the low rating in 2013. Osman's response was: "I felt like there was an objective assignment that she had been given, but clearly didn't complete. And it wasn't a matter of training; it was a matter of choice, because she had done it before, so I rated it minimally or satisfactory or needs improvement, sorry."

"When did you notice this deteriorating performance; what did you do?" my attorney asked.

Instead of providing a simple answer to the question, Osman gave a second disjointed response, a lengthy spiel about the initial meeting in April 2013 and the assignments, his weekly follow-up emails, the assignment he gave me to complete during my leave, and the "miscommunications with my leave plan."

Osman had no real reasons for my poor performance rating. I felt sick as he attempted to justify the low ratings. Osman was truthful when he stated that he never spoke with me regarding any alleged performance issues. Instead of talking with me about any "declining" performance issues, he decided to speak with George Fox, who wasn't even in my performance rating chain.

My attorney wanted to know what the communication between Osman and George was like regarding my declining performance. Again, he presented a third dissertation beginning with when I first started working at DBC. I was unsure what that had to do with his conversation with George but I sat in silence.

He began again by saying, "I needed her to be the voice of the agency budget offices."

At this point, I wanted to laugh out loud, but I kept my composure. That's news to me, I thought.

He continued by saying, "She was an agency budget officer, a supervisor as an agency budget officer. She had that perspective, and we needed that in DBC. But, yeah, when I called her into meetings during 2013, she really wasn't engaged, and so I went to Mr. Fox in—I think it was late October, early November, I don't remember which—to see if there was a possibility of finding somewhere else in OCM that she might work."

According to Osman's testimony, after talking about my alleged poor performance, George Fox volunteered to audit my computer. But there was simply no reason to do this. The conversation between Osman and my attorney at the MSPB went as follows regarding the audit:

Ms. Grant: "And what was your response?"

Mr. Payne: "I asked him to go ahead, that would be good. That would be good information to have for her performance appraisal."

Ms. Grant: "And do you know if he did?"

Mr. Payne: "He did."

■ ■ ■

Lynching in America was a widely supported phenomenon that was used to enforce racial subordination and segregation. People who participated in lynching were celebrated and acted with impunity. Lynching reinforced a narrative of racial difference and a legacy of racial inequality. This is not only readily apparent in our criminal justice system today but also in organizations, even in federal government agencies like the DOL.

As I sat in the MSPB hearing, tears fell from my eyes as I listened to the testimony. I felt as if I were experiencing a workplace lynching and there was no one there to seek justice on my behalf. The conversation between Osman and my attorney continued:

Ms. Grant: "And do you recall, was it right around the same time, this October timeframe?"

Mr. Payne: "Yes, it was, you know, the same conversation, or in follow-up later that day."

Ms. Grant: "Okay. And then what happened?"

Mr. Payne: "He, as part of the follow-up, he came to me and said, you know, these folks need to know some idea of what they might be looking for. They can go in and take a look, but it's going to take forever. And I noted to him that Jean from the very get-go was very interested in education training. She had completed her PhD the previous year. And from what I could tell when I walked by her cube, she was on the Internet. I couldn't really tell what websites or not; but it occurred to me that it could've been her pursuing another PhD or additional education or certifications. And so, I recommended that they actually look at educational-type activities."

Ms. Grant: "Did you ever get any preliminary results regarding this inquiry?"

Mr. Payne: "The only results, as I remember—I don't remember who it was, if it was Mr. Fox or somebody else saying that it did look like there was some activity in there, that they would get me a final report."

Ms. Grant: "And did you ever get a final report?"

Mr. Payne: "I did, yeah, I did, mid-December."

Regarding the alleged declining performance Osman also said that he didn't confer with HRM. Instead, he had spoken with George Fox about my performance based on an alleged "objective" that he stated I didn't complete. At the MSPB, Ed claimed that Osman approached him about a job opening. I had never before heard that claim. It also makes no sense, as a month earlier they had denied me a job even after my physician had asked them to move me to a less stressful position.

Osman would also identify a few other off-the-wall reasons for auditing my computer such as: "I knew she had just gotten her PhD, and I thought she was working on another PhD." and "She looked busy." These are poor excuses to audit an employee's computer, even if they were true. All of this leads me to believe my computer was audited to intimidate me.

I submit to you that auditing an employee's computer is never an action that an organization takes to probe the alleged "declining performance" of an employee. That was unheard of! George also testified his version of the decision to audit my computer. He couldn't even bring himself to say that I had committed any misconduct. He said it was a "possible misconduct."

I believe the leadership had concocted the storyline and followed through on it. If Osman had admitted to receiving the original training plan, he would have had to find another reason why he was inclined to audit my computer.

At the MSPB hearing, George Fox was asked to give his side of the story. According to him, the conversation with Osman began with an inquiry about a job, a job they had denied me one month prior to their conversation. This occurred immediately after the DEBS online training initiative meeting. The conversation supposedly segued into poor performance issues, performance issues that Osman could not prove. The conversation finally morphed into "let's audit her computer for educational websites." The very same sites Osman said were a good idea and approved researching in developing a similar online platform for a new training initiative.

I believe this all stemmed from my filing of the formal EEO complaint against Osman on September 12, 2013. In my view, their actions were nothing less than brazen retaliation.

The following conversation occurred between George and my attorney on May 1, 2015:

Ms. Grant: "Why didn't you ask them to review her work before her detail?"

Mr. Fox: "I don't have a good answer for that other than I knew she had just returned. She had been gone for six months. I presumed there wouldn't be anything in that six-month period to look at."

Ms. Grant: "Oh, okay. But, what about before the detail?"

Mr. Fox: "It didn't seem germane to the moment to me."

Ms. Grant: "Did you think that it was odd that he was recommending this employee to you whose productivity was poor?"

Mr. Fox: "It's not odd, and I'll try to explain. I think he was very clearly conveying to me that this person wasn't working out very well. I had done—I do this for people from time to time, and others do it for me.

Ms. Grant: "So going back to your audit request, what was the subject matter, recommendation that you made to the OCIO?"

Mr. Fox: "Mr. Payne did say to me that he knew that Dr. Francis had an interest in pursuing her academic, I'll say career, for lack of a better word. So, I did mention that to the OCIO staff to say, 'That's something you should look for.'"

George Fox gave the green light to audit my computer based on alleged "declining performance" reported by Osman. When asked if it was normal for him to give the green light for auditing an employee's computer for declining performance, he gave an incoherent answer. I had the following conversation with George while representing myself as pro se on March 16, 2017:

Me: "Did you ask Mr. Payne if he confronted Dr. Francis about her work product, or did he counsel her or talk to her before coming to you?"

Mr. Fox: "No, I didn't—I didn't ask him that."

Me: "Did Mr. Payne provide evidence of the work product that he wasn't receiving from Dr. Francis?"

Mr. Fox: "No. I didn't ask him for it either."

Me: "But obviously, you did take his word at face value?"

Mr. Fox: "I did."

Me: "So late summer of 2013, did Mr. Payne identify the work products he was giving to Dr. Francis?"

Mr. Fox: "No, nor did I ask."

George never answered the question regarding if it was normal for him to audit other employees' computers for alleged poor performance. Instead, he said he didn't "follow" the line of questioning. According to him, he had taken Osman's claim for alleged declining poor performance at face value, and he launched a request for auditing my computer. Osman didn't reveal the DEBS training initiative and research he had approved.

Not only did George give the green light to audit my computer, but my profile was also changed to "allow mapping to my computer hard drive remotely." It was as though they believed I was a criminal or that I was selling government secrets. The CIO actually took over my computer, and George, the manager, requested that the chief information officer (CIO) IT specialists focus specifically on "educational websites." It sure appeared that these folks were pulling out all the stops in making sure they developed a solid smoke screen to distract from the real issue—my discrimination and retaliation EEO complaint.

If this was truly a performance issue, wouldn't he have liked to know all the sites an employee was accessing? Osman reported to George exactly what to look for after the meeting on the DEBS online training initiative and in turn, George was precise as to what the IT personnel were to look for, according to Chang Ming's (one of the IT personnel assigned the auditing) testimony at the MSPB hearing on May 1, 2015:

Ms. Grant: "And who made this request?"

Mr. Ming: "My supervisor at the time, Toya Williams, who was the chief information security officer."

Ms. Grant: "And did Ms. Williams inform you who had made the request of her?"

Mr. Ming: "Yes, Mr. George Fox."

Ms. Grant: "And who is that?"

Mr. Ming: "He has many titles. The one that I refer to him is our departmental operations manager."

Ms. Grant: "Did Mr. Fox specifically tell you to look for educational websites?"

Mr. Ming: "Just education, correct."

You may recall the yearly March Madness activities that employees engaged in at the DBC. I brought this up, but my revelation was ignored. During the MSPB hearing, my attorney asked Mr. Ming if the department had ever audited the computer of any person who had engaged in gambling activities while at work. He couldn't answer the question. The agency's consul interrupted the line of questioning by my attorney, who argued that the use of work computers for March Madness activities wasn't "similar to what" I had done.

My attorney asked Ming if he had ever been asked to audit an employee's computer on sporting events at DOL. Unfortunately, the agency's counsel objected to her line of questioning. So, Mr. Ming wasn't allowed to answer.

No other DBC employee's computer was audited, even though other employees were taking courses on their government computers around this time. Additionally, others were also watching movies at their desks, and perusing the web for various, clearly nongovernment-related reasons.

■ ■ ■

The MSPB judge ultimately ruled in favor of the agency on my removal case. I was devastated and disappointed, but not surprised.

Discovery and presentation were important in my case because I bore the burden of proving my affirmative defenses and I was entitled to depose witnesses who could support my affirmative defenses and prove that the agency's removal claims were false. On May 8, 2015, my attorney filed a petition to the MSPB board for review, and the petition was denied. However, the board's recommendation was for me to file my case in the district court to have my discrimination and removal case heard. And once again, I was prepared to do just that.

■ ■ ■

But despite the setbacks in my professional life, my personal life went on. There was so much to be thankful for. On May 21, 2015, I was scheduled to attend the prayer breakfast event at the Capitol. Interfaith and Congressional leaders were to join in solidarity at this event to support military and veteran caregivers in the Kennedy Caucus Room of the Russell Senate Office Building, in Washington, DC.

The event was planned by the Elizabeth Dole Foundation, of which I was a member. And I accepted the invitation to attend. The focus at the event was to provide spiritual support to the nation's military and veteran caregivers, but I was also empowered and motivated. At the end of the event, I had the honor to greet many of the attendees. It was quite exhilarating. I left with my faith fully intact and filled with hope and strength to keep on fighting for justice despite the odds.

Standing with Ms. Nancy Pelosi

Standing with Joel Osteen

Chapter 33

I call on each one of us to speak out and stand up to racism,
wherever and whenever we see it happen.

—Nelson Mandela

On April 25, 2016, through my attorney, I filed my civil case number 1:16-cv-00763 in the US District Court, District of Columbia, against the DOL for actions arising from prohibited personnel practices, of discriminatory and retaliatory actions, pursuant to Title VII of the Civil Rights Act of 1964, 42 USC. My case was assigned to Judge Rosemary M. Collyer. I asked for my day in court to present my case before twelve jurors. It would later be denied.

On July 28, 2016, I appeared at the first court session. I was representing myself without a lawyer because he had withdrawn from my case because of a disagreement with me. Despite the setback with my attorney, I kept my case moving. When Judge Collyer walked in the courtroom, she said, "Hi, Damien." Damien was representing the agency and he responded in kind. I thought, *Wow, they know each other on first name basis.* The judge proceeded to set the parameters for the case.

Halfway through her directives, she said to Damien Baron, "Are you going to submit summary judgment?" He said "Yes." I was appalled because I didn't believe that was something the judge should have asked the defendant's lawyer in front of me. I thought that showed bias at best. I was disappointed after the short proceeding. Despite the occurrence in the courtroom, I gave the judge the benefit of the doubt to review the evidence and to rule justly in my case.

I immediately began searching for a new attorney to represent me in my lawsuit. I contacted the Baltimore NAACP, DC Bar Pro Bono Center, the Legal Aid Society, and the American Civil Liberties Union's Washington legislative office to assist with handling my case pro bono. I knew it would be challenging, if not impossible, to convince an attorney in any of these agencies to take the case when I had no money for a retainer's fee. However, I believed in my case, and so I tried. Unfortunately, I was unable to locate an attorney in any of the agencies during the early stages of my lawsuit.

Hence, I began representing myself. I was confident that I could do this, and I began preparing myself by reading every legal document and guidance I could find. I selected the court reporter and planned for the depositions for all the DOL personnel I wanted to depose. I prayed for strength and guidance in the process, and I moved forward in faith with my questions and exhibits in hand for the depositions.

From March 2017 through April 2017, I conducted the discovery phase of my lawsuit, particularly in the removal aspect of my case, as pro se. I was nervous about serving as my own attorney because this was out of my league. However, I committed myself to researching how to conduct depositions and how to file my motions with the court. I found examples and began creating my own. I believed I was prepared to move forward.

I also researched court-reporting companies in my area and selected one of the companies to transcribe the verbatim record at the depositions. As pro se, I deposed Osman Payne, Rob Briar, Fachnan Ellis, George Fox, and Hue Hoang. I recall one day after a deposition, the court reporter said, "I have never recorded a proceeding where an individual represented him or herself in the deposition process, but I must say that you were excellent in the entire process." I thanked her. I knew no matter how the story ended that God was with me.

Osman was last in the process, and his deposition lasted over eight hours on March 16, 2017.

Osman had begun my termination process based on his assertion that he had requested the report following the 2013 performance review because "the results for work assigned during the performance period weren't congruent to the amount of time the complainant was busy at her desk during work hours."

I was greatly astonished by Osman's statement and wondered if there was a memorandum of assigned tasks that I had missed. From my recollection, Osman didn't assign any other work after April 2013 and those assignments were completed and submitted to him. I wanted to get to the bottom of this and allow Osman, in his own words, to describe the assignments to which he was referring and that had led him to the actions he had taken against me.

I was doing well until I began asking a line of questions about the assignments he was referring to after April 2013 that had led to my termination and the moment that was before me. The following conversation ensued between Osman and me at his deposition:

Me: "Did you provide any assignments in August?"

Mr. Payne: "Other than the ones we've just discussed; those were the ones that were still in place."

I wanted to stop at this question, but this wasn't when he proposed the audit, so I continued my questioning.

Me: "In September, did you assign any work?"

I was hoping that he would speak about the DEBs initiative he had assigned.

Mr. Payne: "Again, I recall the ones that were consistently in place, but no specific ones other than those."

At this point in his responses, I was overcome with sadness because in September, I had already submitted all the frivolous assignments by the due dates as he requested, and this was when he requested to audit my computer claiming that he wasn't getting "the work."

Me: "How about October?"

Mr. Payne: "I don't recall," he said.

His response pierced the depths of my wounded, broken, and depressed spirit. Tears welled up in my eyes, and I buckled in my chair. I continued to question him as I held back more tears.

Me: "How about November?"

Mr. Payne: "I don't recall."

Me: "December?"

Mr. Payne: "I don't recall."

Me: "How about January?"

Mr. Payne: "I don't recall."

Me: "And February?"

Mr. Payne: "I don't recall."

Me: "So, you don't recall any assignments from June 2013 through February of 2014?"

Mr. Payne: "Except for the standing assignments of reviewing policy documents, working on customer assistance, and the things we've already talked about."

I plowed on, now more composed.

Me: "Okay. How about March 2014?"

Mr. Payne: "Same."

I was saddened at this point, but I wanted Payne to speak the truth in his own words. Sitting in front of my accuser who claimed he was "not getting the work" from me—work that in his own words he couldn't even "recall," I was left speechless and full of pain but glad I held firm throughout the interrogation.

Me: "And April and May 2014?"

Mr. Payne: "Same."

■ ■ ■

At this point, there were so many emotions stirring up in me. I asked the reporter to end the deposition proceedings so that I could take a break. I went to the lady's room and let it all out. I did not sense that the truth was being told. To me, this was truly a moment of reflection in a very difficult way. The institution would protect itself and forget about the principles it was supposed to stand for. I proceeded to wash my face and dry my eyes, and I returned to the conference room to continue Osman's deposition.

Osman was bold enough to state that he had not assigned any work for one full year. His action in this regard wasn't new. Neither did he assign any real work to me during my tenure at the DBC for the four years prior to this. He was protected time and time again after I had raised concerns about this situation my concerns were ignored. Osman was never held accountable for his actions.

He had people in high places on his side at the DOL who covered for him and for the department. I had no one looking out for me.

Then, immediately after conducting the deposition proceedings, I located an attorney. On June 5, 2017, Kofi Abimbola, filed his formal appearance as the lead attorney in my case. We worked together for several months in developing the case and providing all the necessary evidence to bolster my case and refute the agency's fabrications. I shared the depositions and all documents in my possession.

Damien Baron, assistant United States attorney, who the judge in my case knew on a first name basis, represented the agency. He was at the deposition and would constantly object when I asked Osman hard questions, claiming they were "argumentative." I felt the questions were appropriate, and I turned to Baron and told him that Osman needed to answer. In response, he would tell Osman, "Answer if you can." I felt bullied by Baron, but I stood my ground.

Baron deposed me on or around the first week of April 2017. I didn't have an attorney present. He began asking questions relating to my tenure with at the ESA and ending with DBC. It was difficult for me to rehash those experiences. But what concerned me during the process was when Damien Baron began asking questions about Lionel: "Where does your husband work? What is his grade? What does he do? What is his salary? How many children are at home?" I was livid!

I believe Damien Baron was in violation with his line of questionings about Lionel and my other personal affairs. Baron proceeded to ask me personal questions about myself: "Where do you work? How much do you get paid? How many students?" After giving Baron the information regarding where I worked, I lost my job one month later.

Then, in answering to the agency's request for information on September 26, 2016, Damien Baron from the justice department and representing the agency responded to my "request for relief" in this manner:

This paragraph contains Plaintiff's request for relief, to which no answer is required. To the extent answer may be deemed required; the Defendant denies that Plaintiff experienced any unlawful employment practice and denies that she is entitled to relief under the facts of this case. Consequently, the Defendant requests that the Plaintiff take nothing by this action, which should be dismissed.

I was at a loss for words at his response, but I wasn't surprised. Damien and the judge assigned to my case knew each other. In my view, the outcome was already decided. One thing is for sure, though: there is a Judge above all judges. He sits high and He looks low, and He is the one who will bring me the relief and the justice that I deserved. And I believe He will do just that!

Finally, despite the statements that A. Wiley Thornton, Osman Payne, George Fox, and Rob Briar had made under oath, they could not provide a shred of evidence to support their claims of my alleged poor and declining performance and teaching on the job; and despite the depositions and number of documents that I had filed in court that proved their statements were false, on April 18, 2018, Judge Collyer granted the summary judgment in favor of the DOL.

In essence, she dismissed my lawsuit by ruling that I had failed to create any genuine issue of material fact, and therefore the agency was entitled to summary judgment on all my claims. There were no words to express my emotions. I was utterly stunned after learning that she had ruled against me. But I quickly remembered the proceedings at the first court appearance in my case, and I wasn't surprised at the outcome.

I was still devastated when I heard the news. My family and friends who had followed me every step of the way throughout my legal process were also dumbfounded. I decided to keep my lawsuit moving and filed an appeal. However, at this phase of my legal proceedings, I had exhausted my savings and was entirely out of funds.

My attorney recommended that I file my appeal in *forma pauperis*, which would allow my appeal to be taken without prepayment of fees and costs by a party who makes an affidavit that he or she cannot pay those costs. According to USC §1915(a) and Fed. R. App. P. 24, this means that appeals courts are authorized to waive the fee for the application often referred to as "Fee Waiver Applications" or *in forma pauperis* petitions. My current attorney wasn't an appellate attorney; therefore, he was unable to help me through the process.

■ ■ ■

It's difficult to appeal a summary judgment in a discrimination case. Before moving forward with my appeal, I prayed about the process and asked for three signs. The first sign was that I would find a competent attorney to represent me in the appeals process; the second was that I would be granted an extension to find the lawyer, and third, that God would provide the required five-hundred-dollar fee to file the Notice of Appeal. On the week that I was to file the Notice of Appeal, God blessed me with the exact amount to file the appeal after facilitating a course at APUS. Additionally, my attorney Mr. Kofi Abimbola, emailed me that same week to remind me that the date for filing the appeal was coming due.

On May 28, 2019, I completed the appeal forms, signed, and emailed them back to Kofi, and he drove to the courthouse and placed them in the drop box in a timely manner. He also advised me to mail the check for filing the Notice of Appeal to the US Court of Appeals for the District of Columbia the following day. I did. Because I was still searching for an attorney and couldn't meet the July 8, 2019, date for submitting the initial documents, I filed a motion for the court to grant me a thirty-day extension to file the Entry of Appearance form, procedural motions, and dipositive motions. My request was granted. The new date was now August 8, 2019.

In my search for an attorney, Alan Lescht responded to my inquiry and agreed to represent me in the appeals process. On June 25, 2019, Alan invited me to his office for the initial consultation. He briefly reviewed the summary judgment motion, as well as the response to the agency's proposed removal. He said, "Based on the judge's motion, you deserved to be terminated; however, based on the response to the proposal to remove that is not the case." He further stated that he would represent me and began drafting the retainer agreement.

Although I had received the appeals filing fee and found the attorney, I had no idea how I would get the money for the retainer fee.

God provided the retainer fee in a phenomenal way. When I returned to sign the retainer and make the payment, the secretary facilitated the transaction. I never heard from or spoke to Mr. Lescht again. Moreover, I was convinced that he would be the one representing me with the appeal proceedings, and I asked the secretary to confirm. She went back to his office to confirm and returned by saying he told her to tell me that he and Susan Kruger would be handling my case. I never heard from either of them.

Susan Kruger never communicated with me regarding my case or addressed what the next step would be. Nicole, who was an associate attorney, was the only one who communicated with me throughout the entire process letting me know what Susan's next step would be. It appears I wasn't good enough for her to speak with directly. According to Nicole, they were looking into whether they could supplement the lower court's record with evidence that my former counsel obtained in discovery. I immediately thought that wasn't the direction to proceed. Moreover, I thought it would be a waste of money. After all, an abundance of document production—the agency's answers to my interrogatories and transcripts of all deposition—were already in the record.

On September 24, 2019, I received an email from Nicole stating that she and Susan had filed a Motion to Supplement the Record for my case. In response, the agency's counsel had filed an Opposition to the Motion to Supplement the Record. I'm not an attorney but the Motion to Supplement the Record because my former counsel inadvertently didn't submit to the lower court evidence that was obtained in discovery didn't sit well with me. In the lower court's records, thousands of documents, depositions, and affidavits were filed by my attorney and me with each motion submitted. I believe that a brief would be more beneficial to explain why the lower court made a mistake in deciding my case. I waited in earnest for the judge's decision.

On January 08, 2020, a panel of three circuit judges denied my attorney's motion to supplement the record and denied my summary affirmance. In essence, the judges declared that through my attorney, I didn't put forth sufficient evidence for a reasonable jury to find the DOL's asserted reasons for my "negative performance rating and termination pretext for retaliation for protected activity." The judges determined the evidence provided wasn't enough. Additionally, the judges claimed that I didn't present sufficient evidence for a reasonable jury to find that I was subjected to "discriminatory intimidation, ridicule, and insult that is sufficiently severe or pervasive to alter the conditions of the victim's employment and create an abusive working environment." The judges in my case had found that the agency had done nothing wrong to this Black professional woman, based on the evidence provided to refute its claim.

Simply put, the three judges of the US District Court and District of Columbia Circuit of Appeals Court seemed to ignore much of this evidence and waved the rest away. In this regard, I join almost half of Americans polled in believing that the US justice system is indeed corrupt. In both of my cases, the justice system had determined that the DOL and its tolerance of unethical, racist, discriminatory, and retaliatory practices had done nothing wrong.

■ ■ ■

In the judge's order filed on January 8, 2020, I was granted the opportunity to file a petition for hearing or petition for rehearing *en banc*. I wanted to file the petition on my own. It was due on or around March 3, 2020. I began researching the process of developing the petition, as well as determining the most critical issues I needed to prove to the three-judge appellate panel. On day one, as I began gathering the files and other material to begin the process, a still small voice said, "Write your book." I ignored the small voice and continued gathering my documents in preparation for developing my petition to meet the March deadline. On day two, again, the still small voice returned and whispered again, "Write your book." I had no intention of writing a book about my employment history; it was never on my radar. At least, that's what I thought.

Then, I looked at the vast number of documents, files, and depositions. Even if I did want to write a book, I had no idea where to begin. The task was just too great. Instead, I returned to the task of preparing to develop the petition. I also researched others who had represented themselves pro se in the appeals process, and I stumbled upon a woman named Joyce Hutchens. Her story and experiences with her employment discrimination mirrored mine. She had represented herself pro se on appeal and had won, and she had written a book about it. I immediately purchased her book, *How a Pro Se Won Justice*, and I called and emailed her regarding my case and whether she might be willing to speak with me.

Again, as I was waiting for Ms. Hutchens to return the call or email, on day three, the still small voice returned and said, "Write your book." The third time hearing the faint voice got my attention. Instead of locating and researching files to begin developing my petition, I was looking for books and stacking them up to begin the writing process. Honestly, I didn't know where to begin. I prayed and asked God to guide me if He was indeed directing me to write a book. The week prior to beginning the book-writing process, I had bought several books and one was Willy Jolley's newest book titled *Turn Setbacks into Greenbacks*. This book was a part of my stack of books; however, the still small voice returned and reminded me that some years ago I had bought his book titled It *Only Takes a Minute to Change Your Life*, and I needed to have this book, too.

I ignored the voice because I had no idea where I would find the book. I didn't even remember what the book looked like. I prepared to begin writing my manuscript; the still small voice returned and convinced me that I needed to find the book. For three days, I searched for the book and finally found it stacked in my library. Happiness seemed to come over me once it was found. Curiosity set in as I sat and immediately prepared to open the book and flip the pages. I wondered what on earth would be in that book that I needed to use for my book and what was the need to find it? I turned a few pages, and nothing jumped out at me; however, when I turned the page one last time, to my surprise I found a neatly folded piece of paper tucked in between the pages of the book. It was pristine.

Gingerly, I opened it and to my surprise, it was the timeline of my life goals that I had written nineteen years before on that day when I'd arrived early to the office in 2001. As I read the timeline, I was amazed at the level of detail, and the fact that I had accomplished every milestone as indicated on the piece of paper, except for becoming a senior executive service employee.

However, the most astonishing entry on the list was the one stating that I would retire from government service at age fifty-five. I almost fell over in my chair when I read it. On May 9, 2014, the day that George Fox had concurred to remove me from my federal service, I was fifty-five years and eleven months old. This wasn't an official decision on my part to retirement at the time, but I left government service at age fifty-five, nonetheless. It was no coincidence that this aligned with the milestone I had written on my timeline nineteen years before. Right then and there, I knew God was in the details. During my crucibles at the DOL God was silent. But He revealed to me, through a nineteen-year-old piece of paper, what I needed to know and what I should do.

It was also interesting that prior to leaving at age fifty-five, I had visited my doctor at Walter Reed, who was interested in my health and how I was fairing on the job. After telling her my story, she said, "I believe you should cut your losses and leave." She was right. I had been ready to move on for years.

All the signs pointed to it. As I read my timeline written nineteen years earlier, I knew that this was God's doing and that it was meant to be. The recorded timeline of my life and career path has since helped me to confidently rest in God's providence and promises because He has shown me in every situation of my life that He is indeed the master strategist; hence, I know that my victory is guaranteed.

On April 1, 2020, I also applied for my federal retirement benefits for my twenty-five years of service, which ended on May 9, 2014. According to Office of Personnel Management (OPM), the process would take only ninety days. However, as of July 2020, I still had not received a letter confirming receipt of my application and retirement claim number. I called OPM, Retirement Programs in Boyers, Pennsylvania, and spoke with a service specialist regarding the status. She apologized for the delay in forwarding the verification of annuity and said I should receive it in a few days.

On or around August 12, 2020, I received a letter dated August 5, 2020, as the specialist indicated. I opened the letter, which read:

The following information is provided in response to your request for verification of your retirement benefits under the Civil Service System or the Federal Employees Retirement System. The Monthly gross monthly annuity, $0.00; and net monthly annuity, $0.00. The annuity of a retired member terminates on the day the member dies or the date of other terminating events provided by title 5, US Code, Section 8345(c), et seq.

I didn't know what to make of the letter. One thing I know is that the specialist can only forward the information placed in the system. I called the next day and spoke with a retirement service specialist at OPM. She quickly told me to ignore the letter because the specialist who mailed it should not have done so. She assured me that they were computing my retirement benefits and that it would be completed in a few weeks. On October 1, 2020, I began receiving my retirement annuity. This was after I had applied for a refund of the contributions I had made during my working time to the civil service retirement fund. My goal was to invest the proceeds into a Fidelity Retirement Account; however, the DOL agency refused to return the form to OPM on several occasions. I had left the DOL; however, I was still experiencing the wrath of my previous employer.

Based on my three highest salaries calculation, the monthly amount

I received as my retirement annuity wasn't adding up. There was a difference of at least $200 per month. I called OPM and asked for a calculation on how my annuity was derived, and I was told that I would receive the information in approximately two months. Two months had passed, and I hadn't heard anything. When I called to inquire why I had not received the information requested, I was told to forward my request in writing along with my supporting documents. I did. Currently, I wait with patience for a resolution because I'm determined to receive every penny of my annuity based on my twenty-five years of government service. During my tenure, the DOL leadership may have controlled my work assignments, training, and the conditions of my work environment. It appears that they also want to control my annuity by calculating what I receive based on my lowest three years of salary instead of the highest three years. Not on my watch.

■ ■ ■

Going through my legal battles for many years was challenging. It didn't seem that life could get much worse. But let me tell you that despite the challenges, there was so much to celebrate from year to year in my personal life. My family and I were blessed, and no man could have taken that away. During my civil case debacle, I took a mental break to share in the joy of helping our daughter, Jeanelle, develop and finalize the plans for her wedding day. Planning for this event had been one of the most exciting and rewarding endeavors of my lifetime.

It was wonderful to see our first daughter grown up, getting married, and starting her own family. For Lionel, being the father of the bride was a big deal. He has been a doting father of our daughter since her birth. For me, her wedding was arguably one of the most special events I would get to experience as a mom. I was all in with helping her to plan for her big day.

On July 5, 2016, I was bursting with joy and excitement when our daughter walked down the aisle, beautifully radiant, and leaning on her father's strong arm, to meet the man she'd take as the chosen love of her life. My heart was full of unbridled happiness and bursting with excitement for them both as family and friends gathered to celebrate love and life itself. The wedding was wonderful and filled with sheer joy. My hope is that I had been an exceptional example in all facets of my life for my daughter to emulate—and one who would seek justice, love mercy, and walk humbly with her God. At the end, of the celebration, the evening was filled with fireworks. I pray that the fireworks of their love will remain continually.

Then, on October 11, 2016, Lionel and I decided to celebrate our thirty-fifth wedding anniversary. It was a beautiful milestone despite the legal woes we were facing. We still had each other and took the opportunity in pulling out all the stops for celebrating our love with family and friends. Our day was absolutely beautiful. After the celebration and before we checked in to our hotel, we made a quick stop at our local Whole Foods store. I proudly walked down the aisles in my gown. I was happy and feeling regal. Everyone congratulated us on our wedding day and commented on how beautiful I looked as we walked elegantly from aisle to aisle. We smiled and thanked everyone for the kind words.

It was one of the most joyous days of my life—one that lifted my spirit and put a smile on my face despite my circumstances. When we got to the checkout, everyone who was there congratulated us on our wedding day. My husband was giddy with joy as I stood by his side smiling in wonderment. "We are celebrating our wedding anniversary" he smiled and said. To this revelation, the elated crowd cheered even more. The cashier gleefully interjected, "Your groceries are on the house." Everyone clapped. We were stunned. It was an exceptional anniversary gift among other things—complements of our local Whole Foods and God's favor.

On June 8, many years ago, I filled my lungs with air for the first time and cried. My mother was elated. Many other milestones had passed through the years. On June 8, 2018, I approached a milestone of threescore years. I was excited and begin researching and planning the perfect location to make my day unforgettable. I chose to celebrate in San Francisco—one of the places on my bucket list. My husband accompanied me, and my birthday was a smash. We decided to take a ride on a streetcar to Market Street. The sightseeing tour was breathtaking along the way, and we had fun. No experience is more uniquely San Francisco than a cable car ride. I couldn't have chosen a better location to celebrate my huge milestone.

On our second day in San Francisco, we headed to the Golden Gate Bridge. We were going to walk across the bridge starting at the Welcome Center at the south end of the bridge, which is 1.7 miles one way. I was mentally and physically ready to walk. My shoes were cute but not ready for the journey—they were not walking shoes.

At the end of the walk across the spectacular bridge and back, both of my feet were blistered, and walking was painful and uncomfortable. *Not on my birthday*, I thought. Moreover, we had a reservation that evening to attend a dinner show and we were concerned that we may have to cancel the event. I was intentional about attending despite of my blistered feet. After returning to our hotel, I prepared myself for the evening's event. It was there that Lionel had to carry me over the threshold and to my seat because of the excruciating pain. But I had a fabulous birthday despite my condition.

As if my birthday travel was not enough, Lionel, children, and siblings planned a magnificent surprise party a few months later. Surprised? I was! My family left me speechless, indeed. I had the time of my life celebrating at the event and looking royal. I wished Mom had been there to see me. Truly, family is everything and everything is family. I felt like a queen that evening—compliments of Lionel and family. With them, I am extremely blessed.

■ ■ ■

Keep laughing. He who laughs last, laughs best! This was my late uncle's favorite phrase that has also resonated with me throughout my life. My late uncle's name was Fred, and he was a man of few words. I never heard or saw him laugh. He was my father's brother, and was vision impaired in one eye. But he didn't allow his vision impairment to keep him from what he loved to do.

As kids, my brother Lemuel and I would visit Uncle Fred on weekends at regular intervals. Whenever we visited, he was always cooking rice and the meat of the day. The aroma was tantalizing but the rice was always soggy. My brother and I would laugh at Uncle Fred's rice, which seemed as though the water would never soak in.

The look on his face would tell me that he wasn't happy with us laughing at him and his food. With a serious expression on his face, Uncle Fred would turn to us and say, "Keep laughing. Who laughs last, laughs the best." We thought his words were funny, and as kids we laughed even more. My uncle never told us kids whether he had had the last laugh. In my adult life, much like my grandmother's favorite phrase, I got what Uncle Fred was trying to say.

I share this story because I couldn't help but see a distinct similarity between this imagery and my situations experienced at the DOL. The day after Osman proposed my removal, I saw Osman and Stormi walking down the hallway laughing. I couldn't help but notice how happy they were. I could imagine Osman revealing to her that they had been vindicated, finally. I had been fired. As I observed their behavior that day, I also remembered when Hattie and Stormi laughed me to scorn when they had demoted me and reassigned me to a cubicle in front of her office. In my uncle's voice, I say to Osman and his accomplices, and to Hattie, Stormi, and their posse, and to all those who laughed at my unfortunate plight at the DOL, "Keep laughing. Who laughs last, laughs the best!"

Today, my life is beautiful minus the DOL. Even though I didn't win my cases as I had hoped, I remain grateful that God gave me the strength, grace, and tenacity to fight the good fight for justice. My fight is not over, and I look forward to affecting change as I share my story. I'm also confident that God will restore to me the years that the locust has eaten and the cankerworm and the caterpillar have destroyed. I'm convinced that my best days are still ahead, and I'm so excited about it.

All smiles with daughter on her big wedding day.

Lionel and me on my 60th birthday on the #22 Trolley in San Fransisco

Epilogue

God knew there'd be unfair situations. That's why He's already arranged a comeback for every setback, vindication for every wrong, and a new beginning for every disappointment."
—Vicky Zugah

I walked out of the DOL for the last time on May 9, 2014 as a government employee. That day I was tired, distraught, confused, and overwhelmed yet confident about my future. One thing I knew for sure, I was walking out with my dignity intact. Knowing that I no longer had to sit in a cubicle day after day and experience Osman's or any other DOL unethical and incompetent leadership abuse. I left with the resolve to fight for justice, no matter how long it took.

On my way out, I passed a member of the DBC administrative staff and told her that it was my last day. She was surprised. I saw tears come to her eyes. She hugged me and said, "You are going to be all right."

I smiled and said, "Yes. I will be." I turned and walked out the front doors, knowing that for the first time in my seven-year battle, I was finally free. I felt as though a heavy burden had been lifted. This may have been how Christian felt when he came to the end of his tumultuous journey in the *Pilgrim's Progress* allegory.

I remember stopping at our local CVS on my way home just like it was yesterday. As I was waiting in line to pay for my purchase, a conversation ensued between me and the customer standing behind me. He told me that he was distraught because of an event that had happened to him that day. I encouraged him in his time of need and told him that I had just been terminated from my employment as well.

He looked at me and said, "And you're in such a good mood?" I smiled because I didn't realize my mood was "good," but a stranger seemed to think so.

Things in my professional life were crumbling, but things in my personnel life balanced out the professional chaos. I began focusing

on myself, reassessing my wants and needs, and setting new goals for
the future. It was also a welcoming experience to sit in my sunroom
each morning—carefree—with a cup of tea, as the morning sun rays
warmed my skin.

I attended my first Woman Thou Art Loose Conference in Atlanta,
Georgia in early October. The conference was created to empower and
educate women all over the world and is a top attraction for Christian
women worldwide. To be transparent, I never thought of attending
these events because of my work and busy schedule. However, this year
was different. I felt like a woman who was loose, and I talked myself
into going.

My friend Annette, who lived in Atlanta, also attended and was
good company for me. Sermons and motivational thoughts during each
session spoke to the needs of the thousands of attendees and brought
hope and encouragement for the future. During the lunch break,
as we stood in line to purchase our food, many women shared their
experiences as we befriend each other in solidarity for a common cause.

I shared my experience of how I was terminated from my
employment after twenty-five years of service and the women
surrounding me empathized with me. As we mutually shared, I listened
to the pain of each woman. I realized that no matter the differences in
our personal and professional lives, there is something that connects us
all—pain. And each of our pain comes in different form. At the end of
the conference, I made the decision never to hold on to my past—to
live for what each day has to offer and not for what yesterday has taken
away. My hope for you is the same.

■ ■ ■

In an earlier chapter, I stated that I felt the DOL owed me a new career
because through the accusations of its leaders, my career had come to a
screeching halt. Now let me tell you how God turned it around.

On February 16, 2021, I received an email requesting that if I was interested in submitting an Artificial Intelligence Academy (AI): Computer Programming with Python applicant assessment, to do so no later than March 1, 2021. After considering the request, I decided to complete the program because it was a free Data Scientist Apprenticeship program, and I would receive a certificate of completion in eighteen months through North Carolina State University.

All applicants were required to attend the orientation before beginning the program, and I attended. However, to my surprise and amazement, I discovered that the program was funded by the DOL. What a surprise indeed! On January 17, 2023, I received my credential of Artificial Intelligence Associate for completing the course at the end of December 2022 in the AI Academy.

I'm a witness that God can turn your wrongs to right. So don't take it on yourself to repay a wrong. Tell your truth, trust the Lord, and watch Him make it right.

Today, the field of AI has a tremendous outlook. The US Bureau of Labor Statistics expects that employment in this occupation will grow 11 percent from 2019 to 2029. I currently have the credentials to meet the increased job needs for data scientists and mathematical science professionals, which are crucial to AI. And the DOL fully funded my certification—by default.

God did that! And I want you to know that He will right every wrong in your life and compensate every loss that you've had.

One Last Message!

You either walk inside your story and own it, or you stand outside your story and hustle for your worthiness.

—Brené Brown

During my tenure with the DOL, I experienced what was clearly to me the pangs of systemic racism in the US government. For far too long, the DOL's culture has been rife with cronyism among a good ol' White boy network, often leading to unjust treatment of—or at the very least extremely insensitive behavior toward—employees of color. The leadership at DOL retaliated when I complained about the injustices I felt I was suffering. It has done the same to others I've known.

No one dreams of entering a lion's den, but in retrospect, the DOL was mine. My tenure at the DOL was a stark learning experience; many hard-won lessons came from my seven years there. I believe that these actions were directly and indirectly inflicted against me due to my unwillingness to work on my Sabbath, which is how it all started. This is shameful in the US government. As months turned into years at the DOL, my life felt like a long tedious journey with no foreseeable exit sign. I suffered much for what I believe. However, given the same opportunity to speak out about my religious beliefs, I would make the same choice.

No one should have to endure such deplorable treatment in a government organization or anywhere else. The perpetrators should not be given a free pass. My hope is that one day they will be held accountable. I shared my story to speak truth to power and affect change. The truth is slow, but like a brilliant light, it will eventually illuminate brightly even the darkest corners of justice.

I also believe that everything happens in life for a reason, and that every trial in life comes with a lesson to be learned and a blessing to be earned. These lessons will stay in my memory forever and the blessings earned will be shared continually. I want to share a few of the lessons I have learned through my journey with you:

Employment discrimination cases are very difficult to win. Even after supporting evidence is provided, it's often an uphill battle. This, sadly, is particularly true when the case is against a government office under the protection of the Justice Department. I hope you will never have to file a discrimination lawsuit against your employer. I wish this nightmare on no one. There will be a long and lonely road ahead if you do or are currently in the process of filing a claim. I encourage you to never give up. Stand your ground if you believe a wrong has been perpetuated against you. If no one listens to you, tell your truth. People are waiting to hear your story. Never be afraid to speak truth to power. Remember, like me, you were born for this.

Take time to reflect and destress. The process of taking time to reflect on where you are and finding ways to de-stress after losing a job is important. Self-reflection is a good way to give the brain an opportunity to pause amid the chaos or loss, and to be attentive to self-care during this difficult time. Although it's important to update your resumé and begin applying for jobs, it's also productive to take as much time as you need to recover. Make reflection and self-care a priority. Also, be mindful of depression.

Sometimes, depression can slowly and quietly take hold of us. Other times, it strikes quickly after a draining emotional event like the loss of a job or loved one. If you're a person of faith, know that depression is not a sign of a lack of your faith. Depression happens to the best of us. But don't stay there. Seek help if you need it. Finally, stay positive in the process. Remember, tough times never last but tough people do!

Learn to find teachable moments. There are always lessons that can be learned from every situation, including workplace discrimination, retaliation, and termination. My biggest lesson learned is to be consciously aware of interview nightmares that are filled with alarming red flags. After what I have been through, I'm careful not to accept any and every job offer but to decline politely and professionally offers with alarming red flags.

Your workplace is where you spend most of your time during the day, eight hours or more to be exact. It should be one of the best places for you to be in and a good fit for you. If you face or are facing a toxic work environment, remember that the emotions arising from that environment will bleed into every aspect of your life. Get out! No job, no matter the pay, is worth your health and that kind of misery.

Use your talents and skillset to serve others. If you have not experienced job loss, you may fear the very possibility. During job loss, you may not be able to help others financially; however, on a personal level, you can look for ways to employ your talents and skills by helping others in your spare time. For me, Lionel and I held the title of marriage ministry leaders in our church. I had the opportunity to plan various events for the married couples that I truly enjoyed doing. This was a welcome opportunity for me to use my planning and organizing skillsets. Additionally, I also served as treasurer for three years with the Executive Woman in Government (EWG) organization to help prepare, promote, support, and mentor women for leadership positions in the Federal Government.

The support I provided to EWG was rewarding. I also engaged in the Christmas party events, conferences, and visit to the White House with the leadership. Our time together was always educational and enjoyable. I was humbled to be a member of such a phenomenal organization and professional group of women.

Don't be afraid to start over. Even if you are afraid to start over in your career, just do it—and do it scared. But remember, as Sarah Jakes says, "This time you are not starting from scratch, you are starting from experience." This is a good place to begin again. I submit to you that even God had to start over by sending a flood during Noah's time.

In starting over, His expectation of you does not change—be fruitful and multiply using your talents and skillsets in your new venture. We serve a God of multiplication. Let me tell you about how I've multiplied since DOL. I've started my own business, and I am confident that I'll be successful in providing goods and services to my customers while creating generational wealth.

I am confident that I will be an exceptional leader because the DOL leaders have taught me what not to be in my leadership role. Then I became an author of not one but two books. My hope is that my books will encourage, motivate, and inspire others and in making a difference. Finally, I've also started my very own learning institute where young entrepreneurs desiring to become exceptional leaders can learn and grow in getting to results. And I've only just begun the multiplication concept based on the talents God has entrusted to me. Finally, I want you to know that yard by yard, success is hard. But inch by inch, it's a cinch. Don't give up! God has endowed you with all the talent and skills you need to be successful on your own.

Prepare to walk the journey alone. If you want to find out who is a true friend, go through a challenging time and see who sticks around. I found that to be true in my journey. The day I received the news that Georg Fox had concurred with my removal; I received a call from an individual I had supervised in the past at ESA. I answered the phone. At the other end, he was laughing hysterically and said, "Boom," in my ear, then hung up the phone while still laughing.

This was an individual who I had provided my name as a reference for his job search; one for whom I had given a good report for a position he had applied at another agency. I dismissed the tomfoolery because one thing I have learned in life is that, as Socrates once stated, "No human condition is ever permanent; never be too overjoyed in good fortune or too scornful in someone else's misfortune."

In the coming weeks, months, and years, I reached out to friends and coworkers who I had worked with regarding employment opportunities moving forward. After empty promises, I never heard back. I found a mixed bag of sympathy and support, judgment, and joy about my pain. Most offered empty or shallow comfort. Additionally, I specifically remember walking into my church the first weekend I was removed from my position and a few of the ladies greeted me. I felt their good wishes were genuine as we laughed and chatted. Afterward, I turned and walked away.

Another lady greeted me on my way out and said, "How are you doing?"

I responded by saying, "I'm doing fine, thank you."

She replied, "But you're not working for the government anymore." She smiled and walked away.

I didn't know how to feel. This was a sister in my church for crying out loud. I wasn't sure what her intent was for saying that at that moment. But her comment is certainly unforgettable.

There were others who were giving the side-eye as though I had committed an unpardonable sin. I felt the chatter. One of the church brothers would approach me with a puzzled look on his face on a weekly basis and say, "How can you be fired from the government?" I wanted to tell him that if he had walked in my moccasins, he would have found the answer to his question.

However, I repeatedly dismissed his query. Still others would try to tell my story to others, like they were there! No one can tell my story; that's my story! I thank God for Lionel, who has been my staunchest supporter. He comforted me, stood by me, and motivated me on my journey day after day. For this, I'm truly blessed.

But I've also learned that having friends in the difficult seasons of life is rewarding. They are like sisters and brothers we never had, and the exceptional ones remain by our side through the ebbs and flows of life. According to an old Irish Proverb—*A good friend is like a four-leaf clover: hard to find and lucky to have.*

I have found such a friend in Ms. Mattie Hawkins—an exceptional friend who I lovingly call "Sister Mattie." She has been a constant friend in my life since my mother's passing. There's never a birthday or special day that she has not remembered me by sending me a card with a gift to help me celebrate my special day. And not only for my birthday, but a card from Sister Mattie consistently arrives in my mailbox during holidays and special days. My heart often melts in appreciation and gratitude for her loving and thoughtfulness towards me. I could never reciprocate the kindness fast enough—she is always days, if not weeks ahead of me.

In addition, she calls me on a regular basis just to ensure that I am doing well, getting plenty of rest, and taking care of myself—what a blessing she is indeed. For example, I spent my birthday in Hawaii last year, and who would call be on my birthday from Maryland? Sis Mattie. She wanted to wish me a happy birthday and to inquire if everything was going well. What a friend she has been to me! And for her friendship, I am grateful. But not all friends or acquaintances are like sister Mattie. So be thankful if you've found such a friend.

I had decided to apply for a position that caught my interest. The position required a background check for which I had to provide names of individuals who knew me. My husband recommended two elders in our church whom we had known for over twenty years. They would not have been my first choices; however, he convinced me otherwise. Immediately, I messaged both gentlemen asking if it was okay to use them as references.

The first one said, "No problem, Jean, I will let you know after I speak with the person." The other said, "Be happy to help!"

I informed them that I was using my first name, Daphnie, on the application so that they would know that I was the applicant when they received the call. The call and interview for one of the positions took a while. The two elders were called as references after I was offered the job. Elder A told the HR representative that he only knew me at church. Elder B said he didn't know me. Words can never express how I felt when the HR representative told me about her conversation with the elders. I apologized for the inconvenience, and she moved on with another candidate.

I shared that story because I have learned that in my hour of crisis, God remained the only constant. He was my provider. I never lacked.

He always provided right on time. When the Psalmist said, "I have been young, and now am old; yet have I not seen the righteous forsaken, nor his seed begging for bread," I concur, because God favored me by providing all my needs and throwing some wants in on the side. Most importantly, in my times of need and distress, He reminds me daily that my struggle is "not against flesh-and-blood, but against evil rulers and authorities of the unseen world, against mighty powers in this dark world, and against evil spirits in heavenly places" (Ephesians 6:12). He has allowed me to see firsthand the evil rulers and authorities in high places.

To them I say, as Chaplain Barry Black would declare, "Once to every man and nation comes the moment to decide; in the strife of Truth with Falsehood for the good or evil side." Confess, and tell the truth.

■ ■ ■

Why do I tell this story? What do I hope to accomplish? Am I just an angry, bitter person wanting to rant against the establishment? Well, the truth is, of course, I'm angry, but it's righteous anger. The types of injustices perpetrated against me have been happening to people of color for centuries. Our voices have been muted; our experiences invalidated; neither is religious discrimination limited to me. Countless Muslims, Sikhs, Jews, and even some Christians experience persecution and discrimination that not only threatens their work, but their very lives. I don't think my experience is unique; and that's the problem. This happens too often to too many people, and this cycle must stop.

Yet some may say that I am an angry and frustrated Black woman who wrote my book as a means of catharsis—a way to drag seven years' worth of exasperation into the open. Because I would continue to drag that sack of melancholy wherever I went. This is far from the truth. Then, again, what happened to me at the DOL needed to be in the open. But I never thought about writing a book.

Most importantly, with God's favor and blessings over my life, dragging seven years of frustration wherever I go is not an option. It is not what I do. On the contrary, I am a strong Black woman who lives by three requirements. That is, to seek justice, to love mercy, and to walk humbly with my God. And as if that weren't enough, I read where God called me "a chosen" and adapted me into His royal priesthood" (1 Peter 2:9). Hence, I lived like I am chosen and have royal blood running through my veins! I was born for this.

Yet, I didn't write this story only to highlight the injustices I experienced. I wrote this story because I want to encourage anyone that may be going through a similar situation. I encourage them to find that source of strength and hope that works for them. Whether that's God, family, nature, a hobby, or something else, we must have something that takes us outside of ourselves and our situation. For me, it was my God and my faith community that were sources of strength. I knew that I was in God's hands no matter what and I lived my faith like my grandmother had taught me.

Every Sabbath was a high day for me, despite the struggles on the job or with the justice system. I always arise early and dress as though I was going to meet the King of the universe. The Sabbath is a day that I seek to motivate and encourage others the most, and it is that day that I am motivated and encouraged the most. I don't look defeated or like an angry Black woman. I look like a highly favored child of God who does not reflect on the outside what she is enduring on the inside.

Therefore, in your time of pain, sadness, and heartbreak, I encourage you to crawl into your Abba's lap and allow His love and promises to comfort you. He didn't say when, but he does say you will shout again for joy.

This is not to say there are not still struggles. I still wrestle with the repercussions of my experiences today. The health issues that accumulated during this time are still with me, as are some of the mental and emotional after-effects. What I experienced was traumatic, and trauma always carries beyond the immediate event. I want to say to those who have experienced trauma because of toxic work environments, don't be afraid or ashamed to get help. Talk to your doctor, go to a therapist, or talk to a religious leader in your community.

Too many people, particularly in minority communities, are so hesitant to reach out for help, but I'm here to tell you that I wouldn't have made it without it. Please don't try to take all that weight on alone. We weren't meant to carry these kinds of loads alone. By nature, we need other people. We must have someone to lean on—someone you we can trust.

I often tell my family that I curse the day I applied for and accepted a job with the DOL. Throughout my life, I had always made wise and sound decisions; this wasn't one of them. However, I also believe everything happens for a reason, and in time that reason will be revealed. I stand for all those who have been discriminated and retaliated against and are fearful about coming forward and speaking truth to power. Now, I fully understand the pain and I stand in solidarity with you.

My mission with this book has been to tell the naked truth to the world because no one is above the law. And, by using the words of my accusers to refute their claims, I want to set the record straight. My hope is that I can affect change not only at the DOL, but in organizations everywhere.

The late Myles Munroe once stated that "The graveyard is the richest place on earth, because it is here that you will find all the hopes and dreams that were never fulfilled, the books that were never written, the songs that were never sung, the inventions that were never shared, the cures that were never discovered, all because someone was too afraid to take that first step, to keep with the problem, or determined not to carry out their dream." I've taken the first step in writing my story. Perhaps my story will inspire you to tell your own truth.

As Maya Angelou said, "There is no greater agony than bearing an untold story inside you!"

The EWG Leadership Team at the White House tour

Rejoice
IN THE LORD ALWAYS!

Dressed and ready for Sabbath worship each week where I am
motivated and Inspired to endure another week

Acknowledgments

As with everything that I have done in my life, this memoir would not have been possible without the love and support of many people. Through the years, many have shared ideas, mentored, and supported me in ways that have impacted my life, each in a different way. It's impossible to thank everyone and I apologize for anyone not listed. Please know that I appreciate you greatly.

First, I would not be who I am today without the sturdy hand and unconditional love of my late mother, Viola Estella Lake. Before her passing, she had always been a prayer warrior on my behalf. To my mother, I dedicate this memoir. She was one of my staunchest supporters and always provided guidance and support during my entire DOL debacle. My mother's strength, stamina, and fighting spirit are part of who I am today. There is not a day that I don't think about her.

Second, my husband, Lionel, my love, my best friend, my partner for forty years, my staunchest supporter, and the most loving and committed father to our children. You have been to me the life partner that a girl could have only imagined. Ours is quite a love story, and it's still evolving. I'm so excited about our future because our best years are yet to come. Thank you for the guidance, funding, help, and support with my book. You are truly the love of my life.

Third, to my children, Jeanelle, Latisha, and Lionel Jr., thank you for being my supporters, my motivators, and for making me a mother and giving me so much purpose in my life; you are the best kids a mother can have. Thank you for your love!

Fourth, to my brothers and sisters—siblings truly share one of the best relationships of all. Thank you for your love, support, and the contributions to my memoir. If it weren't for each one of you, I would not be the person I am now. You taught me what it means to be a big sister. Having each of you as brothers and sisters is a gift I will always treasure.

Finally, there is absolutely no way that I could have completed this memoir in my lifetime without my incredible editors. Thank you for your positive feedback. I'm forever grateful to each of you for the enthusiasm, energy, and passion you bring to the editing process. I hope that this is just the beginning of a lasting friendship.

Ingram Content Group UK Ltd.
Milton Keynes UK
UKHW012130280623
424228UK00002B/27